"Old Slow Town"

"Old Slow Town"
Detroit during the Civil War

PAUL TAYLOR

Wayne State University Press
DETROIT

© 2013 by Wayne State University Press, Detroit, Michigan 48201.

17 16 15 14 13   5 4 3 2 1

Library of Congress Cataloging-in-Publication Data
Taylor, Paul.
    "Old Slow Town" : Detroit during the Civil War / Paul Taylor.
        pages cm. — (Great Lakes books series)
    Includes bibliographical references and index.
    ISBN 978-0-8143-3603-8 (cloth : alk. paper) — ISBN 978-0-8143-3930-5 (ebook) (print)
    1. Detroit (Mich.)—History—19th century. 2. Michigan—History—Civil War, 1861–1865. I. Title.
    F574.D457T39 2013
    977.4'3403—dc23

                                                    2013007474

∞

Endsheets: Civil War and Reconstruction era street map of Detroit (author's collection).
Designed and typeset by Westchester
Composed in Trump Medieval LT Std

To the memory of
Robert Fisher Taylor
and Russell Willard Fuller,
two Detroit fathers
sorely missed

Contents

Contents

Acknowledgments

Over the course of the past five and one-half years, numerous individuals have helped me transform a rough idea into this finished book. Whether they work at university libraries or other public institutions, or volunteer at local historical societies, these dedicated professionals bring a high level of commitment to their task that shows through to the various researchers they encounter every day. Though there are no doubt more names than I can recall, a few individuals do stand out for the generous assistance they rendered.

Gail Lelyveld helped me overcome time and distance by assisting me with research within the various record groups at the National Archives in Washington, D.C. At the National Archives' Chicago branch, archivist Glen Longacre sent me considerable reference material in advance of my planned visits, which allowed me to make the most of my research time during several journeys to that facility. Once I arrived, Glen provided significant suggestions regarding potential areas of research.

Closer to home, Karen Jania and her reference staff at the University of Michigan's Bentley Historical Library were always cheerful models of efficiency during my many visits to that repository. Historical research involving any facet of Michigan history must always include visits to the Bentley. Likewise, my appreciation is given to the staff at the Archives of Michigan at Lansing for many useful tips and suggestions during my time spent at that facility. Similar thanks are given to Jonathan Boegler of the Howell Area Historical Society for delving into its holdings to uncover an image of George W. Lee.

Acknowledgments

The same gratitude is given to John Fierst of Central Michigan University's Clarke Historical Library for his research on my behalf. I must also thank Mr. Shawn West, who graciously allowed me to use his image of Colonel Fabian Brydolf.

Of course, *the* cornerstone for any Detroit-oriented research is the Burton Collection at the Detroit Public Library. Named after its creator, Clarence Monroe Burton, this collection has, for almost one hundred years, housed thousands of manuscript collections, photographs, newspapers, books, and pamphlets pertaining to the history of Detroit. I am indebted to its always-helpful staff who graciously addressed my many queries over the past years.

Detroit's very own Wayne State University Press seemed to me the obvious home for this book, and I am grateful and appreciative that it agreed. Acquisitions editor Kathy Wildfong and her team were a delight to work with and always very helpful and informative. It was a consultative partnership that I will warmly remember. I must also acknowledge Robin DuBlanc, who copyedited the manuscript's final version. Her suggestions regarding style and word flow were a great benefit, resulting in a better book than the one I originally submitted.

Last but certainly not least, I am again indebted to my wife, Miriam, for her undying patience with my avocation. In this particular instance, however, her support blossomed into multiple roles. My appreciation and love go out to her not only for reading over the manuscript's first draft and making many useful critiques and suggestions, but also for serving as a translator. As she is fluent in German, she translated a number of German-language Civil War–era letters from the Bentley Library collections into English.

As any author will attest, all of these individuals, and I'm sure many unmentioned ones as well, all contributed to the finished product more than my mere words of thanks can say. If this labor of love achieves the level of success that I hope for, it is due in no small part to the contributions and assistance offered by those mentioned here.

Introduction

The Northern home front during the American Civil War was far from unified regarding the need for war in the first place or the ongoing merits of the conflict as the war progressed. Though there was ample flag waving from one end of the North to the other in the days immediately following the attack on Fort Sumter, schisms in thought soon began to appear about the legitimacy of Federal troops marching into Southern states once it became clear that the war was not going to be the bloodless, ninety-days' affair many had initially envisioned. The most vocal antiwar bloc of the public was led by what became known as the "Copperheads," a boisterous faction of the Democratic Party whose goals and motto were "the Constitution as it is and the Union as it was," which would ideally be achieved through a negotiated settlement to bring the Confederacy back into the Union. Such a settlement would, inevitably, maintain the preservation of slavery. With the announcement of Lincoln's Emancipation Proclamation in September 1862, the political divide in the North ruptured even further, for what had ostensibly been a war only for the restoration of the Union was now viewed by many as a war primarily for the emancipation of the black slave. The workingman's fear of conscription caused by the March 1863 Enrollment Act only added fuel to the fire.

Most Northerners abhorred slavery. However, the belief that blacks were the intellectual and moral inferiors to whites was a conviction every bit as widespread in the North as in the South. Accordingly, forcing white men to shed their blood as well as spending immense amounts of national treasure to free the slaves was viewed with disdain by much of the populace. Driving this antipathy in the North was the great fear that these uneducated blacks, once freed, would stream into Northern cities and compete with white workingmen for the available manual labor jobs, thereby pushing wages ever downward. Moreover, the prospect of the inevitable public socialization that would occur between blacks and whites further increased Northern racial angst.

Northern social prejudices and anxiety were not limited to racial animus toward blacks but often extended across ethnic lines to European immigrants, in particular the poor Irish of Catholic faith who had come to America seeking a better life. To many native-born, Protestant white Americans, the uneducated Irish were of a moral state barely a notch above that of blacks. To those same Irish, however, regardless of their economic lot in life, the very fact of their "whiteness" offered them a rung on the caste ladder firmly above that of blacks. Much of the social strife in the North during the war was the result of the Irish striving to maintain that higher rung.

Though situated in what was known as the Old Northwest, far removed from Southern battlefields, Detroit was not immune to this war-related potpourri of political, racial, and ethnic conflict. The city was for the most part a Democratic island surrounded by a sea of Michigan Republicanism, though it should be stressed to the modern reader that the Civil War–era Republican and Democratic parties often held political opinions and social beliefs that were practically the opposite of their positions in the early twenty-first century. With the exception of the years 1860–61, Detroit's mayor was a Democrat from 1858 through 1871, while throughout the war, Detroit's Common Council (the forerunner of today's city council) tilted Democratic as well. Michigan, however, was a state solidly in the Republican camp throughout the war. The state went for Abraham Lincoln in both the 1860 and 1864 presidential elections. From 1861 through 1865 the governor's chair and both U.S. Senate seats were occupied not by mere Republicans but by ardent Radical Republicans who favored the immediate abolition of slavery and a firm-handed prosecution of the war against Confederate soldiers and civilians. The state legislature was, with few exceptions, a Republican stronghold from the late 1850s through the 1930s.

Why were Detroit's politics so different than the rest of Michigan's? Detroit's Democratic political makeup was due in large measure to an immigrant community that by 1860 represented close to one-half of the city's total population. This was in stark contrast to Michigan as a whole, where the number of immigrants statewide represented just under 20 percent of the state's total population. Most, but of course not all, of these ethnic newcomers aligned themselves with the values and beliefs of the Democratic Party.[1]

Detroit's civilian and military leaders, unlike those in the rest of the state, had to deal with the consistent fear of social unrest for much of the war, which was brought about by three primary issues: the intense divide over the war's purpose; the debate regarding who was to blame for the conflict; and the question of who, precisely, was going to fight the war. This book contends that the anger generated by these questions within Detroit's diverse political and ethnic communities drove Civil War Detroit to become a city nearly torn in two by the division between pro-Union and antiwar (Copperhead) sentiments, the latter being led by the virulently anti-Lincoln and anti-black *Detroit Free Press*.

The real and feared strife in Civil War Detroit was fueled in large measure by competing journalistic beliefs as to what the fundamental purpose of the war should and should not be, with the city's newspapers striving to shape public opinion on the ultimate legitimacy of the war. These conflicting editorial opinions were echoed among Detroit's various native-born, ethnic, and immigrant communities, seen through the prism of their different cultural backgrounds. In order to understand why much of the political, journalistic, and social strife in Detroit occurred as it did, this book will also demonstrate how and why Detroit's diverse residents came to occupy the specific social stations that they generally held during the Civil War era, and how this affected their beliefs about the war.

Although Detroit was far from the war's killing fields, the conflict brought significant economic change and heartache to much of the city's populace. Price inflation was a particularly sinister enemy, causing many staples to more than double in price over those four years of war. With male labor generally in short supply, rising prices coupled with a demand for more humane working conditions gave rise to the organized labor movement in Detroit.

With their men off fighting, women often bore the brunt of the suffering. When husbands and fathers no longer filled the traditional role of breadwinner, anxiety over how women were to survive economically was a concern faced by every major urban area in the

North, and the work that many women performed to secure an income in an era of limited opportunity was an important aspect of day-to-day life in Detroit. Their legacy is an important early contribution to the labor unionization in the city.

As the war progressed, the continued economic growth brought to the city by its growing role as a Great Lakes shipping hub helped transform Detroit from a frontier town primarily dedicated to agriculture, mining, and lumber to a modern city driven principally by the manufacturing industry in the latter half of the 1860s and beyond.

What transpired in Detroit during the Civil War and what life was like for its residents are subjects that have been only lightly touched upon in general histories of Detroit. These past works may mention the recruiting efforts at the war's 1861 commencement and perhaps the 1863 riot or the *Philo Parsons* affair. There has never been, however, a book-length work devoted solely to the military, political, and social aspects of this critical period in the city's history. Through the use of previously overlooked military correspondence from the National Archives, soldier and civilian diaries and letters, and period articles and editorials from Detroit's Republican and Democratic Civil War newspapers, along with a fresh, judicious synthesis of secondary sources, this work closes that long existing gap in Detroit's written history.

Chapter 1 examines the ethnic, social, and commercial growth of Michigan and Detroit from the end of the War of 1812 up to the eve of the Civil War as well as Detroit's role as a minor military town in the second quarter of the nineteenth century. How Detroit's Civil War–era military forts and posts came into existence is presented in this opening chapter. It will also explain how and why Detroit's native-born and immigrant population grew over those decades, especially during the 1850s, when Detroit began to slowly change from a frontier town into a city that was on the cusp of becoming an urban industrial center. The story of the freed black community in antebellum Detroit, and the racism it endured at the hands of Detroit's anti-black newspapers, is also discussed. The key result of the city's immigrant and black population growth was that at the beginning of the great rebellion, the ethnic and political makeup of Detroit was significantly different from Michigan as a whole; therefore, this chapter will lay the groundwork and historical context for understanding how such extensive cultural diversity led to the political, racial, and ethnic discord that occurred in Detroit during the Civil War.

Chapter 2 illustrates how, once war came to the nation, Detroit, the state of Michigan, and the North as a whole were initially united in their belief that the Union must be preserved. This chapter will also show how Detroit responded to the tremendous needs of Michigan's soldiers and quickly became the primary training and supply center for those departing for the front. By the fall of 1861, however, antiwar voices were being heard throughout the North.

Though the narrative as a whole generally progresses chronologically, chapters 3 through 6 are more topical, with each subject being discussed over the entire four-year time frame of the Civil War. Chapter 3 explores the growing fear that many Northerners had of so-called secret societies that purportedly operated within the North and were alleged to be sympathetic to the Confederacy. How that angst manifested itself in Detroit is fully examined. Moreover, there was a growing resentment toward blacks, especially following the 1862 announcement of Lincoln's Emancipation Proclamation, when it now seemed to much of the populace, especially conservative Democrats, that what had begun as a noble war for the sanctity of Union had now become a war for the emancipation of the black slaves who, in the eyes of many Northerners, were members of a degraded race not worth the white man's blood. The chapter examines how such anger in Detroit erupted into a fiery newspaper war of words, which peaked over the creation of Michigan's first and only "colored regiment."

Chapter 4 studies how national conscription and the attendant fear of the draft affected Detroit. No single issue had a broader impact across the Michigan and Detroit home front, for the possibility of being forcibly drafted into the Union army was a fear that transcended across all economic, ethnic, and class-based lines. This chapter looks at the perceived unfairness of the draft system and explains how working-class Detroit men became convinced that they were to be the Union's mandatory cannon fodder for a war in which many did not believe.

Chapter 5 presents an economic and labor portrait of Detroit during the war. With so many men off fighting, male labor became scarce, prompting new opportunities for women. Indeed, with their husbands, fathers, and brothers off fighting, many women were forced into the Detroit workplace to ensure their families' survival. The challenges that these unskilled women were forced to overcome in a patriarchal society are discussed. The chapter also analyzes two additional and unfortunate consequences of the war that affected all Detroiters: rampant price inflation and a substantial increase in street crime.

From nearly the onset of the war, many of Detroit's civilians wanted to assist the war effort in some form. Chapter 6 explores the myriad charitable organizations that grew within Detroit over the next four years, all with the intent of providing relief and sustenance to Michigan's boys in blue or for the widows and orphans left behind.

The Civil War came almost to Detroit's doorstep in the fall of 1863, when the Federal government learned that a Confederate plot to seize the Union navy's lone warship on the Great Lakes and then terrorize port towns had been thwarted. Chapter 7 explores how and why that plot and other such schemes to bring terror into the North came about in mid- to late 1864. In fact, Detroit was often feared to be high on the Confederates' target list. As most of these Confederate plans emanated from a supposedly neutral Canada, the diplomatic fallout from these planned raids along with the attendant fear and military responses they created within Detroit are also discussed.

Chapter 8 concludes Detroit's Civil War story, describing the soldiers' return home. Though the muskets had fallen silent, this chapter explains how pens replaced guns in the ongoing battle over the role of freed blacks in Detroit society. Meanwhile, though now home, many of the war's veterans did not wish to forget the sacrifices they had put forth for the nation, which led to the formation of the Grand Army of the Republic, the largest and most important of the postwar fraternal organizations. These men knew their service had been a trial by fire that, for many of them, had transformed their lives forever. In the years that followed, many could not remember or conceive of what life had been like before the war. In a sense, the same was true for the city of Detroit, forever altered by the Civil War.

"A pleasant Protestant, no *smell* of Irish about her but respectable German"

The Ethnic and Commercial Development of Detroit, 1815–60

The population and commercial growth of Detroit in the first sixty years of the nineteenth century is a rags-to-partial-riches story that would have been incomprehensible to a Detroit resident in 1805. Serially a French Catholic–dominated fur-trading outpost, a British-controlled village, and an American town, Detroit had existed for over one hundred years by 1805. In that year, Detroit was all but wiped out by a fire, forcing those few residents who remained to rebuild the town. When the War of 1812 concluded a decade later, the picture that emerged of Detroit was still not an attractive one to potential settlers. Soldiers returning to their eastern homes reported that Detroit was good for Indians and disease but little else. Another guest described it as "a town calculated to make but poor impression upon travelers," its "streets full of Indians and doubtful looking Frenchmen."[1]

The U.S. surveyor general remarked in an 1815 public report that the southeastern Michigan territory was riddled with swamps and lakes. Though the report was later shown to be erroneous, it hardly stimulated the interest of many American settlers. In any event, just getting to Michigan from the East Coast was no easy feat. The Great Lakes water route from Buffalo to Detroit was deemed difficult and even dangerous. Those attempting to arrive by land from Ohio had to contend with the Black Swamp, a soupy wetland in northwestern Ohio that extended as far as northeastern Indiana. In addition, the area between Ohio and Detroit was a dense wilderness, thickly wooded and wet, without any road through it or any bridges across its numerous rivers and streams. All these various obstacles meant that much of the burgeoning westward expansion was bypassing Michigan in general and Detroit in particular.[2]

Facing these challenges, Michigan authorities came to the conclusion that if their territory was going to grow and prosper, promoting farming would be their best course, as they believed the profitability of the fur trade was slowly diminishing, even though the region's agricultural capability was still primitive at best. It was apparent that the scores of destitute Indians and the majority of French residents had little skill for farming and even less desire to learn, with one writer claiming that their "aspirations seldom extended beyond the possession of a canoe, a spear, and a few hooks for fishing, with a rifle, and a half-dozen dogs." Michigan's territorial governor, Lewis Cass, even pleaded for Federal assistance since he felt that the "moral character" of the local French was well below that of true Americans. He held little expectation that Michigan's civilization could properly advance until a sizable number of Americans migrated to the state, in the process enhancing the territory's moral fiber. To overcome the territory's negative image, Cass began a publicity campaign aimed at attracting newcomers by touting the area's desirable features.[3]

The most important aspect of those promotions was the opening of a state land office in Detroit, from which public lands were put up for sale. In fact, the real beginning of Detroit's growth took place in 1818 with these sales. With land priced at bargain rates, these offerings were meant to attract new settlers who would provide the necessary stimulus for Detroit and Michigan to prosper in the areas of agriculture, trade, commerce, and manufacturing.[4]

At the same time, the ease and speed of traveling to Detroit from the East improved dramatically with the arrival of the *Walk-in-the-Water*, the first ever steamship to sail between Buffalo, New York, and Detroit. When the ship first dropped anchor in Detroit on August 27, 1818, its voyage from Buffalo had taken forty-four hours as compared to the two weeks usually required for the schooners that had previously made the trek. Such an increase in speed helped enhance Detroit's status as an attractive destination. More significant travel improvement came in 1825 with the completion of the Erie Canal; a ten-year feat that marked a significant milestone in Midwest development. This 363-mile man-made waterway ran east to west from Albany, New York, on the Hudson River to Buffalo, New York, at Lake Erie. In the process, the canal overcame the rapids and waterfall obstacles east of Lake Erie. The canal immediately cut transportation costs dramatically.[5]

Coupled with an increasing number of steamboats on Lake Erie, the new canal helped to foster a population surge into the upper Midwest by New Englanders and, to an even greater extent, by the children of New Englanders who now lived in western and upstate New York. These new settlers were known as "Yankees" and nowhere in that great western migration did they dominate population growth to the degree that they did in Michigan, to the point that Michigan became known as the "third New England," the second being New York. As one historian described it, "The opening of the Erie Canal acted like an open sluiceway to drain off the population of New England." The migration of these New York and New England settlers into Michigan continued throughout the 1830s and 1840s, due in large measure to continued public land sales. By 1850, the "Yankees" represented Michigan's largest ethnic group, accounting for 41.3 percent of the state's total population.[6]

When Michigan achieved statehood in 1837, state officials realized that, as in the years following the War of 1812, the fledgling state's future would be determined by whether the state could attract sufficient numbers of newcomers. It was not, however, merely a question of numbers; state officials wanted to attract what they deemed to be the "right" kind of immigrant. That assessment was determined in large measure by the Yankees' influence in Michigan and the societal values they brought with them. With a staunch Puritanical religious background that was reflected in an uncompromising solemnity and a distrust of inherent human goodness, Yankees vigorously sought to impose their values regarding proper individual behavior and societal order wherever they went, buoyed by their strong sense of cultural superiority and self-righteousness. When they arrived in Michigan, most of them had been young with little money, the type of individual who would have been attracted to the frontier's spirit of equality, and therefore would also have a natural aversion to slavery and the South's rigid societal caste system. In the years to come, their fervor for religion, education, and societal reform put them in the vanguard of the abolitionist movement and made the transplanted Yankee a vital factor in the birth of the Republican Party.[7]

Since the state's territorial days and even into statehood, it was such Yankee men, who had immigrated to Michigan early in their lives, who dominated Michigan politics. Between 1805 and 1870, twelve of Michigan's fifteen governors were Yankees. Concurrently at the local level, almost 77 percent of all officeholders in the southern part of the state were of New England descent. What this dominance meant was that Yankee principles and values influenced many of Michigan's governmental institutions and the decisions that emanated from them, such as a focus on which immigrant groups would be deemed most desirable. The result of this focus would help Michigan build its desired economic and social model.[8]

This chapter will explain how these specific efforts, together with food shortages and political turmoil in Europe, helped to spur rapid immigrant population growth in Detroit during the late 1840s and up to the Civil War. In spite of some resentment by native-born Americans toward the newcomers, matched with desires to stem the immigrant tide, the end result was that Detroit's ethnic character was substantially different from Michigan's as a whole in 1860. Such a diverse ethnic and cultural makeup of Detroit, coupled with the antiwar and anti-black emotions held by much of the city's immigrant and native-born population, helped contribute significantly to societal strife in Detroit during the 1861–65 Civil War.

Michigan state authorities viewed the German immigrant as hardworking and industrious; therefore this group was considered particularly attractive and stood near the top of Michigan's wish list. The initial German immigrants to Michigan in the 1830s and early 1840s were generally from the poorer, uneducated working class, who came to the new land to improve their economic life. They had seen firsthand the lack of social or economic advancement in their homeland, which prompted the search for a new life in America. As many were of the Catholic faith, Detroit's century-plus history of Catholic dominance provided a welcome familiarity to many of these working-class German immigrants. By 1848, those Germans already in Detroit and its environs had significantly impressed their neighbors with their hard work and prudence as farmers, prompting the state to prepare in 1849 a pamphlet entitled *Der Auswander Wegweiser: The Emigrant's Guide to the State of Michigan*, which was printed in both German and English. The pamphlet was stocked with a wealth of commercial, economic, and scientific data and served as Michigan's formal invitation to Germans seeking to immigrate to the state. The result was that the first half of the 1850s marked the peak of German migration.[9]

The success of the 1849 pamphlet was underscored in large measure by the political unrest in Germany[10] and the rest of Europe, which had been seething for years and had come to a head in 1848. Following the failure of their revolution for various social reforms, which included a desire for more open and democratic government as well as enhanced human rights, scores of educated Germans had left their homelands to come to America. Known as "Forty-Eighters," these were men and women who were generally more wealthy, free-thinking, and skilled than their immigrant predecessors of one and two decades before. Once in America, many Forty-Eighters vigorously stood against nativism and, of course, slavery. Such activism was in keeping with the liberal ideals that had prompted them to flee Germany in the first place. This progressive though small class of German immigrants would prove valuable to Republican Party ideals during the Civil War.[11]

Nevertheless, by the eve of the Civil War, Michigan's working-class and farming Germans had remained far more loyal to Democrats than to Republicans. Those Germans who identified with the Republicans were generally the Forty-Eighters and a minority of working-class Protestants. The majority of German Protestants, however, still voted Democratic. These Democratic-leaning Germans viewed themselves as deeply religious and therefore resented the liberal and freethinking Forty-Eighters. A Republican Party preference for alcohol temperance also offended many working-class Germans, for whom drinking beer was an integral part of their culture. This was not a minor issue in that community. When the state legislature passed a law in June 1861 disallowing the sale of any type of alcoholic beverage in less than a five-gallon container, Detroit's Germans formed a uniformed "Anti-Liquor Law Brigade," which stood ready to defend any German arrested for the sale of lager beer. Moreover, apart from the relatively small number of Forty-Eighters, most Germans were not strong antislavery proponents. Within Detroit's wards where the German population was highest, Democrats retained control throughout the Civil War.[12]

Though immigrants came to Michigan from many different European countries, the British Isles and especially Ireland provided the other great wave of immigration into nineteenth-century Detroit. Throughout the 1800s, English landowners in Ireland had been slowly evicting Irish peasants from their small farms in order to use that land for more profitable sheep and cattle grazing. Meanwhile, what little beef those same English landlords had produced on their own farms was destined for England as export. Forced evictions followed by starvation became commonplace, as these Irish peasants could no longer pay their rents and had no means of feeding themselves. The final nail in the coffin for the poor Irish was the potato famine of 1845–49, which devastated that country's population as the potato crop, the principal food of Ireland's poorer masses, rotted in the ground before it could be properly harvested due to a disease known as "late blight." Nevertheless, the English land-owning class did nothing. "There is a very prevalent feeling among the landlord class," wrote Irish revolutionary John Mitchell in 1847, "that the people of Ireland ought not to be fed upon the grain produced in this country . . . and that it is desirable to get rid of a couple millions of them." Close to 25 percent of Ireland's population perished as the famine forever altered the country's demographic and social landscape. While Irish immigrants had been coming to America for years, the late-1840s famine sent hundreds of thousands of Irish immigrants to America in search of a new start, with Detroit and Michigan receiving their fair share. Among them were John Ford and his twenty-one-year-old son William, grandfather and father of Detroit's legendary Henry Ford. Detroit's growing industrial base and Catholic-friendly roots provided ample appeal to the new immigrants, the latter standing in stark contrast to the semiorganized anti-Catholic prejudices and even outright hostility the Irish had experienced upon their arrival at most eastern seaports. Such hostility had included mob attacks on Irish Catholics in Richmond, Charleston, and Philadelphia in 1844–45, and even the burning of a Massachusetts convent in 1834. Since Detroit possessed a burgeoning immigrant Irish population that had been growing throughout the 1840s, the city's leading residents decided to join in a national effort under way to help those Irish still starving on the Emerald Isle. On February 25, 1847, a committee was formed in Detroit to begin a relief effort that ultimately resulted in over two thousand barrels of provisions being sent to Ireland.[13]

Unlike earlier Irish immigrants, however, who were often of some means and education, the new wave of Irish into Detroit were primarily from its lowest social class, meaning they were its poorest, least literate, and certainly the most unaware of their new surroundings. It was said that on any given Saturday night in Detroit, you could spot an Irishman just off the boat by his tall beaver hat, "high-water" trousers, and short, stubby clay pipe. Surprisingly, and unlike any other foreign-born ethnic group, more Irish women than men immigrated to the United States in the decades following the famine, which led to many Irish enclaves containing more females than males.[14]

As had been the case for immigrants in the earlier part of the century, traveling from the East Coast to Detroit still proved financially problematic for many newcomers, though the Erie Canal had certainly improved matters. Still, for many who arrived in America with hardly a penny, the cost of traversing across the country could prove overwhelming. Not having any funds to buy land, either, many of these immigrant poor ended up settling in Detroit rather than Michigan's outlying areas due to the available manual work. This contributed greatly to the aforementioned disparity in immigrant population percentages between Detroit and Michigan as a whole at the start of the Civil War. For many of these immigrants, Detroit's growing commercial and waterfront environment provided them with their best chances of obtaining any type of unskilled, manual labor jobs. A fortunate few were able to choose self-employment. One common field was that of a drayman, with sons and brothers working alongside the wagon owner. They would haul wood, coal, or other freight to and from Detroit's docks to the rail yards.[15]

Those Irish immigrants who made it to Detroit in the mid-nineteenth century mostly settled in wards 1, 5, and especially ward 8 on the city's west side, a part of town that was quickly to become known as "Corktown," so named after Ireland's Cork County. For Irish newcomers, that neighborhood helped provide a feeling of home, as it offered a Catholic church and fellow countrymen who shared a common culture yet was close enough to the available work opportunities. The eighth ward had been subdivided in 1835 and by midcentury, its housing sat on what had once been French farmland that ran from the river northward "as far as a horse could plow in a single day." Its eastern and western boundaries were Third and Eighth streets, which placed the ward's housing reasonably close to the jobs provided by Detroit's burgeoning riverfront. By 1850, the eighth ward claimed 1,864 Irish Catholics out of a total ward population of 4,188, an amount equal to 44.5 percent of the total.[16]

Like the Germans, most of the Irish immigrants to Detroit initially aligned themselves politically with the Democratic Party. Many immigrants were attracted to the Democrats by the very sound of the party name; it epitomized the spirit of America and the free western masses. Most but not all of these immigrants were poor and had labored as farmers or small artisans in their home country. With little chance of improving their lot and enduring poor economic conditions at home, many had set sail for the land that they felt offered them a better chance for success. Having lived their entire lives at the bottom of the social and economic ladder, most immigrants to Michigan and Detroit quickly associated themselves with the Democrats, for that was the party that was deemed most amenable to the immigrants' social and economic interests and the party that was striving to curb the powers of the "aristocratic" class. Along with the Catholic Church, the Democrats espoused a dogma of "whiteness" that reassured the lowly and poor Irish that their lot was certainly not on the civic level of blacks.[17]

This was a crucial distinction to Irish immigrants. As a means of asserting their "whiteness," poor Irish welcomed any description of American nationality that emphasized the importance of race, placing them safely within an Anglo-Celtic racial majority. This crucial racial status as a "free white person" was paramount to becoming a true "American." In other words, the Irish immigrants' racial inclusion was overwhelmingly reliant upon the racial *exclusion* of the black race. This prompted most Irish to subscribe to a racist view of the Negro that bordered on paranoia.[18]

Meanwhile, as most of the Irish and some Germans were poor and illiterate, Michigan and Detroit Whigs, as well as later Republicans, viewed them as a boorish and ignorant class of people who were not ready for the vote. As early as 1833, Detroiters were openly worrying about the influx of such immigrants, whose cultural traditions changed "the general character of our city, as regards order and sobriety," especially the number of beer halls that seemed to be mushrooming in the ethnic parts of town. When the city investigated the matter a year later, it was shocked to discover that there was one saloon for every thirteen families in Detroit. This Whig/Republican disgust toward the Irish came as no surprise to Democrats. Simply put, from the Democratic perspective, the Irish were a people who tenaciously clung to their religious faith and Democratic associations, which therefore opened them up to ceaseless scorn and attack from the opposition. "The refined Puritan [that is, "Yankee"] of the 19th century," alleged Democrats, "allowed no opportunity for a demonstration of hatred to escape." Nothing had changed by the eve of the Civil War. Voicing an opinion that had existed for decades among many of the nation's native-born population, the Republican *Detroit Daily Advertiser* referred to the Irish immigrants in 1858 as "miserable rowdies who had not the right to vote in their own country, and who were brought up like swine." This view was no different from that traditionally held by the English, who for generations had viewed the Irish as savages ever ready to convert the Anglo-Saxon to their malicious ways.[19]

Abstinence from alcohol and the corresponding temperance movement also created tension in Detroit. Led by Catholic bishop Peter Paul Lefevere, temperance in Detroit was strongly advocated by the Catholic Church throughout the 1840s and '50s, finding what support it could muster within the Democratic-leaning Irish community. In fact, nearly all of the names of members of the Detroit Catholic Temperance Society in the 1840s were Irish, though most Irish were not supporters of this movement. German immigrants, along with other European immigrants such as Poles and the French, were generally hostile to the notion of total abstinence. The Republican Party's position on the liquor question was certainly not agreeable to many Germans. One German liberal wrote to his parents regarding the conundrum some faced: "Our choice in politics leaves much to be desired, slavery on the one side, the temperance humbug on the other." As a strident antislavery man, this German chose what he considered to be the lesser of two evils and voted the Republican ticket despite the "temperance humbug." With the rapid increase of European immigration to Detroit in the 1850s, the temperance issue became a source of conflict within the Catholic Church. Outside the church, nativist thinking often viewed alcohol consumption and the social ills brought with it as a troublesome issue that could easily be laid at the feet of Detroit's steadily growing foreign population.[20]

With the poor Irish generally relegated to the most menial of jobs and the hardest of labor, they quickly came to view free blacks not as fellow sufferers but as competition for those unskilled labor jobs. In short order, the black man was seen as a threat to the Irishman's own tenuous economic situation. In observing this paradigm, *Harper's* magazine reported that "no class of our foreign population is as jealous of its own liberties as the Irish, and there is also none which more strongly resents every liberty accorded to the Negro race."

Northern blacks quickly showed equal disdain for the Irish, and in time the phrase "white nigger" was coined to describe the sons and daughters of Erin, or for that matter any white worker who was engaged in the hardest of unskilled labor or in a perceived subservient role.[21]

Concurrently, Irish women were looked down upon because of their willingness to embrace domestic servitude as a means of income. Such a cultural willingness to serve strangers in a strange home stood in stark contrast to Protestant, native-born American girls and women, who found the notion of serving another so demeaning to one's sense of self that they were willing to accept work that paid much lower rates in order to avoid the label of servant. As more and more Irish women flooded into that field, domestic service became associated with "Irish work," thereby becoming even more odious to American females. This antipathy toward Irish women, coupled with a greater respect for Germans, was illustrated by Mrs. Elizabeth Stuart of Detroit, who wrote to her daughter Kate in April 1851 expressing delight that Kate had been able to find "proper" domestic help: "I am happy that you have a *woman*," she proclaimed, "and not a headlong, Irish, heedless animal." Six years later, she expressed similar sentiments in a letter to her son, informing him that she had been through four servants in the past three weeks but kept the fifth because she was "a pleasant Protestant, no *smell* of Irish about her but respectable German." Such sentiments firmly tied in with the long-standing Michigan belief that the German female, with her stereotyped reputation for order and cleanliness, was a particularly desirable immigrant.[22]

❀ ❀ ❀

UNLIKE the New York and New England "Yankees" who began immigrating to Michigan en masse following the completion of the Erie Canal, and then the scores of European immigrants in the decades following, relatively few American-born blacks could be found in Michigan from its earliest days. Bondage did exist in Michigan, but native Indians initially made up the bulk of the slave population. Those black slaves found in Detroit in its early days were generally those who had been captured by Indians during raids into the South and then traded to Detroit's white residents. As introduced by the French, the role of the slave was solely domestic in nature and never played a significant economic role within Detroit or Michigan. Importing slaves into Michigan was abolished by the Northwest Ordinance of 1787; however, it was not until 1837 that slavery was formally abolished by the then new state's first constitution.[23]

Nonetheless, slavery was fully legal in the Southern states, so Detroit officials did have a legal obligation to return runaways to their Southern masters. As late as 1827, advertisements seeking runaway slaves were appearing in the *Detroit Gazette*. There was, however, no formal treaty between Britain and the United States that dealt with returning runaway slaves, so any runaway slaves who made it across the Detroit River to Windsor, Canada, knew they were gaining freedom.[24]

How whites in Michigan felt about blacks in general was often a measure of their attitude toward the slavery issue. Since most whites who had not been born in Michigan were immigrants from either New England or western New York, they were largely unaware of the racial characteristics of the so-called low blacks prevalent on Southern plantations. Most Michigan whites rarely, if ever, saw a black person and if they did that individual was most likely to be trained for "proper" domestic service. By 1850, there were only about twenty-five hundred blacks in all of Michigan, and many of these were free men and women, considered highly "civilized." In fact, significant numbers of Michigan's antislavery radicals had wanted as early as 1835 to amend Michigan's constitution to allow black males the vote.[25]

The growing antislavery movement in Michigan led to the creation of a statewide antislavery society in 1836, formed by a group of Quakers, Methodists, Congregationalists, and Presbyterians who met in Ann Arbor. The Detroit Anti-Slavery Society was then organized in 1837 as an auxiliary to the state society. Its mission was to keep the abolition message in front of the populace with its core message that blacks should be recognized as people fully entitled to personal liberty. Within a year there were nineteen such societies, usually led by primarily Protestant clergy and professional men, while small rural farmers made up most of the members. As what might be known in today's political world as single-issue groups, their questions to politicians and candidates centered on how they viewed the slavery issue. The dominance of the slavery question and its feared expansion soon led to the creation of the Liberty Party in 1840, a single-issue and short-lived party devoted to the abolitionist cause.[26]

Of course, the most important and best known antislavery activities throughout the nation were the actions of the many who participated in the Underground Railroad, the famous secret network of individuals with safe houses who helped escaped slaves fleeing northward from bondage to freedom. Usually these safe houses, or "stations," were situated one night's journey apart. The owner of the house, or "conductor," was a trusted man or woman who could be counted on to feed and clothe the runaway slave while providing concealing shelter by day. Many of Detroit's leading citizens who aligned themselves with the Liberty Party in the early 1840s were participants in these "railroad" operations. Indeed, Detroit's proximity to Canada made it a crucial terminus of the Underground Railroad. Once in Detroit, escaped slaves would be hidden in various safe houses until it was deemed safe to cross the Detroit River to freedom in Canada. Most but not all of the Underground Railroad safe houses in Detroit were in the third ward. One of the most famous belonged to Seymour Finney, who ran a hotel at the corner of Woodward and Gratiot. Many slaves were routinely hidden in his barn at the northeast corner of State and Griswold. Other important shelters in Detroit were the basements of the Second Baptist Church and the First Congregational Church, then located at the corner of Fort and Wayne streets.[27]

With the exception of these staunch abolitionists, however, it must be stressed that Michigan's general aversion to slavery did not translate into a belief that the black race was the moral or social equivalent of the white. Black children, for example, were not allowed in the public schools, nor were they welcome in "white" churches. Such racist views persisted across the North as a whole. "I have no special love for the African, any more than for the low-class Irish, but don't want to see either imposed upon," was a typical region-wide sentiment written by one New Englander who considered himself anti-slavery. While many Northern and upper-class abolitionists took a more romanticized view of blacks that cast them as created in God's image and sharing a common humanity with whites, most Northern whites viewed blacks as innately inferior and probably of a separate creation.[28]

Despite its small black population, Michigan nevertheless insisted on passing a series of what were known as "Black Laws," as evidenced by the Act of April 13, 1827. Thus Michigan maintained the region's tradition of closing its doors to black refugees and subjugating those free blacks who already resided in the state. The new law closed militia service to blacks and enforced racial segregation in the area of public education. Furthermore, the laws dictated that after May 1 all "colored persons" had to register themselves in the county clerk's office. No blacks were allowed to reside in the Michigan territory unless they could produce a certificate that stated they were free. The document was to be placed in the public record, at a cost to the black man or woman of 12 ½¢. To add insult to injury, these free blacks were also required to file surety bonds within twenty days in the punitive sum of $500 to ensure their "good behavior." If they were unable to support themselves, then the bondsman would be required to pay for their support. If any aspect of the act was not obeyed, the black in question would be sent out of the territory. The law was overtly racist, but at first of little consequence; no real attempt was made to enforce it until after the Blackburn riot of 1833.[29]

The 1833 Thornton and Ruth Blackburn affair illustrated that Detroit's free blacks were more than willing to stand up for their dignity as well as what they believed to be their natural rights. Thornton Blackburn was in his late twenties when he and his wife, Ruth, escaped from their Kentucky mistress, Mrs. Susan Brown of Louisville, in 1831. Both were described as mulattoes, which meant their skin color was light enough to help them successfully make their way north to Detroit. At the time, Detroit had a population somewhere between 4,000 and 5,000 which included about 275 blacks. After the Blackburns had peaceably resided in Detroit for two years, three slave catchers from Kentucky arrived in Detroit seeking to recapture them, and accordingly made their claim before a Wayne County justice of the peace. The claim was approved and resulted in the couple's arrest on June 14, 1833, as fugitive slaves, which of course caused a great stir within the black community. After the Blackburns appeared in court for what appeared to be a pro forma trial, the judge directed an officer of the court to deliver the couple to the claimants. While these proceedings were under way, a crowd of free blacks had gathered outside the courthouse and loudly proclaimed that resistance to a negative decision would be forthcoming. Nevertheless, in the event the Blackburns were taken to jail after the verdict and the crowd dispersed. The agents for the purported owner of the slaves demanded on the following day that they be handed over, but the jail keeper, fearing a disturbance, declined to do so.

Throughout that day, a number of Detroit's black residents were allowed to visit with the Blackburns in their jail cell, while many others gathered nearby with clubs, threatening a jailbreak. One black woman stayed in the cell till after dark, at which time she switched clothes with Ruth Blackburn, allowing the latter to escape, much to the outrage of the slave catchers. The next morning brought more of the same; a black mob armed with clubs and even pistols gathered near the jail threatening violence if the sheriff attempted to take Blackburn to the docks, where a steamboat waited to take him away. Unlike on the previous day, however, Detroit's sheriff was now determined to carry out his duties. A carriage was brought up and Blackburn put in it. The carriage had hardly left the jail before it was attacked by the crowd. In the melee that followed, the sheriff was brutally assaulted and beaten senseless while attempting to turn the carriage around and escape back to the safety of the jail. Meanwhile, Blackburn was whisked away by the crowd to a waiting boat, which took him across the Detroit River to what all thought would be safe asylum in Canada. Once on the other side, however, Blackburn was quickly arrested by Canadian authorities and placed in the Sandwich jail. Meanwhile, Michigan authorities quickly began extradition proceedings. The antislavery Canadian authorities, upon learning the full story, ultimately set Blackburn free, refusing on a legal technicality to return him to Detroit, despite the pleas of the state of Michigan. As part of their decision, the Canadians asserted that the Detroit sheriff had detained Thornton Blackburn not in his official capacity but merely as an agent for the slave owner, and that the law did not provide him with such authority.[30]

Despite residents' fears, editorial opinion following the episode was mixed. The *Detroit Courier* editorialized most sympathetically toward the Blackburns: "In common with the whole community our sympathies have been enlisted, and whatever may be the abstract right given by the constitution and laws of our country to traffic in human flesh, we have found it a difficult task to divest ourselves wholly of the spontaneous prepossession in favor of natural liberty which gains a foot hold in the breasts of most men on viewing and appreciating the necessary consequences of legalized slavery." Concurrently, the weekly *Journal and Advertiser* took a more common anti-black tone by asserting that Detroit's colored residents "have little or no stake in our community. . . . Ignorant and vicious, they have been tolerated thus far." Such anti-black attitudes in Detroit had not diminished in the least by the start of the Civil War; if anything, they became more inflamed as many believed blacks to be the cause of the war in the first place.[31]

Though many blacks were convicted for riotous activity, the sentences handed down to those involved were remarkably light, especially considering that Detroit's sheriff was so severely beaten that he never fully recovered and ultimately died within the year. Such open aggression from blacks against white authority coupled with the relatively minor judgments suggested that Detroit's recognition of injustice to blacks rose above the era's obvious racial prejudice. Further, as historian David Grimsted pointed out, "When Northerners saw blacks who risked all to be free and those like the Blackburns who had long since proven their ability to care for themselves and their family, despite the ever-present racism, arrested by Northern officers on Northern soil, it became impossible to pretend that slavery was only the South's business." Such empathy was further evidenced by the fact that all of Michigan's "Black Laws" were repealed prior to statehood in 1837, in stark contrast to the neighboring states of Ohio and Illinois, where "Black Laws" were maintained until after the Civil War.[32]

The elimination of the "Black Laws" in Michigan helped make the state a relatively desirable destination for decades to come for free blacks from Virginia cities such as Fredericksburg and Richmond, where a stringent black code remained in place. Black migration to Detroit began to increase noticeably throughout the 1840s, and the black community had reached a population of 587 by 1850. Initially, Detroit's black community settled in the third ward, near the foot and to the east of Woodward, just above the Detroit River. Even though the community would continue to grow and expand eastward in the antebellum period, few blacks moved west of Woodward. As the community moved east from Woodward, it also steadily moved north from Jefferson Avenue, which was the city's first commercial street. By the end of the 1850s, blacks had migrated to and lived mostly in what were known as wards 3 and 4, near the docks and commercial quarter but well away from the industrial sector. Despite these positive migration trends, Detroit's blacks realized that they were still considered second-class citizens. They were given the lowliest of jobs and were not allowed to send their children to public schools. Suffrage was open only to white males over the age of twenty-one, as was jury duty, while militia service was likewise deemed off limits to blacks. Concurrently, another state statute forbade marriage between blacks and whites.[33]

Blacks were still generally not welcome in Detroit's white churches, but unlike in other Northwestern states, they were allowed to start their own. Because of this type of discrimination, thirteen former slaves now living free in Detroit resigned from the white-dominated First Baptist Church to form the Second Baptist Church in 1836, which became the town's first black church. As Norman McRae noted in his history of blacks in early Detroit, this act laid the foundational cornerstone for a permanent and growing black community within Detroit. Three years later, the church opened Detroit's first school for black children. Prior to that first school, blacks in Detroit had educated their children at home, as was the case in most Northern free black communities. Because of such proactive organizing, by 1846 Detroit's black community could claim a literary society, a library, a temperance society, and three churches, the basements of which often served as schools for black children and as meeting halls for black women's benevolent societies. Concurrently, the chapels also served as political rally sites. The growth of such cultural organizations coupled with black mutual aid continued to increase throughout the end of the 1840s and into the 1850s, which only enhanced the vibrancy of a growing black community within Detroit.[34]

❀ ❀ ❀

DETROIT'S growing industrial reputation was generated in large measure by the discovery of vast quantities of iron ore in Michigan's Upper Peninsula in the early 1840s. Within a few years, iron furnaces, smelters, foundries, and sawmills were appearing in Detroit, and these operations were able to employ more and more people. Maximizing the economic importance of seemingly limitless natural resources such as iron ore and the state's vast forests was the completion in 1855 of a pair of twin 350-foot-long shipping locks on the St. Marys River at Sault Ste. Marie, Michigan. This engineering marvel now allowed ships to overcome the natural twenty-foot rocky drop off between Lakes Superior and Huron, thereby eliminating the need for ships to unload and reload their cargos via the portage system, as had been the case ever since cargo ships had first sailed these lakes. Now the largest vessels could sail unimpeded from Lake Superior to Detroit and other port towns, where their full cargo of raw material could be unloaded and converted to finished products. These new developments made Detroit a regional transportation hub and ended its frontier town status. No longer did Detroit's factories only process the raw materials; now Detroit became a manufacturing town as well. The production of railroad cars, stoves, steam engines,

and cigars became just a few of the city's burgeoning factory industries. Detroit's growing population base and these new industries
would soon provide ample job opportunities for Irish, German, and
other European artisans and laborers arriving in Detroit. Such a growing industrial presence helped Detroit to more than double its population during the 1850s, from 21,019 in 1850 to 45,619 in 1860.[35]

Detroit's military importance at midcentury was considered to
be little more than a far-flung garrison at the western edge of American civilization, though the town's military history could hardly be
considered insignificant. Because of its prominent role in the War of
1812, much of its early history was associated with military conflict,
and its soldiers had been engaged in every American war to that point.
Its sole active military installation in the early 1840s was known as
the Detroit Barracks, a three- to four-acre facility located on the old
Mullet Farm at the corners of Gratiot Avenue, Russell Street, and
Catherine Street, and whose construction had begun in 1830. Prior to
its construction, troops stationed at Detroit were housed in an old
government warehouse at the foot of Wayne Street, which was hardly
suitable for such a purpose.[36]

Armed conflict and the prospects of war again came to Detroit's
doorstep in the late 1830s due to the internal Canadian rebellion
known as the Patriot War—though, of course, to the ruling British, the
"patriots" were merely pirates or brigands. At that time, Canadian
insurgents and their American sympathizers from all along the border had allied themselves in an attempt to free Canada from British
rule, not unlike the American Revolution some sixty years earlier.
From a certain American perspective, there were those who eagerly
viewed Canada's formal separation from Great Britain as a mere
question of time, at which point its entry into the American union
would be desirable.[37]

From the outset of the squabble, however, the American government's position was one of strict neutrality and it was prepared to
use its military in an attempt to stop any American volunteers from
participating. Yet Detroit's and Michigan's isolation from Washington often made American assistance to the insurgency relatively easy.
The fact that Americans were assisting the patriots prompted consistent reports on the Canadian side of an attack originating from
Michigan, including one rumor that warned of a thousand men with
artillery gathered at Mount Clemens. If that were true, Canadian
and British authorities knew there was little they could do, for the

approximately 150 troops at their command could only monitor what they termed "the Detroit rabble." Throughout 1838 there were incidents all along the Detroit River and western Lake Erie, including skirmishes at Fighting Island, the large uninhabited island that lies in the Detroit River between Ecorse and Canada. The final "battle" of the conflict took place at Windsor on December 4, 1838.[38]

Canadian (that is, British) government troops had soundly defeated the patriots in every skirmish, which resulted in about three hundred insurgents fleeing to Detroit. Canadian authorities issued warnings that they would pursue the insurgents into Detroit and sack the town unless they were rounded up and handed over. Such foreign threats were sufficient to raise eyebrows as well as Detroiters' ire, which resulted in many townsfolk offering to aid and assist the refugees. When three Canadian officers visited Detroit in May 1838, they were pelted with eggs and stones in an attempt to provoke the officers into drawing their swords.[39]

Such warnings from across the river also made the Americans realize that there was no fortification anywhere near Detroit that might offer sufficient defense against a British attack. Of particular worry was British-held Fort Malden, located across the Detroit River just south of Windsor at Amherstburg. As a result, Congress appropriated funds in 1841 in accordance with the Great Lakes Defense Plan to build a chain of forts stretching from the East Coast to the Minnesota Territory, including a new fort at Detroit. After all, Detroit and its older residents had not entirely forgotten the British attack on the town and its subsequent humiliating surrender to the redcoats in the War of 1812. A further consideration was that Detroit's population was less than twenty thousand when construction on the new fort started, yet much of that number was comprised of people of foreign birth, with a good number of those foreigners being loyal British subjects.[40]

Construction of the new star-shaped bastion began in 1843 near the intersection of Jefferson and Livernois avenues, which was about three miles west of Detroit's city center. It was a logical point strategically, for that location also happened to be at the narrowest point of the Detroit River. When it was completed eight years later at a cost of $150,000, it was Detroit's third fort and the first to be built solely by Americans. The complex was christened Fort Wayne, in honor of General "Mad Anthony" Wayne of Revolutionary War fame. During wartime, Fort Wayne's primary roles were to act as support for any ground operation, guard the river, and protect the town; however, it was admitted that the fort could not resist a protracted siege.[41]

The 1842 Webster-Ashburton Treaty with Great Britain greatly relaxed tensions, however, and ultimately put an end to any immediate threat of a Canadian/British attack against Detroit. Nevertheless, both sides seemed to sense that there was an ongoing undercurrent of mistrust driven by competing interests in North America. That mistrust would again rear its head during the Civil War, once more prompting concern in both Detroit and Windsor of possible attack from just across the river.

When the Mexican War came in 1845, the Detroit Barracks again served as the mustering point for Michigan volunteers. As the 1850s began, the Detroit Barracks were occupied by the Fourth U.S. Infantry and commanded by a young lieutenant named Ulysses S. Grant. One local who worked alongside Grant at the barracks described him as "always the gentleman, quiet and retiring, never obtrusive." Despite being a very simple and modest man himself, Grant was generally unimpressed with the fledgling town when he first arrived there in April 1849. In a letter to his wife, Julia, Grant described Detroit as a "very dull" place and complained that he had little to do. Such a sentiment was not limited to the future general and president; future Detroit mayor John C. Lodge recalled that as a young boy he often heard antebellum and Civil War–era Detroit derisively referred to as "old slow town" by Chicago visitors, despite its growing industrial prowess. The derogatory nickname apparently stuck, for it was still being used by businessmen forty years after the war.[42]

The 1850s brought whirlwinds of contention and controversy to the national stage that had been brewing for years. Leading the way was the slavery issue: should slavery be legal in any new territories or future states? The two combatants in this issue were yet to be classified as blue and gray, though North and South were certainly contesting the matter and had been for decades. On the political stage, the two dominant political parties in the 1850s were the Democrats and the Whigs. The Democrats had held dominance for two decades, espousing the egalitarian belief that equal rights should be afforded to all *white* men while eschewing privileged rights for the few. Believing in a simple agrarian lifestyle with small, limited government, Jacksonian Democrats were mistrustful of the burgeoning capitalistic ideals epitomized by central banks and especially the notion of a monied and educated elite that would lead the less informed. Their

Jefferson Avenue, Detroit, circa 1850 (Burton Historical Collection, Detroit Public Library).

Michigan leaders had been those who represented the interests of the masses and those who wished to "defeat the machinations of the aristocracy of wealth centered in [Detroit's] Jefferson Avenue."[43]

The Whig Party began in Michigan in 1834 as a coalition of groups whose overarching common bond was opposition to the policies of Democratic president Andrew Jackson. So named in an attempt to call to mind recollections of the anti-monarchial party in England, the Whigs were favored by small businessmen in urban centers and the well-to-do, for they believed strongly in the power of capital markets, internal improvements financed by the Federal government, and protective tariffs. Industry, sobriety, and personal responsibility exemplified by thrift were their hallmarks. Accordingly, this group was well represented in east-central Michigan and especially in Detroit. Many of Detroit's Whigs had enjoyed the advantages of wealth and prestige back in New England or eastern New York prior to arriving in Michigan. Yet in its early years in Michigan, the Whig Party was dominated by a strong Protestant intolerance to Catholics that alienated practically every other demographic group in the state; the result being that with the exception of 1839–40, the Democratic Party maintained control in Michigan through 1854.[44]

In an attempt to stave off the growing sectionalism over the slavery issue that was dividing the country, Congress passed what was known as the Compromise of 1850, a series of legislative acts that purportedly gave the North and South some but not all of what they were seeking. By far, the most contentious part of the compromise in the North was the Fugitive Slave Act, signed into law on September 18, 1850, by President Zachary Taylor. This law declared that runaway slaves could be forcibly returned to their masters regardless of where in the country they might be found. Even former slaves who had escaped years earlier could now be arrested and sent back into bondage. The act further stipulated that blacks alleged to be runaway slaves had no right to a trial by jury and could not testify on their own behalf. Whites in the North who assisted a runaway could be fined up to $1,000. With the passage of the act, Northern abolitionists essentially found themselves now responsible for enforcing the terms of a Federal law they abhorred. The new act radicalized Michigan's anti-slavery activists, especially because of a provision that declared any person could be deputized to assist in the capture of runaway slaves.[45]

Within days of the act's passage, Southern slaveholders began filing claims in Northern courts, including Michigan. Detroit soon became a magnet not only for the oppressed seeking freedom but for the slave hunter as well. Nevertheless, according to Mrs. Elizabeth Stuart of Detroit in a letter to her daughter, Detroit appeared "very calm upon the fugitive slave bill." But that was certainly not the case in Detroit's black community. Northern free blacks had always viewed slave catchers as nothing more than kidnappers and now, in acts reminiscent of the Blackburn affair, they stepped up their vigilance, even to the point of arming themselves. Violence was narrowly averted on October 8, 1850, only weeks after the act's passage, when a black man named Giles Rose was arrested as a fugitive slave in Detroit and sent to jail for over a week to await the arrival of the evidence against him. Soon after his arrest, hundreds of armed blacks appeared in the streets and threatened to rescue the prisoner. Three volunteer companies of troops were called in to protect the peace and though no blood was shed, several rocks were hurled at the marshal's carriage. Before matters got out of hand, the slave's freedom was purchased for $500 because, according to Mrs. Stuart, "They would never allow a Runaway to go back among the plantation folks and the Master went home without the Niggar [*sic*]."[46]

The Rose matter galvanized Detroit, as the city now witnessed the true effects of the Fugitive Slave Act. On October 14, the *Detroit Advertiser* wrote, "A very deep excitement pervades this community in reference to the fugitive slave bill. Its terms and provisions meet with general reprobation by a majority of our citizens, independent of all party distinctions, and the utmost surprise is felt that any man could have been found arrogant enough to give his support to the measure, while *pretending* to represent the feelings and wishes of citizens of Michigan."[47]

Not all were against the Fugitive Slave Act, however. The Democratic and very conservative *Detroit Free Press* blasted critics by alleging that their real "hue and cry" against the act was that it multiplied the means by which runaway slaves could be recaptured, and in reality had little to do with habeas corpus and trial by jury. "It compels Marshals and their agents to do their duty," asserted the paper, "and it punishes with heavy fines those who obstruct the execution of this law for the restoration to the people of the Southern states of their property." From the *Free Press*'s perspective, slavery was constitutionally legal and therefore righteousness and morality were secondary matters "if we intend to maintain and preserve the Constitution." Despite changes in ownership, that newspaper's anti-black sentiments would continue up through and well beyond the end of the Civil War. In a portent to sentiments that would divide Detroit just over a decade later, Michigan senator Lewis Cass justified his vote in favor of the compromise by declaring, "I would have voted for twenty Fugitive Slave Laws, if I had believed the safety of the Union depended upon my doing so." Now that it was the law of the land, Cass promised that it would "never be touched, or altered, or shaken, or repealed" by any vote he might cast.[48]

Some of the act's unintended consequences seem inevitable in retrospect. Less than a month after the act went into effect, Henry R. Mizner of the U.S. Marshal's Office in Detroit was reporting how corrupt speculators were falsely warning Detroit blacks that over a hundred writs for the arrest of "fugitive slaves" had already been issued and were now in the hands of law enforcement officials. The purpose of the duplicity, according to the marshal, was so these shady opportunists could then purchase black-owned homes and other property at bargain prices, as many blacks hurriedly began relocating to Canada.[49]

In keeping with its antislavery origins, Michigan responded to the Fugitive Slave Act by enacting its own Personal Liberty Law in 1855, which made the capture of runaway slaves a state crime. Nevertheless, Michigan's antislavery initiatives had little effect in the ongoing battle for black equality. The 1850 Michigan Constitutional Convention and its subsequent popular referendum denying blacks the right to vote, while granting it to detribalized Native American Indians, left black Detroiters with little doubt as to the reality of a steady white racism.[50]

Despite Michigan's aversion to slavery in the philosophical sense, freed blacks living in the North were viewed with disdain by most native-born whites. Job competition was the main reason, for many poor and working-class white men feared that the only types of work they were suited for would be taken by the new immigrants or blacks arriving in Michigan. This "nativism" was exemplified by the new American Party, also known as the "Know-Nothing" Party, which had grown from a secret band of forty-three followers in 1852 to a national organization boasting over 1 million members only two years later. Its primary tenet was a nativist opposition to all immigrants and Catholics. Certainly Catholicism was nothing new to Detroit, with its French heritage; however, until the late 1840s that segment of the population was minimal and had been dwindling. Nevertheless, staunch conservatives in both the Whig and Democratic parties found fellow travelers in those who feared a foreign takeover of America via either immigrants or Catholic papal loyalties, not to mention civil liberties for blacks. When questioned by police about destruction of Catholic property, their infamous reply was "I know nothing," thus giving the party its moniker. The party's core assertion was that un-skilled immigrants were driving similarly unskilled, native-born Americans into poverty. Such discontent only increased with the ever-escalating influx of immigrants, which led to nativists loudly complaining of diminishing opportunities, a lowered standard of liv-ing for American workingmen and, perhaps most important, declin-ing wages as factory owners adjusted their pay scales downward to the point that they would only secure immigrant labor. This fear of unskilled "others" taking "white *American* jobs" would show itself to be a core emotion of the antiwar Detroit press in the upcoming Civil War.[51]

One Know-Nothing tract, written and published by a Detroiter in 1854, put forth all of these opinions. As an example, the tract alleged that in Cincinnati, the city government was composed of so many Catholics that it was impossible to obtain a civil judgment against a Roman Catholic in a court of law. When its author rhetorically asked how such matters stood in Detroit, he replied that "the same influ-ence is at work here under the sanction of the church of Rome and its Clergy; and the Catholic vote is considered an important consider-ation upon the day of election." Although the party's influence in Michigan never reached the level of other states, in 1855 its candi-date for Detroit mayor garnered 2,026 votes, with 2,798 against. The Know-Nothings also elected their alderman candidates in Detroit's first, second, fifth, and sixth wards, one half of the whole number.[52]

Meanwhile, Joseph Warren, the antislavery editor of the pro-Whig *Detroit Tribune*, pushed for a new coalition that would be formed "ir-respective of old party organizations, for the purpose of agreeing upon some plan of action that shall combine the whole antislavery senti-ment of the State upon one ticket." Antislavery emotions remained a strong force in Michigan, whereas Know-Nothing sentiment began to diminish.[53]

Viewing the elimination of slavery as their primary goal and plat-form, a gathering of antislavery Democrats and Whigs met outdoors in an oak grove on July 6, 1854, in Jackson, Michigan, in what would become the first formal gathering of a new political party. Over fifteen hundred men attended the creation of what became the Republican Party, so named because the party stood for personal freedom and "against the schemes of aristocracy." Moreover, the Republicans stood in opposition to the 1854 Kansas-Nebraska Act, which created the territories of Kansas and Nebraska and further allowed settlers in those territories to determine by popular vote whether they would allow slavery. The party's aim was to stop the expansion of slavery, and it soon emerged as the dominant force throughout the North.[54]

Though Michigan's Republicans may have been concerned with the spread of slavery, initially few seemed to concern themselves with the practice where it was already in place, and they were always ready to reassure their constituents that they were protectors of Northern white rights. Still, in a broader sense, as historian Eric Foner has argued, the key ideological traits of the new Republican Party were its belief in "free labor" coupled with the convictions that the North's "free society" and the South's "slave society" were wholly incompatible. The distinctive characteristic of the North's free labor society as opposed to the South's slave society was the opportunity it afforded wage earners to rise to property-owning independence.[55]

Control of Michigan's state politics also began to turn by mid-decade. For the most part, the Democrats had been in control since Michigan's territorial days, but with the advent of the Republican Party, culminating in Zachariah Chandler's election to the Senate in 1857, that monopoly was now broken.[56]

National politics had, of course, worked their way down to the state and city level. To the amazement of all, the new Republican Party successfully elected Kingsley S. Bingham to Michigan's governorship in 1854 and Jacob Howard elected attorney general. Two years later, in 1856, the Republicans took all four congressional seats and retained control of the state legislature.

In retrospect, the political decade in Detroit effectively began in 1851 with the mayoral election of Zachariah Chandler, formerly the owner of a dry goods store. Though his term in office lasted only one year, it successfully served as a launching pad for Chandler into state and then national politics. Chandler was born in 1813 in Bedford, New Hampshire, but like many New England Yankees, he had come to Michigan in 1833 to seek his fortune. He initially invested all his money into a retail storefront as a partner with his brother-in-law but decided to enter the dry goods business as a sole proprietor three years later. In the 1840s Chandler shrewdly switched from retail to

Chapter 1

Zachariah Chandler (Library of
Congress, Washington, D.C.).

wholesale, a move that would soon pay handsome dividends. With
the aid of this and other business interests, Chandler had become one
of Detroit's wealthiest citizens by the late 1850s.[57]

Originally holding Whiggish sympathies, and stridently antislavery from his earliest days, Chandler was one of the original Republicans, present at the initial "under the oaks" gathering in Jackson in
1854. Chandler, future Civil War–era senator Jacob Howard, and future Michigan "War Governor" Austin Blair were all instrumental
in the formation of Michigan's Republican Party and would play important "Radical Republican" roles in the upcoming Civil War.

It was when Chandler was serving as Detroit mayor that he first
encountered Ulysses S. Grant, then an obscure lieutenant stationed
at the Detroit Barracks. In January 1851, Grant apparently slipped on
ice on the sidewalk in front of Chandler's home, suffering a severe
sprain. For reasons unknown, Lieutenant Grant sued the mayor,
which resulted in the feisty Chandler choosing to defend himself
with a trial by jury. During the proceedings, Chandler taunted, "If
you soldiers would keep sober, perhaps you would not fall on people's
pavements and hurt your legs." Chandler lost his case and was fined

a grand total of 6¢ along with court costs of about $8. Both men apparently realized the pettiness of the matter, for neither held a grudge in the years to come. Chandler later served as secretary of the interior from 1875 to 1877 during the final years of Grant's presidency.[58]

By the middle part of the 1850s, Detroit was clearly no longer a small frontier outpost. The town was rapidly becoming an urban center with a nightlife that had developed around a lively hotel trade. With such growth came many of the social and moral problems that plagued those larger eastern cities. As early as 1841, a Common Council resolution appeared to sanction the actions of a city marshal and a "posse of helpers" who destroyed a brothel at the corner of Randolph Street and Michigan Avenue. But by the mid-1850s, such businesses were blossoming more than ever. Of particular annoyance to city leaders were the taverns, bordellos, and dance halls that were becoming prevalent in the downtown business district. Even the more desirable neighborhoods were not immune; often such establishments were right in their midst. In one such case, residents discovered that a church on Jefferson Avenue had been converted almost overnight into a dance hall. Such businesses attracted ever more drunks and rowdies, who were often found loitering on Woodbridge Avenue or frequenting the many saloons and dance halls that had sprung up on Jefferson near Beaubien Street. Such scenarios erupted into the so-called brothel riot of 1857 when German residents on Detroit's east side seeking increased residential space took to the streets to destroy several black-run "houses of ill fame." Three such houses were burned to the ground and a fourth ransacked in an act that again appeared to have the subtle sanction of the city's Common Council. These issues would become ever more problematic once the war began, when Detroit became the primary gathering point in Michigan for Union troops shipping out to either the eastern or western theaters. These new arrivals, coupled with what the city believed to be an alarming number of transients and men avoiding the war, would only add to those seeking out the type of entertainment offered by such establishments.[59]

Despite its steady growth in both population and industry throughout the first half of the 1850s, Detroit struggled in the last several years of the decade due to what became known as the financial crisis of 1857, which affected the entire country. Michigan was one of the hardest-hit states and one of the last to recover. Though financial pressures had been slowly building for months, the crisis exploded on

August 24 with the collapse of the Ohio Life and Trust Company, which was headquartered in Cincinnati and also had an agent in New York. That agent's speculations in railroad securities had led to losses greater than the company's capital and surplus. Since many New York banks were holders of drafts from Ohio Life and Trust, a rush on those banks soon followed. When depositors called for their money, the banks quickly realized that their reserves could not cover the demand. The dominoes started falling and on October 14, many of the New York banks were forced to suspend their operations.

The result was a national liquidity crisis. In Detroit, the banking system and the local economy were almost brought to their knees. Many workingmen were dismissed from their jobs and breadlines became a common scene. Detroiters witnessed the unsettling sight of children begging door to door for food and clothing. " 'They say' such dismal times were never seen as now exist in Detroit . . . the pressure for money is terrible," Elizabeth Stuart had written to her son in late May 1857. Five months later, in October, Mrs. Stuart was now informing her son how foundries and machines shops throughout Detroit had suspended their work; the result being that men, women, and even children by the hundreds were let go from their jobs. "Hunger is a tyrant," wrote Stuart and, with an eye toward Detroit's immigrant masses, she confessed, "I fear violence from this starving foreign population!" Concurrently, Orlando B. Willcox, a Detroit native, lawyer, and future colonel of the First Michigan Infantry, described how the crisis had brought about "the hardest times yet known in my life." Fortunately, the New York banks resumed operations within two months, but the consequences of their suspension was beyond remedy. By the spring of 1858, borrowing money was comparatively easy, but the demand for it was still greatly checked.[60]

The need to keep the public informed of such matters as the financial crisis, local politics, and street crime gave rise to the modern newspaper, although by the middle part of the decade journalism already had a long and varied history in Detroit. In fact, in his monumental late nineteenth-century history of Detroit, Silas Farmer noted that the town had been home to 181 unique and distinct literary properties in the form of either newspapers or magazines. Many of those early efforts simply reprinted news from Europe, but by the 1830s local politics had entered the fray. Antebellum and Civil War–era newspapers often put forth no pretense of objectivity; they existed primarily to promote one particular political party and to disparage all others. They were usually steered by one highly partisan figure who colored what news was reported to fit his party's particular viewpoint. Complimentary toward their own party's positions, these papers often editorialized correspondingly viciously against political foes. Newspaper endorsements for political office were rarely for individual candidates but rather for the entire party slate without exception. Further, these endorsements never appeared only a day or two prior to the election but were trumpeted by the papers for weeks on end as if they were a badge of honor to their particular party's ideals. Each paper saw itself as the official voice of its party and bore the solemn and important task of conveying the party's values and ideals. Thus the relationship between paper and reader was not merely one of service provider and customer; solidarity and self-identification bound readers to their preferred newspaper.[61]

Leading the way in Michigan in this style of rough-and-tumble journalism was Wilbur F. Storey, who arrived in Detroit in February 1853 as the new owner and editor of the *Detroit Free Press*. Storey was thirty-three years old when in he took over the *Free Press*, having previously run the *Jackson Patriot* in Jackson, Michigan. The *Free Press* could trace its beginnings back to 1831, but by the time the paper was sold to Storey for $3,000, it had been floundering for years. The new editor promised readers that the *Free Press* would be "radically and thoroughly *democratic*" and in short order, Storey and his *Free Press* became the official voice of Democrats in the Midwest.[62]

According to William Quinby, onetime employee of Storey and future editor in chief of the *Free Press*, Storey was "stern and silent, often times morose, and very reticent of speech, working sometimes for weeks alongside of his staff with scarcely a word spoken." He was extremely detail oriented; the appearance of the paper, credits, punctuation, capitalization, all had to be just so. In essence, wrote Quinby, Storey was as "inflexible as the laws of the Medes and Persians, unchangeable." Nevertheless, he relied on his staff members' knowledge of his requirements to carry out their tasks properly. As long as things went smoothly, Storey was satisfied and therefore silent. On the other hand, if a long-tenured employee made even a minor error, Storey verbally censured the man no less than if he had been a newcomer who routinely committed mistakes. "Gratitude with him was a lively sense of favors yet to come," recalled Quinby.[63]

Storey's attachment to Democratic Party values and ideas was comparable to that of a religious zealot, and he did not confine himself

Wilbur F. Storey (Frederick Francis Cook, *Bygone Days in Chicago* [Chicago: A. C. McClurg, 1910], 332).

to merely political issues. Like most, if not virtually all, whites of his era, Storey was a committed racist who viewed blacks with contempt and believed white dominance of them was Darwinian natural selection. "No more worthless, vagabond, lazy, good-for-nothing set of mortals can be found than the negro population of the northern states," wrote Storey only one day prior to the bombardment of Fort Sumter. This typical outburst was in regard to a large group of blacks that had recently fled Chicago in two cattle cars in an attempt to reach freedom in Canada. Storey's rampant hatred of blacks cannot be overstated, and it made the *Free Press* the most "Negrophobic" sheet in the Middle West throughout the 1850s. Anti-black commentary was almost a daily occurrence within Storey's newspaper. Furthermore, any race other than Caucasian was also deemed inferior. He considered the Chinese then living in California to be "corrupt" and "thieving," while the "Hispanic-American" races living in Latin America came in for similar treatment. According to Lincoln biographer Carl Sandburg, "Storey cultivated suspicion as a habit, looked men over with a cold glitter of eye, boasted he had no friends, and seemed to count that day lost which brought him no added haters." Anyone of any age or gender who disagreed with his views was worthy only of contempt and derision, and Storey dealt both out liberally in scathing, sarcastic language.[64]

Storey showed little mercy even to Michigan Democrats when they disagreed with him. Though he always argued for a "civil tongue and courteous language," Storey showed no hesitation in attempting to expose as immoral or unworthy any Michigan Democratic paper that dared question *Free Press* editorial policy. These "whelping dogs," as Storey called them, were continually frustrated by the fact that outside Michigan, the *Free Press* was often quoted as representing the true feelings of the state Democratic Party, "whereas at home it is well known to speak only the views of W. F. Storey and Co., (a very small company at that)."[65]

Countering Storey in Detroit during the 1850s were the *Detroit Tribune* and the *Daily Advertiser*, Whig-turned-Republican papers that jousted and flung mud with the *Free Press* on a daily basis. The *Advertiser* traced its roots back to 1836, when it had been founded by George Whitney. Over the years it absorbed a number of smaller publications before becoming the town's preeminent anti-Democrat daily during the decade's early years. The *Detroit Tribune* was an evening paper that espoused the Whig line and had been established in October 1849 under the management of Henry Barns. The editor was Joseph Warren, who had come to Detroit from New York, and it was said Warren could never understand how an all-wise God could allow a Democrat to live. He was "a stern, solemn man, genial in his family, lovable to his friends, but caustic in the last degree to Democrats, to whom he applied the names 'loco-foco's' or 'dough-faces.'"[66]

As the decade wound down, the slavery question was becoming more and more of a contentious issue across the entire nation. With Michigan one of the foremost antislavery states, it was only natural that it would attract the nation's leading abolitionist speakers. Certainly included in that group was Frederick Douglass, the famous black abolitionist, who arrived in Detroit on March 12, 1859, for a speaking engagement. In the crowd that day was John Brown, the fiery abolitionist from Oberlin, Ohio. Brown had arrived in Detroit a few days earlier with fourteen liberated slaves bound for freedom in Canada and five of his own men. He had been a key player in the proslavery troubles in Kansas, where his band had killed five proslavery men with broadswords. Brown had then been driven from his Kansas home after two of his sons were killed by proslavery mobs. Following

Austin Blair (Library of Congress, Washington, D.C.).

Douglass's talk, Brown, Douglass, and several well-known leaders of Detroit's black community met at the home of William Webb at 185 East Congress Street, near St. Antoine, where Brown revealed his Harpers Ferry plan to the gathering. Douglass deemed the plan too risky and urged Brown to forego it. Brown purportedly lost his temper and then implied that Douglass might be guilty of cowardice, though Douglass later denied that such acrimony occurred. Others in the gathering dismissed the plan as well but only because they felt it did not go far enough. Their proposition was to destroy many churches in the South on a Sunday so that all slavery proponents could arrive in hell at the same time. Brown left Detroit without the support he was looking for. His destiny awaited him five months later at the sleepy town of Harpers Ferry in western Virginia.[67]

With the slavery issue at the forefront, Detroit and Michigan viewed the presidential election of 1860 with as much fervor as the rest of the nation. On May 18, the Republican Party nominated Abraham Lincoln as its presidential candidate on the third ballot at its national convention in Chicago. With the die cast and despite initially supporting New York's William Seward, Michigan's delegation, led by Austin Blair, now threw its full support to Lincoln. According to Blair, Michigan would now "marshal behind [Lincoln] in the grand column which shall go out to battle for Abraham Lincoln of Illinois."[68]

Three weeks later, on June 7, Republicans meeting at Detroit's Merrill Hall nominated Austin Blair as the gubernatorial candidate. Blair hailed from Jackson and had been one of the party's original founders. Later that month, Democrats nominated Stephen Douglas at their national convention in Baltimore. Within days state Democrats met in Detroit to nominate three-term governor John Barry of Constantine to be their state standard-bearer.[69]

On the all-important slavery issue, the Republican Party vigorously opposed any efforts that would allow slavery in the new territories. Yet despite their antislavery stance, most midwestern Republicans remained firmly against social equality for blacks. This deft combination of the lofty morality of the Declaration of Independence that all men were created equal coupled with a devotion to white racial supremacy led to sweeping Republican victories in the 1860 elections. In Michigan, Lincoln captured over 57 percent of the vote. Democrats lost even Wayne County, managing to carry only seven counties in the northern end of the state.[70]

The new decade was almost a year old, and the still-young nation was heading into stormy seas. The future of slavery was its most contentious issue, especially among the country's native-born population. Primarily because of the slavery question, South Carolina seceded from the Union on December 20, 1860, with more Southern states likely to follow. Meanwhile, immigrants from all countries in Europe were still arriving at America's Atlantic docks on a daily basis. These were people who desired to build a new life for themselves and their families and generally cared little about the plight of the African slave. Concurrently, many native-born white Americans looked down their noses at the new Irish immigrants, viewing them as a beastly lot and hardly the social, cultural, or moral equal of "true" Americans. This cauldron of resentment against racial and ethnic "others" would fully manifest itself during the Civil War in Detroit as well as elsewhere.

"Truly an old fashioned 4th of July scene"

A City, State, and Nation Initially United for Union

O n January 1, 1861, forty-two-year-old Austin Blair became the new governor of Michigan. Blair was a loyal, antislavery Republican whose political roots traced back to the Whigs. A lawyer by training, Blair had been elected to the Michigan House of Representatives in 1846. When the Republican Party was "born" in Jackson, Michigan, in 1854, Blair had been there and switched his allegiance at that time. Like the president-elect, Abraham Lincoln, Blair had been born in a log cabin, had pulled himself up by his bootstraps to become a self-made man, and was also a fine public speaker. Both men had also served in Congress and placed a high premium on honesty and integrity. Blair's intense aversion to slavery prompted him to hold a more favorable view of the growing "Radical Republican" movement than Lincoln, however. An intense and fervent nationalism moved him to identify with congressional leaders who held a disdainful position toward the South. For Blair and the Radicals, secession was treason and could not be tolerated under any circumstances.[1]

On this matter of secession, Blair was in lockstep with his predecessor, Republican Moses Wisner. In his farewell address, Wisner asserted, "Michigan cannot recognize the right of a State to secede from this Union. We believe that the founders of our Government designed it to be perpetual, and we cannot consent to have one star obliterated from our flag. For upwards of thirty years this question of the right of a State to secede has been agitated. It is time it was settled." Invigorated by such rhetoric as well as its own amor patriae, Michigan's legislature acted quickly and forcefully, issuing a resolution on February 2, 1861, declaring its devotion and loyalty to the U.S. government. In addition to such patriotic piety, the state pledged all the material and military resources it could muster while declaring that concession or conciliation would never be offered to traitors. Michigan's allegiance and willingness to stamp out what it saw as treason were in no doubt.[2]

In Detroit, however, Wilbur Storey was outraged at what he viewed as the headlong rush to war. The same day that Blair was sworn in, Storey's *Free Press* lamented, "Revolution is now a fact. It is no longer in the distance—the phantasy of diseased imagination." As with most social or political problems, Storey blamed the Republicans, accusing them of refusing to sacrifice anything for the salvation of the country. Fuming with self-righteous anger, on January 26, 1861, he wrote what would be his most memorable line: "If troops shall be raised in the North to march against the people of the South, *a fire in the rear will be opened upon such troops.*" Taking aim at his Republican enemies, Storey warned that if they persisted on their war footing, the conflict they were precipitating "would not be with the South, *but with tens of thousands of people in the North.* When civil war shall come, it shall be a war here in Michigan and here in Detroit, and in every Northern state." Though perhaps just another instance of the editor's hyperbole at the time, Storey's threat would in due course be used by critics of the Democratic Party as proof positive of that party's treasonous leanings.[3]

Despite Wilbur Storey, war commenced on April 12, 1861, when Rebel shore batteries in Charleston, South Carolina, opened fire upon Union-held Fort Sumter in that city's harbor. Just over twenty-four hours later, Union commander Major Robert Anderson was forced to run up the white flag inside Sumter. The Civil War had begun.

President Abraham Lincoln responded on the fifteenth by issuing a call for seventy-five thousand volunteers to serve ninety days, the maximum then allowed by the Militia Act of 1795, which was still in effect. It also reflected the belief of most of the country that the war would be a short one, certainly no more than three months. In fact, many believed that one great battle would settle things. To a large degree, Lincoln had no choice but to call on the states, for he had virtually no national army. The regular army numbered no more than twenty-five thousand men and most of those were at distant posts in the Far West. News of the Fort Sumter surrender as well as Lincoln's call had quickly reached Detroit, prompting meetings all over town in public halls and churches. From one end of Detroit to the other, public oaths to "stand by the government to the last" were pledged while Southern treason was condemned.[4]

Those who felt otherwise were in the minority and generally kept their fears to themselves or confided only to loved ones. Included in this group was Henry Billings Brown, then a twenty-five-year-old Detroit attorney who in later life would become a U.S. Supreme Court justice. With clear foresight, Brown glumly predicted in his diary that the nation was at the "beginning of a long war; a war of which no man can see the end." Sixty-eight-year-old Mrs. Elizabeth E. Stuart of Detroit informed her son in a letter just after Fort Sumter that news of the war's commencement "had caused sorrow apparently to every heart, and *all* seemed filled with consternation." Meanwhile, Robert McClelland, Democratic Michigan governor from 1851 to 1853, wrote to his daughter from his home in Detroit that he feared for his country, counseling, "The less you say about it the better." Nevertheless, secession could not be tolerated, wrote McClelland, even though he felt the South had been constitutionally wronged over the slavery issue.[5]

On Tuesday, April 16, one day after Lincoln's call for volunteers, Governor Austin Blair arrived in Detroit to hold a planning conference with the military officers of the state and leading citizens of Detroit and other parts of Michigan. Meeting at the grand Michigan Exchange Hotel, which was located at the southwest corner of Jefferson Avenue and Shelby Street, Blair announced that Michigan had been given a quota of one regiment (generally 750–1,000 men), which was to be fully outfitted with all necessary uniforms, armaments, and equipment. Unfortunately for the state, Blair also made it clear that Michigan's state treasury was virtually empty due to theft. To make matters worse, the legislature was not in session so the issue could not even be addressed. With the state coffers in such a condition, other means of gathering the money would have to be devised.[6]

The conference members calculated that $100,000 would be immediately needed to properly organize and equip the regiment. Given the fiscal realities, John Owen, the state treasurer, helped pass a resolution pledging that the city of Detroit would loan the state $50,000, and the citizenry throughout Michigan would give an identical amount. To get matters started, a subscription paper was circulated among those present, which immediately raised $23,000. Committees were created to solicit further subscriptions in Detroit

Henry Billings Brown (Library of
Congress, Washington, D.C.).

and to aid Blair in his undertaking. Amid all the war euphoria, that
initial $23,000 subscription quickly rose to $81,000, which was sufficient to allow the state to begin recruiting what would soon become
the First Michigan Volunteer Infantry. That same day, Blair issued a
public call for ten volunteer militia companies, instructing the state's
adjutant general to accept the first ten to step forward. According to
Blair's proclamation, each company was to be composed of one captain, one first lieutenant, one second lieutenant, four sergeants, four
corporals, two musicians, and sixty-five privates.[7]

Meanwhile, Detroit's twenty-member Common Council also got
involved by passing a resolution denouncing the rebellious acts and
pledging loyalty to the Federal government in Washington. Within
a week, the council set aside in the budget a fund of $20,000 to help
support the families of men who had or were about to enlist in the
Union army. This gesture was in addition to the "Soldiers Relief
Law," passed by the Michigan state legislature in early May, which
was to provide financial aid to soldiers' families in need, up to a
maximum of $15 per month. Considering that the average annual
wage in 1860 for working-class men was approximately $300 per

year, $15 per month only covered 60 percent of that family income, at best.[8]

Despite the boisterous public proclamations and rampant chest thumping, the hard truth was that Michigan's state forces were wholly unprepared for armed conflict. In fact, this was the case in most Northern states. The state militia had been woefully neglected and therefore looked down on because of that very neglect. For years, the national Constitution's belief that "a well-regulated militia is necessary to the security of a free State" had gone totally unheeded in most of the North, as the typical congressman believed in the years prior to the Civil War that his state had very little real use for a standing militia.[9]

At the start of the war, Michigan's military establishment consisted of twenty-eight militia companies totaling 1,241 officers and men. They were generally poorly equipped with antiquated weaponry and, according to John Robertson, Michigan's adjutant general during the Civil War, were looked upon as "a burlesque of the military profession" rather than an efficient and essential part of state government. In the years leading up to the war, the state's total financial commitment to all these companies was a mere $3,000. "At that time the company got nothing from the State," remarked one militia veteran regarding the years just before the Civil War. "They had to pay for all they got; uniforms and all would have to be paid for by the company. I found the men to be all gentlemen of wealth and prominence, who had joined the company just for the pleasure they would derive by being a soldier." And it was from units such as these that the nucleus of Michigan's first regiments would spring forth.[10]

Despite the sorry martial state that Michigan was in when the war started, by the end of 1861 Michigan's clothing factories had turned out over ten thousand sets of what constituted a full uniform: a cap, two pairs of cotton drawers, two pairs of socks, two pairs of flannel shirts, shoes, trousers, field jacket, and heavy overcoat. Most of these uniforms had been sewn in Detroit through an attempt to employ dozens of poorer women. When it proved impossible for some regiments to purchase adequate quantities of undergarments, the state took it upon itself to provide the necessary cloth directly to Detroit's society ladies, who began sewing them at no charge. Moreover, these industrious women also sewed the linings of the men's blankets as well as a large number of bed sacks and haversacks.[11]

If Michigan and the North were insufficiently prepared, the South, on the other hand, had taken a few preparatory measures, including picking Detroit's military pocket. Much of its war material had been shipped from Northern arsenals to the South. For instance, at the Dearborn Arsenal, eight miles west of Detroit, a few boxes of guns were auctioned off at $1 apiece in the summer of 1860 and the balance sold for a small sum to some mysterious stranger, who was an agent for a Southern state.[12]

For the most part, the burgeoning Michigan militia companies were comprised of young men from all professions and trades, often representing what was considered the "most respectable" elements of society. Perhaps the best known of these militia companies was the Detroit Light Guard, which could trace its roots back to 1836. On April 17, the day after Governor Blair's arrival, the Detroit Light Guard held a meeting at the Detroit armory to consider the governor's proclamation calling for a regiment of volunteers in accordance with the requisition of the president. There was never any doubt as to the outcome. A resolution was passed tendering the Guard's service into the new regiment called for by Blair. Recruits came in by the hundreds, and many were so anxious to enlist with the famed Light Guard that bribe money was liberally offered for the honor and privilege.[13]

Detroit awoke on April 18, 1861, to see Old Glory flying from virtually every building. A Light Guard member recalled, "Omnibus men decorated their vehicles and horses with it; draymen and wagoners exhibited a similar partiality for it; shops, stores, offices, public halls and all like places were festooned with it. Those who did not have a flag were eagerly inquiring for one." In short order, Detroit began to take on quite a military appearance. The city had been a military post for years, and the regular army officers stationed there helped to give practical direction to what was necessary. Martial music was heard almost around the clock, and speeches by prominent citizens were a constant. On April 24, an elderly Lewis Cass rose to assure Detroit that all loyal Americans could and most surely would defend the national flag. Further, Cass asserted, to thunderous applause, there was no middle ground in this fight: "He who is not for his country is against her. There is no neutral position to be occupied." Still, all this red, white, and blue was disturbing to some; a prelude to the tensions that would grip Detroit within two years.

Taking the oath of allegiance in front of Detroit's U.S. Post Office, northwest corner of Griswold and Larned, April 20, 1861 (Burton Historical Collection, Detroit Public Library).

One Detroiter facetiously remarked that the entire city seemed to be suffering from a severe case of Star-Spangled Banner on the brain. In truth, the sheer intensity of such displays was just a bit disconcerting to Wilbur Storey of the *Detroit Free Press;* while reluctantly supporting the war as necessary to defend Union and Constitution, Storey felt that the blame for the war could be laid entirely at the feet of politicians both Northern and Southern, and that the blood lust it engendered among the people was dangerous. "We are a great people," the paper acknowledged, but then chastised Detroit for the current war fever: "Just now we are boiling over with patriotism and enthusiastic admiration of red, white and blue bunting, and clamorous for a fight. If Jeff. Davis or somebody else don't put their dirty fingers on our stars and stripes once more pretty soon, we'll really become frantic. We must fight. We don't know exactly what we want to fight for, but fight we must and will." From almost day one, the *Free Press* was urging peace. "We have had and are having war meetings. Let us have Peace Meetings and the first one may just as well be held here in Detroit as anywhere else."[14]

In the meantime, groups of soldiers were constantly seen marching along the streets going to their respective armories, which had quickly become favorite gathering spots for Detroiters who wished to watch the companies perform their drills. Many businessmen were eager to contribute to the needs of Michigan's first regiment. Two men in the steel fabrication business offered to furnish the government with one ton of grapeshot, fully packaged and delivered free of charge to any dock in the city "for the express purpose of dealing death to all traitors." Concurrently, the Western Transportation Company offered free transportation for the Michigan troops from Detroit to Buffalo.[15]

So great was the response to Blair's call for one regiment that in less than a week, the ten companies designated to become the First Michigan Infantry were raised. The Detroit Light Guard and the Michigan Hussars hailed from Detroit while the other eight companies were recruited in various southern Michigan towns. In command of the new three-month regiment was thirty-eight-year-old Orlando Bolivar Willcox. A native Detroiter and loyal Democrat, Willcox had graduated from West Point in 1847 and then spent the next ten years serving at points in Mexico and throughout the United States. He resigned his lieutenant's commission in 1857 to begin a law practice in Detroit and to, he hoped, advance his secondary career as an author, having previously penned two forgettable novels under the pseudonym of "Walter March." Ultimately unhappy with the way his civilian life had progressed, Willcox eagerly accepted the colonelcy of the new regiment when it was offered to him in April 1861. Yet he, as a veteran military man, knew the conflict would not be a sixty or ninety days' affair as was naively believed by so many others. "Having been intimate with army officers from the South, and stationed long at Southern posts, I knew the earnestness of the Southern people," he later wrote, "and deprecated the anti-slavery agitation and the bitterly uncompromising spirit exhibited on both sides." Willcox was not alone in his realization of what the future held. Other Michigan men, including Governor Austin Blair, knew what lay ahead. "This is to be no six weeks' campaign," Blair predicted solemnly in an address to his legislature. "I do not underestimate the gallantry of Southern men, and they will find it a grave error that they have underestimated ours."[16]

By the end of April, all the men who were destined to serve in the First Infantry had arrived in town after being given fond farewells in their hometowns. Those eight companies formed around the state had been filled every bit as quickly as those in Detroit. William Randall of Ypsilanti recalled the long send-off given to him and several others at that town's Baptist church: "We listened with intense interest to several patriotic speeches which strengthened our hearts for the work before us." At the University of Michigan in Ann Arbor, freshman William Moore left his studies and raced off to grab a last-minute opening in the company being formed in Adrian. When asked by his roommate that night what position he had secured, Moore gleefully proclaimed he was to be a "high private in the rear rank." With all men present, the First Michigan Volunteer Infantry was officially mustered in on May 1 at Detroit's Fort Wayne which, at the start of the Civil War, "commanded a full view of [Detroit] and of both shores as far down as Wyandotte," according to one soldier. Now, with war under way and trained men desperately needed, it would serve as Michigan's primary point for mustering and drilling new recruits.[17]

War fever had hit Detroit, and for the next two weeks at least, watching the First Michigan conduct nine hours of daily drills at Fort Wayne was quite an attraction for the town's citizens, who flocked there continually to watch the new regiment practice its martial skills. Many visitors arrived with the purpose of seeing their soldier friends in the regiment and to bring them reading matter and home-cooked food, which was certainly welcomed more than what was provided by the government. The new recruits were well aware of their audience, and their enthusiasm for impressing Detroit's residents, especially the young ladies, was limitless. After the evening's final parade, all the men would gather around the flagpole and sing

"The Star-Spangled Banner," which signaled the end of another day.[18]

It was not all spit and polish, of course, which was to be expected with a large group of young men away from home for the first time in their lives. Upon his arrival at Fort Wayne, twenty-seven-year-old law clerk Charles Haydon of Kalamazoo quickly determined that "camp life is not much different from what I expected. Card playing, profanity & the stealing of provisions are the most noted characteristics outside of the duties." Another new recruit later explained how he was ordered to Fort Wayne's brig "on account of an over-indulgence of Detroit river water mixed with bourbon. . . . I was taught my first lesson in sleeping on a rock, and had for the first time in my life, a man to walk backwards and forwards before my airy room, with a gun with a spike on the end of it." In fact, so many young men confined together often resulted in a Darwinian self-interest taking hold and what one volunteer bemoaned as the loss of all good manners and graces, "especially where there was none of the opposite sex. This learned me at once how indispensable [are] women to the happiness and refinement of men." Then there were the "bold and reckless" young men who took it upon themselves to escape the cramped quarters and monotony of day-after-day drilling by taking what was described as an unauthorized "French leave of absence" into Detroit. To successfully get back into Fort Wayne, these men attached a long rail to some type of slab, which they would then use to scale the fort's walls at night. Few were apparently ever caught.[19]

Leading the clarion call for Michigan interests in the halls of Congress was forty-seven-year-old U.S. senator Zachariah Chandler, the onetime Detroit mayor and leading citizen. Only five days after the shelling of Fort Sumter, Chandler had boldly informed Secretary of War Simon Cameron, "There is but one sentiment here. We will furnish you with the regiments in thirty days if you want them, and 50,000 men if you need them. . . . There are no [Rebel] sympathizers here worth hunting, and if there were, our population would diminish to the extent of their numbers forthwith." Chandler would quickly show himself to be an aggressive supporter of a harsh prosecution of the war and a leader of what would become known as the Radical Republicans. Only two months before the firing on Sumter, Chandler had exhibited his hard-nosed tendencies by urging Governor Blair to send "stiff-backed" delegates to the ill-fated Washington Peace Conference. Almost as an afterthought, Chandler noted in that letter how some of the Northern states feared the prospect of war, but from his vantage, "Without a little blood-letting, this Union will not, in my estimation, be worth a rush." In the halcyon days of April and May 1861, Chandler and his colleagues were convinced the war would be a short one once the Union army marched into Confederate-held territory. Eager for the "blood-letting" to commence, he informed Lincoln on June 15, "The people of Michigan think the time has arrived to commence hanging & so think I."[20]

Not all the people of Michigan were happy, however. Buried in the papers were reports of dissatisfaction among some of Detroit's ethnic Germans, who felt that their offer of war service had been all but ignored. Further, they noted that not one German officer or company had been selected for the First Infantry. "They are deeply incensed and do not keep the fact a secret," reported the *Free Press*, opining that some German companies' Democratic leanings may have played a part in the decision.[21]

On May 11, a major ceremony was held at Detroit's Campus Martius, where the regiment was presented with its regimental colors, which had been designed and sewn by the ladies of Detroit. With the conclusion of that ritual, the First Michigan's departure for Washington was now imminent, which elevated the military zeal in Detroit almost to the point of religious fervor. Indeed, the martial and spiritual were already crossing paths, based on the political sermons that were being preached from pulpits all across Detroit. For instance, the day after receiving its regimental flag, Company A of the First Michigan attended services at Christ Church, presided over by Benjamin H. Paddock. There the soldiers heard the rector remind them that they had a righteous duty in the field while those left behind had duties on the home front. Rector Paddock also made clear why they were fighting: "The cause in defense of which every heart throughout this portion of the land is stirred to its very depths, is *the Salvation of our Country*." To help advance the cause of Union, Paddock reminded his congregation, "A lofty patriotism is a Christian virtue." No words were spoken about the plight of the black slave, despite the regional differences on the slavery issue that had helped ignite the conflict. Paddock proclaimed, "[Secession] is suicidal if it be permitted to go unrebuked." For Paddock, the supreme issue at hand was the reunification of the country. Continuing, he asserted, "The calm folding of the hands over the claims and doings of the last three months on the part of certain of our brethren, would be the offering

The First Michigan Infantry receiving its colors at Detroit's Campus Martius (Burton Historical Collection, Detroit Public Library).

a premium to revolution, honors and riches to disintegration, and, as with the hand of the entire nation, signing the death warrant of this and every possible future Republic."[22]

The next day, May 13, the regiment was off to Washington, first traveling by boat to Cleveland and then continuing by train for the remainder of the trip. When the First Michigan arrived in Washington on May 16, Senator Zachariah Chandler was there to meet it.

Upon learning that the First Michigan was purportedly the first western regiment to arrive in Washington, President Lincoln is said to have remarked, "Thank God for Michigan!"[23]

Other regiments were now quickly forming as well. The Second Michigan Infantry had been authorized only days after the First, allowing many of the men and even companies who had not been able to get into the First Infantry to now join the Second. One of these was the Kalamazoo Light Guards, which arrived at Detroit near sundown on April 30.[24]

War fever clearly still reigned in Detroit, judging by the pageantry and sense of public pride that greeted the Second Infantry. On Thursday afternoon, June 6, the Second Michigan Volunteers departed for Washington after marching around the city in a dress-parade fashion for close to three hours with full backpacks. "It was perhaps a good show for others but it was rather tough on us," complained the Second's Charles Haydon in his diary. Young women appeared at numerous windows waving flags and even firing revolvers in the air to cheer the men on as they headed toward the waiting steamboats. Other regiments soon followed suit, yet regardless of where the regiment was recruited, a stop at Fort Wayne for an extended period of military instruction before shipping out to the theater of war was often the norm.[25]

As Detroit's first regiments were leaving town, so too was its most acerbic newspaper publisher. Detroit newspaper readers awoke on June 5, 1861, to learn that Wilbur F. Storey had sold his beloved *Detroit Free Press* to Henry N. Walker. In most ways, the reader would see little change, for Walker had promised, like Storey, to keep the paper "thoroughly democratic." He would indeed. Walker was a man of some means, and he, along with twenty-five-year-old William Quinby as lead editor, ensured that the *Free Press* would remain throughout the Civil War every bit as anti-Republican and anti-black as it had been under Storey. Meanwhile, Wilbur Storey was headed to Chicago to take over as the new owner of the *Chicago Times*. Over the next four years, Storey turned that newspaper into the most fierce anti-Lincoln paper in the "Old Northwest."[26]

A month and a half later, on July 21, the first great battle of the war was fought, about twenty-three miles west of Washington, D.C., on the plains of Manassas, Virginia, near a small stream known as Bull Run. For several days prior, Union troops had streamed from Washington into Virginia for what many thought would be the first

and last great battle of the war. Numerous prominent civilians concurred, which prompted many to take their horse and buggies, laden
with picnic baskets, out to the fields to watch the spectacle. Though
the Union seemed to have the upper hand in the early part of the
battle, just-arriving Confederate reinforcements turned the tide later
in the day and ended up routing the Northern forces off the field.
Both soldiers and civilians were soon in full flight back to Washington, leaving the field to the victorious Confederates. The stinging
defeat made headlines all across the North. In Detroit, Elizabeth
Stuart wrote, "All faces seem sad, for most all are indirectly connected with many of the wounded and dead." Detroiters soon learned
that the First Michigan Infantry had performed gallantly, though it
suffered a grievous loss in the capture of Colonel Orlando Willcox,
taken prisoner by the Confederates after he fell wounded on the field.
Willcox spent the next year as a prisoner of war, first at Castle Pinck-
ney in Charleston harbor, then in Columbia, South Carolina, and
last at Libby Prison in Richmond. Unlike their colonel, the men of
the First Michigan were on their way back to Detroit in less than ten
days, their ninety-day enlistment over.[27]

The First Michigan Infantry's return home to Detroit on Friday,
August 2 prompted a boisterous celebration of martial glory and patriotism. Most stores were closed and red, white, and blue was everywhere. In a letter to her son, Mrs. Elizabeth E. Stuart reported that
the city "was truly an old fashioned 4th of July scene. The shops were
partially closed, the city decorated with flags on every building, out
of windows, from sidewalk to sidewalk, large placards met the eye
everywhere on which was written 'Welcome Home to our brave Soldiers of the First, We bitterly mourn for our gallant ones, left behind.'" The First Michigan Infantry had landed at the foot of Brush
Street, and then marched down Jefferson Avenue to the Central
Depot, with the sick and wounded following in carriages. One of the
sick was Private George Farr, a farmhand from southern Michigan.
Like many young soldiers who had been encamped with large groups
of men for the first time in his life, Farr had become quite ill and now
lay prostrate in his carriage, nearly deaf, blind, and unconscious after
contracting the measles. "I have a dim recollection of hearing the
cannon boom as we came into Detroit," Farr later recalled. Over the
next four years, twice as many men would die from illness or disease
as from battle wounds. Once at the depot, the First was greeted with
endless cheers, ringing church bells, the blasts of cannon, and

Address by Lewis Cass at the Detroit & Milwaukee railroad depot upon return of the ninety days' men (Burton Historical Collection, Detroit Public Library).

speeches. Table after table was brimming with home-cooked food for the returning warriors.[28]

The Union disaster at Bull Run served as a wakeup call to many in the North that Southerners could indeed fight and that the war was not going to be the glorious, relatively bloodless event many had envisioned. Just like the weather, the initial public outpouring of support for war began to cool as the summer of 1861 faded into fall. The early thoughts of a ninety-day war had become a distant memory as the true severity of the rebellion began to come into focus. The result was that the early bipartisanship among Republicans and Democrats was starting to fracture, and citizens, the press, and politicians alike expressed dissatisfaction. In a letter to a confidant from his home in Detroit, Senator Zachariah Chandler wrote, "We have had an awful load to carry." Fearing that the Union lacked vigor for aggressively prosecuting the war, the senator complained, "Lincoln means well but has no force of character. He is surrounded by old fogy Army officers more than one half of whom are downright traitors and one half of the other half sympathize with the South."[29]

On Detroit's streets, Mrs. Elizabeth Stuart was certainly noticing grumbling among some Detroiters by the fall. She reported that most of these unhappy townsfolk had relatives who were living in the South and were obviously worried and frustrated that they could not find out if their families were safe or not. "Indeed, some of our own North men," she wrote, "are filled with bitterness to the Government, and have gone so far as to express their opinion in favor of Southern men, Southern Measures, and Southern Institutions."[30]

Though most Michiganders supported the government's efforts, many families were becoming a bit more hesitant about their seeing relatives enlist, especially when the personal costs to families became more apparent. "You know I told you last spring you had better give up the idea," Isaac Beers reminded his brother, who had a young family to look after. Still, Beers assured his sibling, "If I had no children to depend upon me for a living and education I should volunteer to fight for the Stars and Stripes." This reluctance to enlist was especially prevalent among farmers, who had the most to lose financially if they were not at home to work their fields during the fall harvest or spring planting seasons. Laborers or employees would have had less to lose. Such wavering also was apparent in some who had already enlisted; fervent at first, they had developed a case of cold feet by the time they arrived at Fort Wayne in mid-September. With the monotony of daily drill and military life sinking in, some enlisted men abandoned their posts and fled to Canada, the first of what became known as "skedaddlers." "They [military authorities] followed after them but [the Canadians] would not give them up," reported Private Soloman Kroll to his parents, knowing that the British government in Canada would not extradite haven seekers back to either side. "All they had to do was cross the river and they was in Canady."[31]

On January 2, 1862, Governor Austin Blair delivered his New Year message to the Michigan legislature, then meeting in an extra session. Blair was certainly a war hawk who, like other Radical Republicans, urged a vigorous and immediate prosecution of the war. At that time, it was accepted without question that he was speaking for the Michigan people. In his remarks, Blair stressed that Michigan's citizens and soldiers were "no idle spectators of this great contest. They have furnished all the troops required of them, and are preparing to pay the taxes and to submit to the most onerous burdens without a murmur." Yet he was frustrated with the lack of progress and what he saw as the gentle "kid glove" manner with which Rebel citizens were being treated. "The loyal States having furnished adequate means, both of men and money, to crush the rebellion," argued Blair, they "have a right to expect those men to be used with the utmost vigor to accomplish the object, and that without any mawkish sympathy for the interest of traitors in arms." As for Confederate citizens, "Upon those who caused the war, and now maintain it, its chief burdens ought to fall. No property of a rebel ought to be free from confiscation—not even the sacred slave. The object of war is to destroy the power of the enemy, and whatever measures are calculated to accomplish that object, and are in accordance with the usages of civilized nations, ought to be employed."[32]

Though Blair's speech focused on Michigan's place in the war, Detroit's outgoing Republican mayor, Christian H. Buhl, and its Common Council offered barely a mention of the ongoing conflict. In his 1862 New Year address to the council, Buhl spoke of what he considered to be the city's fine advancement in its schools, fire department, public parks, and roads. Detroit's finances also appeared to be in respectable shape, despite the city's need to create a new office and system for the collection of city taxes. As for the war, Buhl's only remark was that "good order and obedience to law have generally prevailed; the people have been loyal and cheerfully offered themselves and their means for the support of our beloved country in this unhappy war in which she is engaged." Buhl was the last Republican mayor in Detroit for some time. For the remainder of the Civil War and even up through 1871, the mayor's chair in Detroit would be occupied by Democrats.[33]

Despite some growing doubts among Democratic citizens and press about the viability or legitimacy of the war, Michigan's Republican-controlled state government was in lockstep with the Lincoln administration. The same could not be said for much of Detroit's populace, despite the fact that it had sent Republican Zachariah Chandler to the Senate. At the start of the war, almost half of Detroit's population was foreign born, mostly Irish and German. Furthermore, most of these immigrants were poor and Catholic, with little use for the abolition, temperance, or nativistic sentiments then popular with much of the native-born, Republican-leaning, Protestant population.[34]

❀ ❀ ❀

THE call for more men coupled with Detroit's preeminence as the state's training center for the burgeoning Michigan regiments required the city to build several more training camps, for Fort Wayne was soon at its maximum capacity. In addition, more military supply space was needed as the town had quickly become the primary rendezvous point for the immense quantity of supplies and food raised in Michigan's smaller towns that was necessary to care for Michigan's men in blue.

One of the first new camps built was Camp Lyon, which was operational by late August 1861 and quickly became home for over eleven hundred men of what was fast becoming the First Michigan Cavalry. The camp had been built near the Detroit River three miles east of downtown Detroit upon an old horseracing track in what was then known as Hamtramck Township which, according to the press, was "a most beautiful place" that had been originally settled by German farmers. The camp's namesake was General Nathaniel Lyon, who had lost his life on August 10, 1861, at the battle of Wilson's Creek, Missouri.[35]

Camp Lyon was a beehive of activity as the heat of August passed into the cool of September. A ten-foot-high, white-washed plank wall had been built around the mile-long oval track, which provided ample space for cavalry drills and maneuvers. Reporters visiting the training grounds observed that the camp "is at present a busy place, everywhere are seen soldiers drilling or lazily lounging, pitching quoits, reading or smoking. Officers in small knots discuss the various rumors of the war that reach them from the city." Two weeks later, additional barracks were still being constructed to house the arriving recruits.[36]

For young farm lads who had grown up with good home cooking, the food at Detroit's training camps seemed to be the biggest and certainly the most unpleasant surprise. One young cavalry recruit at Camp Lyon noted with some dismay that on his very first day dinner consisted of boiled canned beef, "hardtack," and coffee. Next morning's breakfast was a replay of dinner from the previous night, and for his second night's evening meal, he was given bean soup with a piece of fat pork. New enlistee Wilbur Spalding felt a similar scorn, complaining to his diary that "such living as we had while we were there was enough to make a dog sick . . . the victuals were not more than half cooked [and] the coffee tasted more like dishwater than anything else." Spalding certainly wasn't alone in his grumbling, for that foul-tasting coffee was also noticed and later explained by James Rowe. During his fall 1861 training at Camp Lyon, Rowe realized that the camp's water supply for drinking and making coffee came straight from the Detroit River and at the same spot "where we [also] watered our horses and washed our shirts." From Rowe's perspective, those additional additives in the coffee water had a predictable effect: "Such a change from our ordinary diet brought on bowel trouble which was no respector of persons." Not only water, but even something as simple as bread seemed problematic, for Rowe also learned how "the contractor who furnished the bread, in order to increase his profits, used the cheapest grade of flour, and soon 'down with wormy bread and bootleg coffee' became the camp slogan."[37]

The quality of food and drink were not the only problems plaguing Detroit's new training camp during the war's opening months. In late September, thirty-nine-year-old German-born Friedrich Schmalzreid reported to his parents that he and his fellow cavalrymen at Camp Lyon were still without uniforms and that the entire regiment of close to a thousand men had only a hundred horses to work with. "They are kept out in the open and I haven't even touched them yet," wrote Schmalzreid, yet, all in all, the older farmhand was reasonably content, noting that the regiment consistently received three meals a day and that his duties and drill were not very strict.[38]

Another new Detroit site built for up to ten thousand men was known as Camp Backus, named in honor of Lieutenant Colonel Electus Backus Jr., who passed away in Detroit on June 7, 1862. Backus had been an 1824 West Point graduate and Mexican War veteran, though failing health over the years had relegated him to the role of mustering and disbursing officer in Detroit when the war broke out in 1861. Backus was promoted to the colonelcy of the Sixth U.S. Infantry in February 1862, but he never actually joined that unit as his ongoing poor health ultimately led to his death in Detroit that summer. Fully operational by the summer of 1862, Camp Backus was erected on ten acres of gently elevated farmland about one and three-quarter miles from the city center, located off of Clinton Avenue between Elmwood Avenue and the Joseph Campau farm, just across from the current entrance to Elmwood Cemetery.[39]

Still another camp set up on Detroit's outskirts for the new cavalry regiments was called Camp Banks, or the Banks Barracks. This encampment quickly became the mustering and training home for the Fifth Michigan Cavalry. "We were sent out [east on] Jefferson Avenue, about four miles, to camp on an old corn field with nothing to shelter us," recalled the Fifth's Samuel Harris. "The second day after we arrived at the camp grounds, a large amount of lumber was sent to us to build a large barrack. I was the only officer on the ground, and after finding out from the post-quartermaster what kind of a building he wanted put up, I took charge of it, and setting my men to work, soon had a barrack large enough to hold all the men of the regiment." The barracks Harris and his men built was simply one long building containing rows of bunk beds designed for two men in each bed and stacked upward four tiers high. Thus the entire regiment of twelve hundred would-be troopers could sleep in the one warehouse-like building. For some of these young men, many of whom had never been away from home, the experience of being so closely quartered with strangers initially caused frayed nerves and inevitable fights. "We were at this time no more than an awkward squad and many were the small fights caused by some remarks," wrote trooper James Avery. "And what wonder," he continued, "for here was the Yankee with his supposed knowledge of everything, the German whom you must not cross, the keen Frenchman, and the fiery Irishman, all strangers to one another like a lot of new horses together." Soon thereafter, however, the men quickly got to know each other and became good friends.[40]

In the meantime, the Detroit Barracks, located at Gratiot and Russell and Detroit's oldest active military installation, dating back to before the Mexican War, was becoming somewhat of a catchall facility for the city's various military purposes. At any time, it could house paroled prisoners, new recruits awaiting transfer to their respective regiments, captured deserters, and sick and wounded men convalescing at the barracks' small infirmary. The Detroit Barracks was referred to as "a sort of rake, which gathers up the debris, the odds and ends, of the military establishment, and holds them until a proper disposition can be made of them."[41]

The rejuvenated martial fervor in Detroit was heightened in mid-August by the safe return of Colonel Orlando Willcox who, on August 16, 1862, had been exchanged and officially released from a Confederate prison. He returned to Detroit for a brief visit and was accorded a hero's welcome at Campus Martius. It seemed the whole city was there among the specially built triumphal arches that overhung the streets, comprised of evergreens adorned with innumerable red, white, and blue banners. Included among the dignitaries was a detachment of his old First Michigan comrades. Among that group was Thomas Montgomery, who later described Willcox's arrival simply: "He comes as comes a conqueror." Willcox was clearly touched by the welcome, later writing how the crowd's "excited, enthusiastic cheers were the sweetest part of that public reception in Detroit." Within days, Willcox was formally promoted to brigadier general.[42]

The Twenty-fourth Michigan Infantry, also known as the Detroit and Wayne County Regiment, was also being formed in the summer of 1862 and would become Michigan's most famous regiment. With Fort Wayne filled to capacity, the Twenty-fourth trained at the old state fairgrounds, also known as the Detroit Riding Park, which was located between modern-day Woodward, Cass, Alexandrine, and Canfield. The site quickly became known as Camp Barns, in honor of Henry Barns, editor of the *Detroit Advertiser and Tribune* and ardent supporter of the Twenty-fourth. Just as at Detroit's other training camps, a reporter noted, the sounds of fife and drum made "the air resonant with military strains, and the old familiar sound of 'left,' 'left' is again heard as the squads are put through their various marchings and counter-marchings." At 5:00 p.m. on August 29, the regiment began its march from Camp Barns down Woodward Avenue, then up Jefferson, and finally to Detroit's central wharf to begin the long trek to Washington. "Thousands and thousands crowded

Orlando B. Willcox with his general's
stars (Library of Congress,
Washington, D.C.).

the sidewalks and streets," recalled one veteran. "Other thousands
viewed from the housetops, balconies and windows. Continuous
waves of flags and handkerchiefs, and cheer after cheer saluted the
ranks throughout their march." Three days later on September 1, the
Twenty-fourth safely arrived at Washington, though Elmer Wallace,
a British-born hospital steward for the regiment, was clearly not impressed with the Union capital, informing his parents that the city
"does not begin to be as pretty a place as Detroit; there is nothing
worth seeing in the entire city except the government buildings."[43]

Nevertheless, despite the downtown pageantry that marked the
return of Colonel Willcox and the sendoff of the Twenty-fourth Infantry, many on the home front had quietly lost their initial ardor
for war by the time the fall of 1862 came around, which signaled the
breakdown of the volunteer system. This was especially the case for
the wives and mothers left behind, such as Sarah Pardington, who
lamented to her sister, "O Mary what a cruel war this is . . . how
lonely I am since he went away" shortly after her husband, John, enlisted in the Twenty-fourth Michigan. With the stroke of a husband's
pen on an enlistment form, many of these women now wondered how
their family would manage financially and how would they tend to
all the responsibilities that their husbands had previously handled.

Chapter 2

As a new mother with no man at home, Sarah Pardington knew life was about to become much more difficult. Predictably, privations and suffering did indeed come to the doors of some of these women, despite the relative abundance of food and shelter in southeast Michigan. One woman, Archange Lablanc of Ecorse, who was in poor health to begin with, felt compelled to resort to fraud rather than seek admission to the "Poor House" after her husband died in a Confederate prisoner of war camp in May 1863. Having been given a small stipend of $3 per month from Wayne County's volunteer aid fund, Mrs. Lablanc simply wrote a 1 in front of the 3 on her monthly relief voucher, thereby garnering $13. She was found out and arrested, but she was given a suspended sentence on the condition that she try to make restitution after the authorities learned of her pitiable state. Such women as Mrs. Lablanc and their children were entitled to special consideration, opined the *Free Press*, "if not on the score of humanity, at least on the ground of gratitude toward those who have given their lives in our defense."[44]

The financial concerns and fears faced by Sarah Pardington and Archange Lablanc were echoed across thousands of families not only in Detroit but across the country. The war fever experienced by many Northerners in the spring and summer of 1861 had largely dissipated by the time the fall of 1862 rolled around. Lincoln's generally successful call for three hundred thousand more men, however, greatly enhanced morale and patriotism throughout the North. As a result of the president's call, Michigan began raising seven new infantry regiments, numbered from eighteen through twenty-four, though the specter of the nation's first-ever mandatory draft—along with Lincoln's preliminary Emancipation Proclamation in September 1862—raised more than a few eyebrows.

CHAPTER THREE

"Every . . . day laborer . . . will find a rival in a negro"

Fear and Suspicion of
"Secret Societies" and Blacks

Like all Northern cities, Detroit rallied to Lincoln's initial April 1861 call for volunteers when it seemed clear to everyone that the preservation of the Union was *the* fundamental reason for going to war. Circumstances had clearly changed eighteen months later. The preliminary announcement of Lincoln's Emancipation Proclamation in September 1862, coupled with the talk of conscription, began to seriously dampen Northern war fever in some quarters, which lasted all the way through to the president's reelection in November 1864. Those who had opposed the war from the outset kept quiet at first, opting to see how matters played out, but by the fall of 1861 into the summer of 1862 their voices were being heard. These Northern citizens who discouraged enlistments and questioned the war came to be known as Peace Democrats to some, Doughfaces or Copperheads to others (this last moniker a comparison to the extremely venomous snake that makes no rattle with its tail, thus making it all the more dangerous). The earliest known use of the "Copperhead" to describe the Lincoln administration's most vociferous critics dates to the summer of 1861 with an anonymous letter writer to the *Cincinnati Commercial*. The writer further described the Copperheads by quoting Genesis 3:14: "Because thou hast done this, thou art cursed above all cattle, and above every beast of the field; upon thy belly shalt thou go, and dust shalt thou eat all the day of thy life."[1]

Regardless of the epithet, most of these war resisters held to a common belief: that a noble war for the preservation of the Constitution and Union had now become a war *primarily* for the ending of slavery. From their perspective, though abhorrent, slavery was legal; therefore, any attempt to end it by military force was trampling upon the Constitution, not to mention the rights of the individual states. Moreover, the shedding of the white man's blood for the purpose of emancipating what was generally believed to be a degraded race was viewed as an abomination. In short order, the Copperhead mantra became "The Constitution as it is and the Union as it was."

As discussed earlier, Detroit's antislavery roots had run deep for years though, paradoxically, the town's support for and belief in the equality of the black race was always virtually nonexistent. For decades, the town had been the terminus of a key branch of the Underground Railroad. But now, this apparent change in the raison d'être of the war generated immense debate. Lincoln's Emancipation Proclamation did more to change the perception of the war in Detroit and other Northern cities than any other issue, especially within the state's Democratic Party and its chief organ, the *Detroit Free Press*. On September 22, 1862, Lincoln issued an executive order proclaiming a formal liberation of all slaves in any state of the so-called Confederate States of America that did not peaceably return to the Union by January 1, 1863. Realizing the political realities, the act did not cover those slaves in bondage in the crucial and neutral border states of Kentucky, Maryland, Delaware, Missouri, or the soon to be newly created state of West Virginia.

The Copperheads immediately denounced the proclamation, pointing out that not only didn't the act free slaves immediately but, more important, it signaled that the war's purpose was now changed from preserving the Union to emancipation. These Democrats pointed to Lincoln's decree as irrefutable proof that Republican promises that the war was only about Union and not black rights or emancipation were now exposed as the lies that Democrats had always insisted they were. "A practical enunciation of the [Republican] party platform will henceforth color the war," the *Free Press* sadly predicted. Seeing themselves from the beginning as strict and conservative interpreters of the Constitution, the Peace Democrats clearly viewed Lincoln's decree as an unlawful usurpation of power by the executive branch.[2]

Throughout the North, thousands of anti-emancipation soldiers deserted or simply vanished after gaining a furlough. Scores of others in military hospitals quietly decided that their wounds or illnesses were far worse than initially thought and chose to stay put. At the same time, the proclamation was ridiculed by some as freeing the slaves only in those areas where the Union had no power. Anti-black Northerners' greatest fear was that the decree would flood the Northern states with freed blacks, who would inevitably compete with poor whites for the available manual work or else become costly thieves or indigents. Furthermore, whites abhorred the inescapable association between the races that would inevitably occur. From the day the first shells exploded over Fort Sumter, the Peace Democrats' oratory overflowed with allusions to racial mixing, or what became known as "miscegenation," that played on white society's darkest fears and racial prejudices.[3]

According to Montgomery Wilson, a prominent Republican writer of the day, the first commandment of every Copperhead, such as the *Detroit Free Press*, was "Thou shalt hate the Nigger with all thy heart, and with all thy soul, and with all thy mind, and with all thy strength." With the Midwest grappling with an economic recession, such Copperhead arguments played well with members of the Michigan populace who were originally of Southern origin as well as with the poorer Irish immigrants. [4]

The *Free Press*, initially a supporter of the "Save the Union" war aims, now became one of the Lincoln administration's most strident critics. For editor Henry N. Walker, like Wilbur Storey before him, fighting for the sanctity of flag and Union was one thing, but spilling the white man's blood and spending immense amounts of national treasure in order to free the Negro was quite another. Meanwhile, the paper played its miscegenation fears to the hilt, with consistent headlines such as "A Negro Runs Away with the Wife of a White Man," "Miscegenation in Detroit," and so on. So great was the *Free Press*'s "Negrophobia" that within months of Lincoln's announcement it was even envisioning blacks being appointed as general officers in the Union army: "We expect to see Fred[erick] Douglas or some prominent barber buck arrayed in all his glory of twin stars. Let the white volunteers prepare to touch their caps to black generals." Such rhetoric caused unsuspecting black freemen new to Detroit consternation when they realized that the *Free Press*'s name had nothing to do with sympathy or alliance with the black race's plight. "I bought the Free Press, and hired a boy to read it to me, and the boy read it to me," wrote William Webb in his memoirs years later. At that time, Webb was an escaped slave who had just arrived in Detroit. "I thought it was the most curious free paper I ever heard read. It seemed to me that it sided with the rebels, and being in a free state, I was surprised. I could not understand it. I thought the boy had made a mistake in reading it. I thought surely it must be a friend to the colored people, being named the Free Press."[5]

The protection of unskilled labor jobs for working-class white men was a core value of Democrats and the *Free Press*. From the paper's perspective, "the dignity of labor" had been maintained prior to the war simply because the demand for labor had exceeded supply. "But let the country be abolitionized," it argued, "let the north be overrun with negroes, as it must be if the slaves are emancipated, and every wood sawyer, day laborer, servant, porter, or other employee, will find a rival in a negro, will have the bread snatched from their mouths by the sable pets of the abolitionists." This was an economic, social, and inherently racist fear that transcended party lines. When Michigan's Radical Republican and antislavery senator Jacob Howard was informed by a colleague that Michigan's black population would soar to 123,000 as compared to its current 6,800 if the slaves were liberated and then settled in the Northern states in a proportion similar to their white population, Howard dryly remarked, "Canada is very near us, and affords a fine market for 'wool.'" [6]

Though Detroit had garnered scores of European immigrants in the past twenty or so years and had received a substantial influx of newcomers from New York and New England "Yankee" stock, the city's ties to Northern culture were by no means an absolute. Significant numbers of Southern families from western Virginia and Kentucky had also moved northward in the rush for settlement. The Ordinance of 1787 outlawing slavery in the Old Northwest meant that Southerners migrating northward would be of the non-slave-owning class. Their ambivalent attitude to blacks, slavery, and their Southern homeland during the Civil War was evidenced by their cautious reception of the Emancipation Proclamation.[7]

❋ ❋ ❋

DIVISIVENESS began to take hold in the North in the fall of 1861 as it became clear that the war was going to last well beyond the ninety days initially expected. With military success wanting and congressional elections looming, Northern conservative Democrats began pointing fingers at Republicans—especially the Radical Republicans led by Michigan's own Senator Zachariah Chandler and Governor Austin Blair—for their staunch refusal to negotiate with the South as well as their abolitionist leanings. In the meantime, radical elements in the Republican Party began to view any criticism of their party, the Lincoln administration, or their war aims as proof positive of secessionist sympathies or leanings. Bolstered by the belief that there were Rebel spies bent on skullduggery lurking around every corner, rumors quickly sprang up throughout the Northern states of "homegrown" plots to undermine the Union war effort. These nefarious schemes were alleged to be the work of various Southern-sympathizing "secret societies" or, according to Professor Frank Klement, "dark lantern societies," that bore cultish names like the Sons of Liberty, the Order of American Knights, and the Knights of the Golden Circle. Members even allegedly acknowledged one another with secret signs and handshakes.[8]

The Knights of the Golden Circle did indeed exist, as the group had been organized in 1854 by Dr. George W. Bickley in Cincinnati—a city that held the questionable honor of being the birthplace of the Know-Nothings as well as the site of anti-immigrant riots. The Knights, or "KGC," as they soon came to be known, spread to the South and Southwest in the mid- to late 1850s. Initially, the Knights' goal was the annexation of territory from Mexico, for this was the era of "Manifest Destiny," and the prospect of expanding slavery into these lands appealed to many Southern "fire-eaters." In short order, the KGC also became identified with white supremacy, "states' rights," and the Democratic Party, to the extent that that party represented all those interests. When war came, the KGC's focus changed from Mexican escapades to Southern support. With Confederate armies already under arms, Bickley and his Knights realized that they would be best put to use in areas where Southern sympathy remained considerable, such as the northwestern states; however, Federal control of those areas prevented such public expression.[9]

Zealous Unionists soon began seeing Knights everywhere. A thin, anonymously authored booklet appeared in Kentucky, the new center of KGC activity, that purported to be an exposé of the Knights' activities. It included the allegation that the *Detroit Free Press* was one of numerous Northern newspapers "eagerly sought for by the brotherhood in their respective States, and in different States, to indicate the progress of the work, and which are deemed able auxiliaries." Meanwhile, partisan Republican papers soon took advantage of such fears and innuendo by indiscriminately claiming that their Democratic opponents were in league with these societies, even when those opponents were prominent, upstanding members of the community. Irrefutable proof, however, always seemed to be lacking.[10]

Into the midst of such intrigue strode Dr. Guy S. Hopkins of North Branch (Lapeer County), Michigan. Hopkins was a staunch and loyal Democrat who, by late 1861, had become increasingly resentful of such Republican accusations, especially when he read the charge that the Knights had infiltrated Detroit. The *Free Press* deemed the accusation, coming as it did only three days before state elections, unworthy of even a reply. Like that paper, the good doctor was certainly no wallflower. He had spoken out quite loudly in town, proclaiming his vehement disagreement with the policies of Lincoln and the Republicans. One town resident claimed that Hopkins and his associates had erected a flagpole in North Branch from which they planned to run up a secessionist flag. His diatribes became so boisterous that local Republicans accused him of treason while friends cautioned him against further action.[11]

Hopkins reached his emotional limit when he read of a recently concluded several-day visit to Saginaw and Detroit by former president Franklin Pierce. Like Hopkins, Pierce was a devoted Democrat who had strenuously and publicly voiced his disagreement with Lincoln administration policies during his Michigan trip, especially Lincoln's suspension of the writ of habeas corpus and the administration's numerous arbitrary arrests. It was also reported that Pierce had stated he would prefer to see his former secretary of war, Joseph Holt, as president rather than any man living. While in Detroit, Pierce had stayed at the home of Robert McClelland, the esteemed former Democratic governor of Michigan and onetime secretary of the interior in Pierce's cabinet. Pierce had also visited with seventy-nine-year-old Lewis Cass, one of the state's most venerable public figures. Despite McClelland's and Cass's sterling public reputations, Hopkins read in the Republican-leaning *Detroit Tribune* within weeks of Pierce's visit that, while in Detroit, the former president had been "closeted with a select circle who are known to be doubtful in their loyalty." The libelous piece concluded with the stunning allegation, "Our opinion is that Franklin Pierce is a prowling traitor spy." Like all Michigan Democrats who read the story, Hopkins was incensed. Unlike those other Democrats, however, and despite the earlier warnings of his friends, Hopkins decided to gain a measure of personal revenge.[12]

Hopkins's plan was to create a fake letter, written by an "anonymous" member of the Knights of the Golden Circle, that mentioned "Pres^dt P——," a clear allusion to Franklin Pierce, thus purportedly tying him to the society. Dated October 5, 1861, Hopkins's cryptic invention was filled with blanks and riddled with "secret" code and innuendo. Had it been real, it would have been solid proof of treasonous activities. The cornerstone of Hopkins's plot was his conviction that once the phony letter had been successfully "leaked" into the hands of Detroit's Republican newspaper editors, they would immediately print the correspondence (along with howling editorials) as proof positive of Democratic involvement in the Confederate-leaning secret societies. Once the letter was published, Hopkins planned to step forward and publicly reveal that he had, in fact, penned the letter as an intentional hoax, thereby exposing his Republican adversaries in Detroit as naive but vicious dupes who would believe and print anything anti-Democratic, no matter how outlandish. As Hopkins himself later wrote, "It would be sent to one of the treason-shrieking presses and when exploded would produce much fun."[13]

Unfortunately for Hopkins, his prediction that Detroit's Republican newspapers would immediately print the letter turned out to be dead wrong. Initially, Hopkins mailed his creation to a Detroit businessman named Mills who, not knowing what to do with it, showed the letter to Henry Walker, the *Free Press*'s senior editor. The men took the letter to the Detroit postmaster, who then gave it to the editors of Detroit's two Republican papers, the *Advertiser* and the *Tribune*. At last Hopkins's letter had wound up where he intended it to go. Rather than publish it, however, the two editors quietly passed the letter to Federal marshals, who instructed Detroit sheriff Joseph P. Whiting to investigate. Whiting was able to track the letter back to North Branch and to Dr. Hopkins. Meanwhile, the authorities had also forwarded the letter to Secretary of State William Seward. Seward considered the letter legitimate and ordered the immediate arrest of Hopkins. Hopkins and two friends were soon arrested by Michigan authorities and in a matter of days, Dr. Hopkins found himself sitting in a dank jail cell at Fort Lafayette, situated in the middle of New York harbor.[14]

Hopkins never dreamed that his scheme would backfire to such a degree. On November 29, Hopkins wrote a remorseful letter from his cell to Seward admitting that he had authored the "anonymous" letter, but that his "act of inconsiderate folly" was nothing more than a foolish attempt "to play off a practical joke upon the Detroit press."[15]

In the meantime, Seward had already written to Pierce informing him of the anonymously written letter, noting with just a hint of smugness how "it would appear that you were a member of a secret league the object of which is to overthrow the Government. Any explanation upon the subject which you may offer would be acceptable." That Seward would even ask for a formal reply from Pierce outraged the former president, for such a request clearly insinuated that Seward did indeed give the letter some credibility, thereby questioning Pierce's loyalty and commitment to the Stars and Stripes. Pierce's reply to Seward was blistering, first questioning "how any person could give credence to or entertain for a moment the idea that I am now or have ever been connected with a secret league" and then wondering how the extract of Hopkins's letter, which Seward had included, could serve "as a sufficient basis for an official communication." Pierce considered the extract to be nothing more than "the vagaries of an anonymous correspondent" whose words were "incoherent and meaningless," and that the whole affair was a supreme insult considering that it had been officially "sent for explanation to one who during his whole life has never belonged to any secret league, society or association."[16]

Upon receiving Hopkins's mea culpa and Pierce's terse reply, Seward realized he had been deceived, yet chose to hide that fact from all concerned. He sent another letter to the still-fuming Pierce, this time downplaying the whole matter as nothing more than a minor misunderstanding and claiming that his initial communication had simply been poorly worded by an incompetent State Department clerk. While this second letter to Pierce did concede that the anonymous letter writer had been detected and that he had admitted his deed, it still did not contain any formal acknowledgment from Seward that the letter's implied allegations against Pierce were bogus. That omission prompted a second burst of vitriol from Pierce, but there the matter seemed to end. Seward simply filed Pierce's letter away and did nothing further. Hopkins was released from prison on February 22, 1862, after signing parole papers pledging he would "render no aid or comfort to the enemies in hostility to the Government of the United States." He returned home to Michigan chastised and contrite. No more letters passed between Seward and Pierce either.[17]

Yet to the utter surprise of all concerned, and much to the dismay of Seward, Hopkins's hoax letter was published in the *Detroit Tribune* in March 1862 and quickly reprinted throughout the country. Obviously not realizing that the letter was a fake and with elections looming, Republican editors thought ample political points could be scored by again raising the Democrat–Golden Circle specter. Meanwhile, Pierce was indignant that such a ridiculous insinuation against him was now public, forcing him to take steps that would clear his good name. On March 24, 1862, Pierce wrote to Senator Milton S. Latham of California, a close friend, asking that the Senate pass a resolution demanding that all of the Seward-Pierce correspondence be made public. In due course, the Senate passed the resolution, ultimately forcing Seward to relinquish all of his correspondence with Pierce. The secretary suffered some fleeting public embarrassment and Pierce had his name restored, though his criticism of the Lincoln administration never waned.[18]

Detroit's "Hopkins Hoax" quickly became a footnote in Civil War history and was soon forgotten; however, the fear of pro-Southern secret societies fomenting anti-Union and anti-draft sentiment never lost steam throughout most of the Old Northwest up through Lincoln's reelection in November 1864. By 1864, a Union pamphlet from the Bureau of Military Justice put forth that the Sons of Liberty had essentially replaced the KGC and was active throughout the lower Midwest, though to a less extent in Michigan. Its "temple" headquarters in Michigan were reported to be in Detroit, and the organization allegedly had twenty thousand members in Michigan, which was probably a vast overstatement. For the most part, the facts of the Hopkins Hoax case prevented the success of any future Republican assertions of "secret societies" embedded in Michigan. The issue seemed to die down in Detroit and Michigan as 1862 and 1863 wore on, but concerns about "secret societies" were replaced by a new political and highly public controversy: the use of blacks as armed soldiers in the ranks alongside white men.[19]

❀ ❀ ❀

OTHER than the fear of black men taking what were viewed as white jobs, no issue generated more political or racial controversy among Northerners than the question of whether black men should be allowed to serve in the Union army as armed soldiers alongside whites. At the beginning of the conflict, leading men of both the North and the South had seemed to agree that this would be a white man's war. At least as far as being a musket-carrying soldier went, for to put a black man in a blue uniform and give him a musket would imply a level of equality with whites that many were unwilling to acknowledge. Moreover, Lincoln did not want to offend the sensibilities of border states such as Kentucky, which had remained loyal to the Union, prompting the president to opine that arming blacks would cause fifty thousand bayonets that were for the Union to immediately turn against it. Performing heavy manual labor, however, was another story. In July 1862 Congress had authorized the army to employ blacks strictly as laborers at the rate of $6 per month. When the highly racist *Free Press* was then asked by a reader if the paper objected to blacks being used by the army for building entrenchments, digging latrines, cooking, or other forms of drudgery, it responded with a full-throated no. "What we are opposed to," it explained, "is the support by the government of negroes in idleness, the putting of negroes in the ranks beside white troops, and any scheme of general emancipation, which will commit the country to an abolition policy and entail upon the people enormous taxation to colonize the slaves."[20]

As Detroit was a primarily Democratic town, most people seemed to care little about the nobility of blacks serving in the Union army, a topic that was a clarion call for the abolitionist movement. Certainly one of those most interested was Henry Barns, British-born editor of the Republican and pro-Lincoln *Detroit Advertiser and Tribune* who, as a forceful abolitionist and committed supporter of the Underground Railroad, took a very favorable view of efforts to raise a black regiment in Michigan after hearing the vociferous appeals of Detroit's black leaders. In February 1863, only one month after the Emancipation Proclamation had gone into effect, Congress had passed the Negro Regiment Bill, authorizing colored infantry regiments. Soon thereafter, Barns began continually editorializing in support of a black Michigan regiment in the Union army, for he was quite aware that Detroit and Michigan had been slower than some other eastern states in mobilizing support for raising a new black regiment. The paper pointed out how the young nation's two greatest generals to date, George Washington and Andrew Jackson, had never shown any reluctance to use black troops in their respective wars. Furthermore, it noted how England and France, possessors of the two greatest

European armies, thought it no disgrace to utilize black men and accorded them the same respect as their white troops.[21]

Certainly no support for such a venture would be forthcoming from the *Free Press*, which typically vilified the African race as comprised of shiftless men "who do nothing but steal and fight." In an April 1863 editorial, Barns lamented that two hundred black men in Detroit had already enlisted in the Fifty-fourth Massachusetts Colored Infantry, which had become the first black regiment formed in the North. Of this, the *Free Press* sarcastically approved, for every local black enlisting in an out-of-state regiment meant one fewer black living in Michigan. Still, Barns would not be deterred. He appealed to Governor Austin Blair for approval to raise a regiment of colored men; however, Blair lacked the authority to approve Barns's request because Michigan had revised its militia act in 1862 so that only white men could serve. Though he was a staunch Radical Republican, Blair was also likely aware that arming blacks in spring 1863, only a few months after the Emancipation Proclamation went into effect, would be seen as further proof that the war had been transformed into a crusade against slavery, which might have led to even more civil discord. Undaunted, Barns turned to Secretary of War Edwin Stanton and therein found his ally. Stanton informed Blair on July 24, 1863, that the War Department was "very anxious that such regiments should be raised," thus giving Blair the go-ahead to approve Barns's plans.[22]

Barns accepted a commission as colonel in the army and earnestly began the recruitment of his new regiment in Detroit on August 12, 1863. As had been the case just over a year earlier with Detroit's Twenty-fourth Volunteer Infantry, Barns appealed to the patriotism of Detroit's Common Council, urging it to offer a $50 "bounty," or cash bonus, to each colored man who enlisted in the new regiment. He pointed out that given Detroit's Federal enlistment quota, which still existed in part, each black man who enlisted meant one less white man having to serve. In addition, Barns also knew that paying a bounty would stem the flow of Michigan blacks toward out-of-state recruiters. The council was a Democratic stronghold, however and, not surprisingly, denied Barns's request, as did the state of Michigan when Barns came calling to it for some type of bounty. Predictably, Barns's recruitment efforts had little success at first. His potential black recruits, many of whom had families to feed, realized that if they were indeed going to volunteer, why not do so in a regiment where a significant cash bounty was available?[23]

Meanwhile, the *Free Press* went apoplectic at the prospect of such a regiment coming into existence in Michigan in any manner. In an editorial pertaining to Barns's plea to the Common Council, the *Free Press* angrily asserted that there was a "peculiar fitness of things" in Barns having been chosen to lead the new colored regiment. After all, it charged, under Barns's leadership, the *Advertiser and Tribune* had "educate[ed] negroes to *hate* white men, and what, therefore, could be more fit than his selection to be the head of a regiment of negroes to *kill* white men." The *Free Press* referred to Barns as the regiment's "nigger-head" and claimed that his entire motive in building the new regiment was personal financial gain, not patriotism. Almost shrieking, the paper declared that Barns could have enlisted or even formed a white regiment at any time in the past, but now he was strictly playing "a game for plunder, for patronage, for commissions, for contracts . . . for party favorites and to organize and arm a skeleton regiment of whatever negroes can be collected here or from Canada" since so many local blacks had already enlisted in other states' regiments.[24]

Barns's recruitment continued slowly throughout the fall with Detroit's Republican and Democratic newspapers exchanging barbs about the viability and legitimacy of Michigan's first colored regiment every step of the way. Until they were at full strength and ready to muster into the Union army, the new recruits spent their days drilling at the hastily erected Camp Ward, which was named for Detroit industrialist and leading Republican Eber B. Ward. The camp was part of the Union Army Barracks complex located on the city's east side at the present-day site of the now-closed Duffield Elementary School, the same grounds occupied by 1862's Banks Barracks.[25]

It was a cold and miserable early winter for the men of the First Michigan Colored Infantry. Nevertheless, their dreary Thanksgiving season at Camp Ward was brightened for one day at least when they were paid a surprise visit by sixty-six-year-old Sojourner Truth, by then a well-known black antislavery activist. Truth, whose birth name was Isabella Baumfree, had been in Battle Creek, Michigan, where she had gathered up a bountiful Thanksgiving feast for the men of the First as well as much-needed supplies. It was quite a welcome surprise when her carriage drove into the camp laden with boxes and packages containing all manner of delicacies for "the boys." The men were promptly ordered into line for the presentation, which was made by Truth, who then gave a speech glowing with exhortation and best wishes. At its conclusion, the men of the First responded with cheers that could be heard from one end of the camp to the other.[26]

After Truth's visit, Barns took 250 of his unformed men and the regiment's band on a "grand tour" of southern Michigan in December 1863 in an attempt to rally support and find recruits for his cause. Upon their return, the shoddy construction of their Camp Ward barracks, initially built for temporary use, became painfully evident with the onset of what was a bitterly cold winter. The persistently leaky roofs, lack of flooring, and crevices in the walls large enough to let snow in prompted heated debates about the quality and condition of the regiment's housing. Surgeon Charles Tripler, conducting a formal inspection, described the barracks at Camp Ward as "wretched" and generally unfit for humans to live in. "There is not a barn or pigsty in the whole city of Detroit that is not better fitted for human habitation," argued the *Advertiser and Tribune.* The paper also reported, "Fifty men are at present suffering from the effect of having been frozen in their quarters, and that too while fires were burning." The insinuation disingenuously put forth by the *Free Press* was that the regiment had been given substandard shelter due to its racial makeup.[27]

When they were off duty, many of the black soldiers desired to go into town and enjoy refreshments or a meal at Detroit's various saloons and eateries. Despite the fact that many of these taverns had previously refused to serve blacks, the soldiers believed their new blue uniforms entitled them to a measure of respect that had previously been denied them. For added protection and even influence, many of the uniformed men would go out in groups, even taking their arms. This prompted considerable tension and consternation throughout Detroit, especially in the nearby (east side) German part of town, where disdain for blacks was almost equal to that found among the Irish. Fights sometime ensued, and regardless of who was at fault, the *Free Press* continued its anti-black narrative. It bitterly complained that colored soldiers in uniform could be "found parading the streets with arms, to the great annoyance of peaceable citizens," sarcastically defending the white citizen "who may not have sufficient of the necessary ingredients in his organization to make him worship these African gods either singly, or in squads."[28]

Joseph R. Smith, Sr. (U.S. Army
Military History Institute,
Carlisle, Pa.).

In overall charge of handling such military concerns was the regular army's military commander for Detroit, Lieutenant Colonel Joseph Rowe Smith Sr., a sixty-one-year-old "gruff spoken and severe looking, one-armed veteran." After delving into this troublesome matter, Smith concluded there was indeed some merit to what the *Free Press* was reporting. Four days after the *Free Press*'s commentary appeared, Smith wrote to Colonel Barns informing him, "Complaints are too frequent, of the rival demonstrations of the colored soldiers, with arms in their hands, threatening, and attacking colored and white citizens, especially the latter." Smith warned that unless Barns maintained tighter control of his men, "collisions must ensue, which will cause bitter blood between the white and colored soldiers and citizens." Obviously fearing civil disturbances, Smith ordered that for the sake of "public peace and good order," Barns's men should no longer wear their side arms to town. The colonel's small patrols of one noncommissioned officer and three or four men could wear side arms, but in no instance should they carry muskets.[29]

Smith's orders seemed to put an end to the issue, allowing the regiment's recruiting to be finally completed soon thereafter. On February 17, 1864, its 895 young black men were formally mustered into the U.S. Army as the 102nd U.S. Colored Infantry. Though now proudly wearing the blue uniform of the Union army, these black men still felt the direct sting of government-sponsored racism, for while their white brothers-in-arms were paid $13 per month, General Orders No. 163 dictated that "persons of African descent" who enlisted were to be paid at the rate of only $10 per month. Adding insult to injury was the fact that $3 of that amount was to be deducted from their pay for uniform costs, even though white soldiers had to bear no such fee.[30]

The newspaper war in Detroit regarding these black troops continued unabated. The *Advertiser and Tribune* attacked the *Free Press* on March 7, alleging that from day one, its policy toward Michigan's only colored regiment had been "base and shameless"; that it had "abused its officers, vilified its members and slandered its friends." Worst of all, "outrages" *upon* the troops had been presented by the *Free Press* as outrages committed *by* the black men. The *Free Press*, in short, had "drawn upon an imagination, fertile in the false but barren of truth, for material with which to vilify the objects of its traitorous malice."[31]

On March 28, just a little over a month after its formal mustering into the Union army, the new black regiment marched down Jefferson Avenue to the Michigan Southern Depot at the corner of Brush Street, with none of the fanfare or accolades that had been accorded to the white Michigan regiments. There the soldiers awaited the arrival of the train that would take them to Annapolis, Maryland, and then on to the theaters of war in South Carolina and Florida. Most of the men and many of their white officers could hardly wait to leave Detroit, for as one white officer later wrote, "It was a happy day for us when we left old Camp Ward, with its many unpleasant associations. . . . We are now far removed from all those pernicious Copperhead influences which have so long injured us as a regiment." The very next day after the regiment went to war the *Free Press* fired its final racist volley against Michigan's first and only colored regiment: "Its departure secures the peace and tranquility of our city."[32]

CHAPTER FOUR

"One of the most melancholy spectacles it was ever our lot to witness"

Anxiety over the Draft and
Its Consequences in Detroit

The Union armies both east and west were able to procure all the soldiers they needed throughout the first year of the war through the volunteer system, despite the fact that some initial grumbling was heard by the fall of 1861, once it became apparent that the war was going to last well beyond the ninety days initially expected. That change in perception also prompted an increase in Michigan's political partisanship that peaked in the fall of 1862 when President Lincoln announced his preliminary Emancipation Proclamation. Such an occurrence was neither surprising nor unexpected. While Republicans could point with pride to the fact that Lincoln had carried seven midwestern states in the 1860 presidential election, including Michigan, which had been virtually conceded by Democrats from the start, it was also true that his margin of victory had been relatively slim; he garnered only 53 percent of the vote. It was also the case that Democratic strength throughout the 1850s had been relatively strong, as early settlement by upland Southerners had given the Democrats a strong advantage over the old Whig Party.[1]

In an action that was never adequately justified, Secretary of War Edwin Stanton ordered all recruiting offices closed in April 1862 on his belief that the war would soon be over and thus no more men were needed. By late June, Union general George McClellan's recently failed Peninsula Campaign in Virginia clearly showed that was not the case and only highlighted the need for more men. By the summer of 1862, however, patriotic war fervor was diminishing, if not exhausted, prompting the need to again raise voices in favor of the war along with the talk of conscription. The 1862 spring agricultural season and its attendant need for farm workers, coupled with increasing demands for factory labor, only underscored the need. On July 2, Lincoln's call for three hundred thousand more men was disingenuously presented to the public simply as the president responding to the pleas of thirteen Northern governors, including Michigan's Austin Blair, to raise more troops . Of that total, Michigan's quota was six new regiments, with one regiment to be recruited and organized from each of the state's six congressional districts. Those requirements worked out to roughly six thousand men, a figure that clearly had Michigan's leaders worried about the state's ability to deliver.[2]

After Lincoln's appeal, Detroit ale brewer and mayor William C. Duncan was petitioned by leading men of the city to hold a public meeting to help speed up the enlistment process. Duncan responded by calling for a public rally to be held at 7:30 p.m. on July 15, 1862, at Detroit's Campus Martius to extol the virtues of enlistment and urge young men of good health to heed the president's call. Blair had also issued a proclamation laying out his plans to create new infantry regiments, numbered from eighteen through twenty-three, one from each of six new regimental districts that corresponded to the congressional districts. In addition, he proclaimed that a new camp would be built in each district to house and train the new recruits. To help families who might lose their sole breadwinner to the army, Blair explained, each household affected could be eligible for up to $15 per month in financial assistance.[3]

The *Free Press* firmly supported Lincoln's call as well as Duncan's, as long as preservation of the Union and its Constitution was the *sole* purpose in asking for more men. In a "To Arms!" editorial published the morning of the planned gathering, the paper hoped it would be a peaceful meeting of citizens devoid of partisan politics, "but that everyone who goes there will be inspired by the spirit of patriotic devotion to *the Union as it was, the Constitution as it is.*" As previously mentioned, such rhetoric was a clear reference to the conviction that the emancipation of the slave should have no place whatsoever in the current conflict.[4]

What was intended that evening as a pro-Lincoln and pro-enlistment public rally started off well enough, but soon the atmosphere at this, the largest public gathering Detroit had ever witnessed, deteriorated. As each speaker rose to the rostrum, he was greeted with hoots and jeers from agitators dispersed throughout the crowd. When Theodore

Romeyn, a well-known Detroit attorney and a "War Democrat," begin speaking on patriotism, one rowdy yelled out, "Bull Run!" intending that the memory of the disastrous Union defeat would counter Romeyn's assertions. Romeyn shot back, shouting, "Where is the wretch who throws that up as a reproach to his country?" Each speaker faced taunts and, perhaps as a precursor to what would transpire in Detroit almost nine months later, the rally turned ugly near its end. The disorderly mob made a dash at Captain Eber B. Ward, Detroit's wealthiest citizen and owner of the Eureka Iron Works, the city's largest employer, most likely in an attempt to kill the man. That Ward was the main target indicates the class tension in the city over the war's underlying purpose and who—and who wouldn't—be on the front lines. Sheriff Mark Flanigan and a handful of deputies succeeded in rushing Ward and several other speakers to safety at the nearby Russell House Hotel. Ward and the others were in good hands, for Flanigan was not a man that many would dare to challenge. A longtime Detroiter of Irish birth and a butcher by trade, Flanigan was an imposing figure. According to Detroit historian George Catlin, Flanigan "stood six feet four inches tall in his stocking feet and had the build of a Roman gladiator." With their revolvers drawn and at the ready, Flanigan and his men succeeded in keeping the mob at bay. Nevertheless, for the next hour, the antiwar horde seemingly laid siege to the hotel, all the while shouting curses at Ward and the night's speakers who were huddled inside. Other elements of the crowd destroyed the speakers' stand and shredded all the Union bunting they could find. Meanwhile, the elderly Lewis Cass barely escaped with his life after the rioters unsuccessfully chased after his carriage.[5]

In the next day's papers, the *Free Press* merely regretted the previous night's "disposition to give way to an unwarranted expression of dissatisfaction with Captain Ward." However, the pro-Republican *Advertiser and Tribune* had little difficulty in assigning blame. "It was one of the most melancholy spectacles it was ever our lot to witness," it sadly remarked, pointing out that those in the mob were most certainly "ignorant, bigoted persons" who had "been tampered with through their political prejudices." The paper had no doubts who the puppet masters were, either. From its vantage, the near riot was instigated by secessionist-leaning politicians "who are traitors to their country, knaves at heart and assassins in purpose, despised by loyal Democrats, as by every other good citizen who knows them."

Mark Flanigan (U.S. Army Military
History Institute, Carlisle, Pa.).

Eber Ward, for his part, rhetorically asked in a letter to the papers just
why the "drunken rabble" had gone after him in the first place, especially when he had consistently kept hundreds of Detroit's workingmen employed when business slowdowns may have called for layoffs. As for the *Free Press,* Ward likened the paper's "pious pretensions
in favor of law and order" to Maximilien Robespierre, one of the
French Revolution's leading figures, who "was undoubtedly horror-
stricken at the crime of blood-letting when he found his own neck
under the guillotine." The presence of a significant, antiwar "Peace
Democrat" element in Detroit and Wayne County was now clearly
visible to all. This was not unusual, for most midwestern war and
draft resistance occurred primarily in counties where public opinion
had been largely shaped by Democratic editors and politicians.[6]

The Campus Martius disturbance was considered a stain upon the
patriotism of Michigan in general and Detroit in particular. In order
to reverse the embarrassment, the city's leading citizens held a meeting the night after the disastrous rally and determined that in order
to properly show its loyalty to the national cause, Detroit would raise
an additional regiment over and beyond the required quota. Governor
Blair had initially rejected the idea, believing that it might hinder the

raising of the six regiments he was already responsible for. Moreover, Blair believed that it was more prudent for new recruits to fill up the older regiments first, rather than create new ones. From the governor's perspective, a new recruit surrounded by grizzled veterans would quickly learn what was expected of him, while a new regiment filled with green men and officers would bumble around for far too long. Yet in due course Blair relented, and agreed to the one special regiment of volunteers beyond the six Lincoln had requested.[7]

Pro-Lincoln factions planned a huge "war meeting" a week later on July 22 to eliminate from the public memory any vestiges of the debacle of the previous week. Campus Martius was packed with people from one end to the other when the public rally began in mid-afternoon. "It would have been impossible for a person to wedge his way through the dense mass of humanity there congregated," reported the *Free Press*. Nearly every store along Woodward and Jefferson was closed that afternoon so that employees could attend the gathering along with farmers from the country and men from the local factories. A number of Michigan's most prominent leaders were lined up to give speeches in a display that would hopefully illustrate the overwhelming patriotism of most of the city's residents. Among the noted speakers were Judge Henry Morrow and Sheriff Mark Flanigan. These men announced their intention to enlist and were set to become the colonel and lieutenant colonel, respectively, of the forthcoming Twenty-fourth Michigan Infantry, the additional regiment that Governor Blair allowed for. It was to be raised primarily from Detroit and Wayne County men, thereby giving the recruitment credit to Michigan's first congressional district.[8]

Lewis Cass was also on hand, sufficiently recovered from the previous week's scare to deliver one of the last impromptu speeches of his long public life. Much of the day was spent in support of Lincoln's recent call for more volunteers, including the formation of new regiments in Michigan. To further spur enlistments, Thomas McEntee, on behalf of the day's finance committee, announced that the city of Detroit would offer a $50 bounty to any single man enlisting and a $100 bounty to a married man as long as they resided within the city limits. Toward the end of the rally, it was announced that well-known Detroiters had also pledged anywhere from $5 to $10 to each man from their ward who enlisted in the Twenty-fourth Michigan. Two days later, on July 24, Detroit's Common Council pledged $40,000 to help pay the bounties to the city's volunteers. This was the first time that Detroit had ever offered such inducements for military service. By the end of the war, the city had paid out more than $200,000 for such enticements.[9]

From Lincoln's and Blair's perspective, the call for the six new infantry regiments plus the additional agreed-upon Twenty-fourth Infantry had to be considered a public relations success, initially at least. The *Free Press* certainly considered it so by proclaiming in its coverage that "the meeting of the citizens of Detroit yesterday was all that could have been desired." What had been a dispirited Detroit and Michigan populace only weeks before was now reinvigorated with patriotic zeal and commitment that must have resembled the early days of the war. For example, Robert Burns, a draft officer in southwest Michigan looking for recruits for the newly created Fourth Michigan Cavalry, informed his mother in mid-July that "volunteers are as scarce as icicles in this part of the country" and that prior to Lincoln's call and potential draft order, his job was all "uphill work." By the time his new regiment reached Detroit in August for training, Burns was happily singing a different tune. Writing home on August 24, he now told his mother that after Lincoln's directive, his company had filled up in two days and that he'd even had to turn away about eighty applicants. "Many farms have been left," he asserted, "and all have gone or are going to war." It must have seemed that way in Detroit, for Burns also informed his mother that about two thousand men had arrived in the city that very week. Detroit's German immigrant community also chimed in, holding a mass meeting on August 19 in which it proclaimed firm support for Lincoln's call for more men, but again stressed in a resolution that any German men drafted should be organized into companies by themselves and led by German officers. The hoopla and excitement even seemed to give attorney Henry Billings Brown some second thoughts about volunteering. "Civil life is getting stale," he complained in his diary. "Shall I go into the army? The only profession in this country is grim-visaged war."[10]

Despite the veneer of enlistment success in Detroit and Michigan, Lincoln's July call for more volunteers did not result throughout the North in attaining the numbers that were needed. As a backup plan, the Federal government gave itself the authority to draft able-bodied men between the ages of eighteen and forty-five for nine months' service, which Lincoln exercised on August 4, 1862. Lincoln's order directed that if any state failed to furnish its assigned quota of

"Candidate for the exempt brigade": the man on the right refers to a certificate in his left hand, signed by "Dr. Syntax," certifying, "I have examined Adam Cowherd, Esq. and find that he has lost the first finger of his right hand. He affirms that it was cut off while digging post holes. I recommend that he be sent to the Army or to Fort Lafayette" (during the Civil War, Fort Lafayette was used as a prison for political offenders). (Library of Congress, Washington, D.C.).

men under the preceding call for volunteers, the shortfall would be made up by a special draft from the militia by August 15. As it was later noted, this was the first time the Federal government had ever acted on the belief that every citizen owes his country some level of military service to help maintain the security of the Republic. There were, of course, official ways for potential draftees to become exempted, such as missing fingers, toes, chronic illness, and so on. Such ways out prompted a Michigan man to inform his friend, who had already enlisted, of the various schemes afoot in their hometown: "Every man that is between 18 & 45 years of age is sick or going to be, or lost a finger, or a thumb, or a great toe. Anything for an excuse."[11]

Meanwhile, on August 9, the *Free Press* reported that "the exodus was very large" of men fleeing Detroit into Canada, "like cravens to escape the draft." That was hardly an overstatement. Only three days prior, on August 6, Mrs. John Harris of London, Ontario (Canada), had noted in her diary that after one hundred Americans who were fleeing the draft had unexpectedly arrived in her small Canadian town, "the station master [was] requested to send as many empty cars as he can to Windsor to bring the Americans and their families who are escaping from conscription." This 1862 draft certainly helped to dampen the patriotic call, especially after reports of another Union disaster at the August 28–30 battle of Second Bull Run. Authorities soon came to realize that, considering how unpopular the draft would be, some method of policing it and keeping order would be necessary.[12]

When Detroit was first incorporated in 1802, the position of town marshal was created to deal with matters of law and order. That position had continued to exist within Detroit through the decades, though watchmen and constables were added in a somewhat random fashion over the years. As the Civil War years approached, preserving order was the domain of the county sheriff and the approximately ten deputies under him. In addition, each ward had an elected constable who had the authority to make criminal arrests. Neither the constables nor the deputies patrolled the city either at night or during the day on a regular basis, which resulted in the various lawmen always seeming to be in a reactive rather than proactive position.[13]

With no formal police department and Detroit's sheriff now enlisted in the army, city authorities knew that they were shorthanded in the number of men required to maintain the peace. Therefore, to preserve civil order and assist with the upcoming draft, a volunteer infantry company of approximately one hundred men, to be known as the Provost Guard, was authorized by the secretary of war on November 4, 1862. The company, to be raised in Detroit and housed at the Detroit Barracks, was a precursor to the modern military police; its essential duties were to help keep the peace, guard public property, and escort new recruits throughout the city. The unit was mustered into service on January 3, 1863, under the command of Captain Erastus D. Robinson.[14]

This guard came under the control of the new Bureau of the Provost Marshal General, then being created in Washington by an act of Congress, which would formally come into existence on March 3, 1863. The new bureau's mission was to administer, oversee, and enforce any upcoming national drafts, arrest deserters and, in a broad general sense, deal with internal enemies of the government. In charge of this new department was thirty-six-year-old James Barnet Fry, an 1847 West Point graduate who recently had served as chief of staff for General Irvin McDowell and General Don Carlos Buell. Well known in Washington circles, Fry was recommended for the position by his former West Point classmate General Ulysses S. Grant, who later described Fry as "the officer best fitted" to command the bureau. Fry assumed command of the new department on March 17 with the rank of colonel and, according to historian Allan Nevins, from the outset "showed the traits of an efficient martinet." Fry rounded out his organizational chart in April by appointing an officer in each state or group of territories to hold the title of acting assistant provost marshal general. These men would report directly to Fry and be responsible for overseeing the proper execution of all draft-related activities and communications within their state. In that position, each officer's most important responsibilities were to oversee the new Federal enrollment act passed in March, which included maintaining draft-related security in the various locales, capturing and arresting deserters and, perhaps somewhat surprisingly, handling counterespionage. Generally, these men were honorable officers who were unsuited for front-line duty due to past illness or injury. Each state's acting assistant provost marshal general further coordinated department activities within his state by appointing a local provost marshal and an enrollment board for each congressional district or county within his jurisdiction. The enrollment board consisted of the local provost marshal, who was given the rank of captain, a respected surgeon, and a civilian. The board had the power to appoint local citizens who made the actual enrollments of local men for any upcoming draft. Furthermore, each acting assistant provost marshal general served as the official liaison between the main provost marshal general's office in Washington and each state or territorial government.[15]

Thus, with this chain of command, the entire draft apparatus was centralized under military control with civilians, for the most part, holding no positions of importance. An unforeseen consequence of this was the development of a popular feeling that the country was now being subjected to military rule, thereby making conscription quite odious to much of the population.[16]

Major Bennett Hoskin Hill was the man chosen to hold the position of acting assistant provost marshal general for the state of Michigan, with his office to be located in Detroit. In a letter to Michigan

Bennett H. Hill (National Archives, College Park, Md.).

governor Austin Blair introducing Hill and explaining his duties, Provost Marshal General Fry described Hill as "an officer of superior ability and a gentleman of attainments." The forty-seven-year-old Hill had been an 1837 West Point graduate and a regular army veteran with the artillery, having served gallantly in both the Florida Indian and Mexican wars. When secession broke out, he was in command of the U.S. Army's Second Artillery stationed at Fort Brown near Brownsville, Texas. His continual poor health prompted the military to send him to Wheeling, West Virginia, in late August 1861 to serve as an enrollment officer and then on to Detroit in April 1863 where he assumed his new administrative role. In short order, Hill reported back to Washington that he had commenced his duties and had leased proper office space on Jefferson Avenue near Woodward at a price of $12 per month.[17]

❀   ❀   ❀

IN his later history of the Bureau of the Provost Marshal General, Fry correctly pointed out that by late 1862 a radical change was needed for raising troops. Even though Lincoln's summer 1862 appeal for more men had been successful in Detroit, the same could not be said for other parts of the country. Twelve states, mostly in the East, were compelled to administer a draft because the call for volunteers had failed to generate enough men. Roughly speaking, about 60,000 to 70,000 men were actually conscripted into the army that fall, a far cry from quotas that totaled 335,000. It was however, an excellent stimulus for recruiting volunteers, for eventually well over 300,000 volunteers were raised.[18]

Even so, by the time winter approached, a recruiting malaise had infected the entire country. Union reverses throughout mid- to late 1862 had made it quite plain that the war was not going to be over soon. Heavy losses also dictated that any future draft had to dwarf anything previously seen. The steady need for more men in the field simply exceeded the willing supply, thereby exposing the shortcomings of the volunteer system. It became clear that some method of fair, orderly conscription had to be implemented. It was also pointed out that the Confederacy had resorted to such measures in April 1862, its government specifying that all able-bodied Southern men between the ages of eighteen and thirty-five were eligible for three years' service. This prompted many in the North to assert that conscription was the reason for so many of the Rebel successes. With their backs somewhat up against the wall, the Lincoln administration and its congressional allies fervently believed that a national draft would secure a more reliable, regular, and abundant supply of men. Other significant benefits, according to Fry, "would be derived from the adoption and enforcement of the principle that every citizen, not incapacitated by physical or mental disability, owes military service to the country in the hour of extremity." Yet many were not convinced, especially in light of Lincoln's Emancipation Proclamation, which had been announced in September 1862 and then gone into effect on January 1, 1863. That proclamation convinced many that a righteous war for Union and Constitution had now, overnight, become a highly controversial war for black emancipation. Fry also acknowledged that many viewed the draft as a dangerous novelty, something that ran completely against the grain of the nation's traditional military policy, whereby citizen-soldier volunteers were all that was needed. "The people had become more accustomed to the enjoyment of privileges than to the fulfillment of duties under the General Government," wrote Fry, "and hence beheld the prospect of compulsory service in the Army with an unreasonable dread." After lengthy and heated debated that spanned almost the entire session of the Thirty-seventh Congress, the Enrollment Act was passed and signed into law, effective March 3, 1863. The overarching decree was that all able-bodied, single male citizens of the United States and persons of foreign birth who intended to become citizens between the ages of twenty and forty-five were subject to the draft. For married men, the eligible ages were twenty to thirty-five. As practically everyone realized, it was the first time ever that the U.S. government, acting through Congress, had attempted to build a national army without the approval or input of state authorities.[19]

As was the case with the militia draft in August 1862, the new enrollment act and its attendant fear of conscription prompted some Detroit men to immediately flee to Canada. As Mrs. Elizabeth Stuart described it, Canada had become a "scene of Frolicking" and she was concerned that a recent hire had "been overtaken in the frolick." The *Free Press* termed the exodus "the second setting in the tide of Canadian immigration." Only two days after the act was signed into law, that newspaper was sarcastically reporting how the Canadian town of Windsor just across the Detroit River "was becoming as popular a place of resort as a fashionable seaside town during the watering season" since "the influx of skedaddlers fills the hotels and boarding houses." The paper likened the flight to what had happened seven months earlier "when a provost guard had to be extemporized and stationed upon the docks and in the streets to watch every man who walked abroad with a suspicious looking valise."[20]

For any man who did not want to find himself in the Union army, there were a number of ways he could lawfully exempt himself from the draft without fleeing to Canada. For example, a man could avoid the draft if he was the only son of aged or infirm parents who depended on him for their support. The same exemption was available for men who were fathers, but had no wife or mother at home to care for his children. While these types of exemptions were generally deemed reasonable by all factions of the public, what really stoked the ire of working-class white men and their newspaper allies was how any eligible man might avoid the draft simply by paying a fee. Known as the "commutation clause," any man could exempt himself by paying a $300 commutation fee to the Federal government, an extremely handsome sum in the Civil War era that was well beyond the financial means of workingmen and seemed to fly in the face of what democracy in America was supposed to represent. An amendatory law signed by Lincoln on February 24, 1864, dictated that those paying the commutation fee were now exempt for that upcoming draft only, not any future drafts. Nevertheless, so great was the public outcry against the commutation clause that Congress ultimately repealed it in July 1864. The fact that $594,600 in such fees were spent by affluent Michiganders in order to avoid the draft only underscores the resentment that was felt by Michigan's working-class men.[21]

A drafted man could also hire a draft-exempt substitute to go permanently in his place, with the fee being negotiated between "buyer" and "seller." Naturally, the demand for such willing men slowly began to outpace the supply, prompting a rise in the fees these willing substitutes demanded, placing that draft avoidance method likewise beyond the means of most ordinary workingmen. This type of business dealing was aptly illustrated by a Republican businessman in Mt. Clemens, Michigan, who thought he had hired an Irish laborer as a substitute for $200 only two weeks after the conscription act went into effect. After a friend of the Irishman advised him "never to go short of $500 at least," the deal quickly fell apart, with the new price now set at $500. This substitute feature of the draft gave rise to the "bounty broker," a type of middleman who, according to Eugene Murdock, "capitalized on the ignorance and gullibility of young volunteers by arranging for their enlistment and then exacting a large fee for the favor." In essence, these brokers were freelance recruiters who earned generous commissions for each recruit they brought in, often with methods that were questionable at best and illegal at worst, including threats or even kidnapping.[22]

The workingman was not without his means of avoiding the draft either, despite the apparent favoritism afforded to the well-to-do by the commutation clause and substitute hiring. From the time of the conscription act's announcement in the spring of 1863 until the war ended in April 1865, numerous cities and counties often raided their treasuries and used funds collected from property taxes to pay the $300 fee for some of their working-class citizens. From one city to the next, this type of public appropriation spread like wildfire, to the point that many Republican papers were condemning the practice, believing it to be undertaken solely as a means to derail the Enrollment Act. "Wherever, all over the country, there is a Democratic Council," complained the *Advertiser and Tribune*, "they are appropriating money to exempt able-bodied men from the conscription. If this is done as generally as now promises, the government will get very few men under the draft."[23]

In other instances, employers set up a commutation clause fund that consisted of their own contributions as well as a small levy from their workers. One of the more popular means for the nonwealthy to avoid the draft was by participating in what were known as "draft insurance societies" or "draft protection clubs." Any member of the public who was subject to the draft could join. In these societies, members could buy a $300 "insurance policy" to pay their commutation fee if they were officially drafted, or they could use the proceeds toward hiring a substitute after the commutation clause was repealed. The monthly premium for this "insurance" was generally anywhere from $1 to several dollars a month. Other fee structures included an upfront, onetime premium that could run as high as $100. It was this latter example that manifested itself in Detroit in mid-February 1865 when citizens of the west end ninth ward met to form their own society. Twenty members joined on the spot, all paying a $100 fee for the privilege. That same week, residents in the second and sixth wards also took out classified ads in the papers announcing their "clubs." One month later, residents from the heavily Irish eighth ward banded together for the same purpose, though in this case the fee was limited to $50. Much of the time however, the working immigrant was too poor to raise $100 or even $50.[24]

The new draft law extended Federal power into communities as never before. Most people's prior contact with the national government had simply been through the U.S. postal system. For working-class native-born and immigrant whites who had chosen not to enlist for one reason or another, conscription was viewed as a form of bondage and therefore compared to slavery. It was clear to such men and their families what was now transpiring. They were to become the mandatory cannon fodder that the Union army seemed to be lacking. Unable to afford $300 to buy a commutation or substitute, these men were to be forcibly drafted into the army to fight a war of emancipation that many in Detroit were hostile to.[25]

The draft was certainly not popular in Michigan. One galling reason was that it was applied selectively, only in those towns or counties that had failed to furnish enough volunteers through the quota system. As one man described it, being drafted "robbed [men] of their patriotism and branded them as unwilling defenders of the nation." Yet paying the requisite fee for a substitute seemed to be the preferred option for most. Charles Cleveland of Adrian wrote of this mindset in his diary in February 1865 when he noted that the quota

"Don't You See the Point?" (*Harper's Weekly*, August 29, 1863).

for his town's fourth ward was twenty-eight men, which would require raising about $9,000 or $10,000 to obtain that number of willing substitutes. "It comes hard to pay so largely as we are doing," grumbled Cleveland, "but better be done than to stand the draft." Within the week, Cleveland observed during a day trip to Detroit that the draft was "the absorbing topic" in that town and how Adrian "was filling up with country boys, who come from towns that pay no bounties."[26]

Most people could see that the reason for the draft was the fact that the Lincoln administration had felt for months that the volunteer enlistment system was no longer supplying the army with enough men. And for many soldiers and most Democrats, the reason why was simple and straightforward: Lincoln and his "Black Republicans'" Emancipation Proclamation had turned the war's cause from one of preserving the Union to freedom for the black race. On that perceived turn, Corporal Marion Munson of the Sixteenth Michigan

Infantry spoke for many soldiers when he wrote in February 1863 that the only way to achieve peace was by "the destruction of slavery on every foot of soil in the Union." Paradoxically, however, Munson was also adamant that "to shoot down white men to do it is a mean and Barbarous act." In his opinion, his current and potential comrades did not want "to go through the rough life of a soldier and perhaps get shot for a d——d nigger." A soldier in the Fourth Michigan Infantry who considered himself a staunch Democrat went even further on what he described as "the niggar question," declaring in a letter home that after attending "a Negro prayer meeting" in Virginia, he became "well enough convinced that they are better off in bondage than they would be free."[27]

Even worse, according to the *Free Press* and other stridently anti-black papers like it, if the white man did not lose his life on the battlefield fighting for the black slave, he then faced the likely prospect of freed blacks streaming into his hometown and taking his job, not to mention the racist fear of those same blacks perpetrating sexual transgressions against his wife or daughters. According to Matthew Kundinger, the *Free Press* repeatedly used racial rhetoric to create a meme that portrayed blacks as simultaneously inferior yet always threatening to white, working-class society. Its use of disparaging racist jokes, such as how blacks smelled, allowed white readers to feel smugly superior, but at the same time the paper attempted to play on white fears and resentment by portraying blacks as threats to white sensibilities on important emotional issues such as manly labor, voting, and sexual morality. The *Free Press* had for years preached an anti-black philosophy to its white readership that, metaphorically, became a keg of dynamite sitting on a shelf. Such racial tensions had blown up into violent altercations for years, including in September 1862, only days prior to Lincoln's announcement of the Emancipation Proclamation, when a black Detroiter was purportedly assaulted by a white soldier in Detroit's downtown market. A week later, a black man was chased by a crowd of whites down Michigan Avenue in the direction of Randolph Street. As the crowd neared, the black man turned and fired a buckshot-loaded pistol at his pursuers, seriously wounding one. He then waylaid a second attacker with a billy club. Meanwhile, another black man in the area was set upon, but was soon rescued by several passersby. Certainly, nothing had changed six months later. The new enrollment act and its perceived intent of forcing poor white men into the army to fight for the black slaves' freedom became the powder keg's short fuse. In early March 1863, Detroit lit the match.[28]

On March 5, a forty-two-year-old, single Detroit man named William Faulkner was brought to trial on charges of "committing an outrage" (rape) against two nine-year-old girls: a white girl named Mary Brown and a black girl named Ellen Hoover. Faulkner, a mulatto, had been arrested on February 26 based solely on the word of the two young girls, who had been in his Michigan Avenue tavern ten days earlier, though the circumstances of the alleged rapes were sketchy at best. Faulkner's skin color was light enough that everyone in the past had considered him a white man; in fact it was recalled that he had even routinely voted, a crystal-clear indication of white privilege, and that he had always chosen the Democratic ticket, no less. Yet during his time in jail, it was alleged that Faulkner was indeed a Negro, which Faulkner vehemently denied, claiming instead to be of "mixed Spanish-Indian blood." As one elderly man had said of Faulkner, "If he thought he had one drop of colored blood in his veins, if he could, he would let it out." The *Free Press* was certainly not swayed, despite its later remark that Faulkner "apparently has but a trifle of negro blood in his veins." *Any* amount of Negro blood was enough for the *Free Press* and other racist papers like it to "condemn" a man as black, for in its daily coverage of the proceedings leading up to and including the trial, and of the events to come, it consistently referred to the accused as the "black fiend" or "the negro Faulkner," thereby slowly converting an innocent-until-proven-guilty man into a black criminal of the type considered the most unspeakable. Meanwhile, concurrent with its reporting of the case, the *Free Press* further stoked the racial embers by describing all the details pertinent to the hated Enrollment Act of 1863, in essence subtly reminding its readers that the white man was now being conscripted to fight for black emancipation.[29]

At the end of the trial's first day, Faulkner was greeted by "a perfect storm of hisses, curses, and threats" as he and his guards exited the courtroom. He was escorted back to the city jail which, then as now, stood at the corner of Beaubien and Clinton Street. During the short trip, he and the deputy sheriffs escorting him were harangued and accosted almost every step of the way by a large crowd of "respectable citizens" that purportedly numbered in the hundreds, all attempting to tear Faulkner away from his guards and lynch him right then and there. The officers guarding him were forced to point their revolvers at the mob on several occasions to maintain the peace. During his trip back to the jail, Faulkner was hit in the head by a large street paving stone, facetiously described by some as "Irish confetti," which knocked him senseless, though ultimately he was placed securely back in his cell.[30]

The next morning, March 6, the same day that the new and hated Enrollment Act went into effect, Faulkner was escorted to the courtroom at 6:00 in an effort to avoid another such scene. Surprisingly, considering the near melee that had taken place less than eighteen hours previously, this was the only proactive security measure the predominantly Democratic city took that day. Later that morning, as feared, a large throng, estimated at close to a thousand, convened outside the city hall courtroom, seemingly intent on bringing mob justice to Faulkner regardless of the lawful court proceedings going on indoors. Many of these people had no doubt read their morning copy of the *Free Press* while sipping their coffee and had learned of the details pertaining to the potential draft. While the trial was continuing inside, blacks who happened past city hall were subjected to "petty persecutions" from the white crowd, including "kicks, cuffs, and blows. . . . Even women and children were not exempt, several of them being abused in a most shameful and outrageous manner," noted a *Free Press* reporter. Despite Faulkner's protestations that he was not a Negro, from the mob's point of view, he was indeed a black man. With the advent of Lincoln's Emancipation Proclamation, which the *Free Press* called an "abolition nigger doctrine," and the new conscription act threatening to force white men to risk their lives for black freedom, many anti-black Detroit Democrats were angry enough to believe just about any allegation against blacks, especially if it involved sexual transgressions. Guilty or not, Faulkner became the symbolic target of their anger and fear.[31]

Faulkner vigorously pled not guilty, his attorney asserting during final remarks that the girls' testimony was "inconsistent, somewhat absurd, and, taken together, unworthy of credence." Nevertheless, the jury found Faulkner guilty on all counts in less than ten minutes, the verdict essentially based solely on the testimony of the two young girls. Only two weeks later, both nine-year-old girls were arrested for larceny, to which they pled guilty. They were sentenced to ninety days in Detroit's House of Correction. Both girls seemed to delight in their conviction and, according to the *Free Press*, "were as expert in the use of low and obscene slang and songs as any of the older depraved ones" within the jail. Meanwhile, back in the Faulkner courtroom, sixty-five-year-old Judge Benjamin F. H. Witherell spent a few minutes pondering an appropriate sentence for the black defendant. At the time of the trial, Witherell was up for reelection as a Democrat and, in spite of a reputation for leniency, he handed down the maximum sentence then allowed in Michigan for rape: life in prison at the state penitentiary in Jackson.[32]

What was now paramount for Detroit authorities was avoiding a repeat of the near lynching that had occurred the previous day; and a lynching is exactly what the mob would have demanded, especially with a guilty verdict for such an "outrage" committed by a black male against a white female. Had someone in the crowd simply wanted to kill Faulkner as a perceived means of just retribution, it would have been easy enough for a marksman with a musket to do so from a reasonable distance or for someone in the mob to fire a pistol. But for those demanding Faulkner's immediate death, such a quick demise would not suffice. As Jonathan Markovitz has noted, lynching was viewed by whites as a metaphor, as a public means of understanding and reinforcing the white-ordained racial order. The gruesome act of public lynching strove to ensure that onlookers, be they black or white, were made well aware of white dominance and the costs of violating the established racial hierarchy. Concurrently, the ritual worked to demonstrate how white men were the gallant protectors of white females. Lynching took on the metaphorical symbolism of white "justice" and power against so-called uppity blacks that no other form of vengeance could obtain. Far from being only the stereotyped Southern method of racial violence against blacks, lynching was a means of execution and public statement that occurred throughout the land.[33]

With no professional police force yet employed in Detroit, Francis Phelps, Detroit's acting mayor while Mayor William C. Duncan was in Lansing on official business, called on Lieutenant Colonel Smith to help preserve the peace and escort Faulkner back to jail. Smith immediately dispatched about seventy-five men from the Detroit Barracks who were serving as part of the recently mustered Provost Guard—the Civil War–era version of military police—to protect and accompany Faulkner on his trip back to his jail cell. Within ten to fifteen minutes and with bayonets fixed and at the ready, the company of blue-uniformed troops began marching Faulkner from city hall down Croghan Street (modern-day Monroe Avenue) toward the jail. In its later investigations, the *Advertiser and Tribune* asserted that the company of soldiers sent was actually only thirty men of the Provost Guard while the other forty or so were made up of members of the Eighth Michigan Cavalry and convalescing soldiers who were also stationed at the Detroit Barracks. Still seeking vengeance, the rowdy crowd began hurling both insults and rocks at Faulkner and the soldiers as the trek continued. According to a black eyewitness, "They were yelling like demons, and crying 'kill all the damned niggers.'"[34]

In spite of the crowd's cries for revenge, Faulkner was safely deposited by the troops inside the jail. Outside the jail, however, the bricks and stones were still flying toward the soldiers. Lieutenant John Van Stan, the officer in charge of the Provost Guard and later described by Lieutenant Colonel Smith as "a man of notoriously intemperate habits," then ordered his men to load a round of blanks into their muskets, as he believed his command's safety was at risk. At Van Stan's command, the rifles were leveled at the crowd and discharged, obviously as a warning. The mob clearly did not get the message, and when it refused to disperse, a live round was then loaded by several soldiers, possibly without orders, and fired toward the crowd. One man, a twenty-four-year-old German shopkeeper named Charles Langer, was shot through the throat and killed instantly. By all accounts, he was an innocent bystander who was merely standing on the sidewalk with his hands in his pockets and his pipe in his mouth. At that point, a riot began in earnest, the mob seeming to realize in unison that from its perspective, a guiltless white man had been shot down so that a guilty black man might live. In the interim, having performed their duty of escorting Faulkner to jail, the members of the still-green Provost Guard then began a swift march back to their Detroit Barracks to halt what was believed to be a potential uprising of new conscripts, leaving the infuriated mob in charge of the surrounding streets.[35]

One of Detroit's best-known militia companies, the Detroit Light Guard, maintained a tight cordon around the jail, so with Faulkner seemingly out of their reach, the rioters decided to seek vengeance on any blacks they could find. As the *Free Press* had repeatedly and vociferously opined, the black man was the source of all national troubles, from the underlying cause of the Civil War to local crime, inflation, and labor issues. To the rabble on the scene, here was an opportunity for the working-class white man to strike back. One man later recalled hearing a rioter loudly swear, "If we are got to be killed up for niggers then we will kill every nigger in this town." John A. Warren, the black preacher at the Lafayette Street African Church, wrote that he saw one white man climb upon a tree stump and boldly declare, "Gentlemen, I am for killing all the Negroes!" "Kill the negroes, kill the negroes!" was the crowd's boisterous reply, according to Warren. The horde streamed south through Beaubien, Antoine, Lafayette, and Fort streets with some carrying axes and others hauling wagonloads of beer; many black residents in this third ward area were fearfully beaten while their homes were looted and set ablaze. Those who tried to flee were pelted with bricks and stones. One black eyewitness reported that he saw a burned man escape from his blazing home and then "when he came out of the door some twenty dirty-looking Irishmen rushed at him with clubs, crying 'kill the nager.'" With Detroit's black population standing at only fourteen hundred, or roughly 3 percent of the entire city, these white rioters probably knew that the local black population was not so great that they had to fear being surrounded in a wholly black neighborhood, the knowledge of this "safety" contributing to their fury. Meanwhile, some frightened blacks were able to make their way to the docks with the intent of fleeing across the river to Canada. Realizing the economic demand that was at hand, ferrymen tripled and quadrupled their normal prices in an appalling attempt to profit from the tumult. Some of those beaten were purportedly Canadian blacks who had the tremendous misfortune to be visiting Detroit when the riot broke out. Apparently some whites chased them back across the border, even beating some. Blacks in Windsor armed themselves and swore vengeance, but were quickly talked out of their plans when it was learned that a white Detroit mob stood at the ready to "exterminate" them.[36]

Throughout the late afternoon and early evening of March 6, Detroit's third ward burned, from Croghan Street down Brush Street and Beaubien Street as far south as Congress. Houses on Lafayette Street between Beaubien and St. Antoine were practically stripped of all furniture and possessions, which were then used as fuel for bonfires in the middle of the street. Meanwhile, word of what was transpiring spread just as quickly as the flames. A young schoolgirl named Mary Bissell who was attending the local female seminary on Fort Street as a day student wrote in her diary that very night how "all the negro houses here are going to be burned by the Dutch [sic] because 2 of the latter were shot this afternoon." Fearing that the flames and violence could easily spread, Mary's father ordered all tubs and buckets in the Bissell residence filled with water once he returned home that evening.[37]

The riot was finally quelled late in the evening by the arrival of more local militia, a detachment of the Nineteenth U.S. Regular Infantry stationed at Fort Wayne, and five companies from the new Twenty-seventh Michigan Volunteer Infantry, which had been rushed to Detroit by special train from their training grounds at Ypsilanti. With the appearance of such an armed force, the rioters seemed to melt away, and by the following morning, all was quiet on Detroit's streets amid the smoldering remains of the burned-out ruins. To help maintain the peace, acting mayor Phelps urged all citizens to stay off the streets and ordered all saloons and taverns to close at 7:00 p.m. for two consecutive nights. The tragic results of the violence included two dead and scores of black men mercilessly beaten, all after the city's Provost Guard beat a hasty retreat to the security of its barracks. Thirty to thirty-five black homes and businesses were burned to the ground while many others were seriously damaged. Yet within several days, Francis Phelps was formally thanking his city's military authorities for their "alacrity and efficiency manifested in the discharge of the duties assigned them."[38]

Who exactly were the rioters? According to the *Free Press*, the participants "were mostly boys ten to eighteen years of age"; no more than twenty to thirty adult men, mostly "rowdies, vagabonds, and loafers," had anything to do with the violence. In his history of mid-nineteenth century Detroit crime and policing, John Schneider determined that of the forty-six men arrested for rioting, at least twenty were Irish, while no more than six were German. Almost half the rioters' names could not be found in city directories, a strong indicator that these men were transients. The *Free Press* decried what it termed "a most lamentable and disgraceful riot" and immediately distanced itself from the unrest, earnestly denying any responsibility despite its inflammatory reporting of the Faulkner case. On the other side of the political aisle, the Republican *Advertiser and Tribune* had no doubt about its rival's culpability, calling the rioters "a *Free Press* mob" composed primarily of Detroit's Irish underclass who had been urged to such violence for months by the *Free Press*'s reckless anti-black commentary. William Spalding, the quartermaster for the Twenty-seventh Michigan, certainly concurred with the

Advertiser and Tribune's assessment after surveying the scene. Spalding had returned to Detroit from Cleveland a few days after the riot and was surprised to find the five companies of his comrades angrily patrolling the town. After talking with his men, he wrote to his wife that the riot "was a scandalous affair, excited and brought about by just such men as we see in the South. The 'Free Press' is in fact at the bottom of the affair and responsible for it." Other Midwest papers agreed, including the *Chicago Tribune*, the *Springfield Republican*, and the *Cleveland Leader*. In explaining the riot's causes, the *Tribune* opined, "The Detroit massacre is the legitimate fruitage of the rebellious teachings of secession newspapers and stumpers," a clear allusion to the *Free Press's* past editorial positions. Detroit's black community held the same belief. In his account of the disturbance to friends in Philadelphia, black pastor John A. Warren blamed "*prejudice* and passion, brought on by the Democratic Free Press, the most reckless sheet that was ever issued from any press."[39]

Despite its denial about having anything to do with the just-concluded riot, the *Free Press* continued to put forth its anti-black warnings. Within months, it practically seemed to excuse the riot by reminding its readers, "The notion that the war for the Union was becoming a crusade for the social and political elevation of the negro at the expense of the white man, could not fail to enlist the fiercest passions of the white population against the blacks." Thus from the vantage of the *Detroit Free Press*, the official organ of the Democratic Party in Michigan, the small black population of Detroit could be blamed for all manner of concerns, including Lincolnian war policy, price inflation, taxation, crime, labor issues, depressed wages, or any other subject well beyond its control. Meanwhile, such memes allowed whites to collectively package their socioeconomic worries, sexual angst, and class grievances into a noble form of racial prejudice.[40]

William Webb, an ex-slave who had earlier made his way to Detroit and was now living on Fort Street, five miles west of downtown, recalled that after the riot "a great many colored people were fleeing out in the country where I was, and some came to the house where I was stopping to get shelter." Fleeing for their lives, these Detroit residents described the white hostility in town. They still did not know whether they had reached safety; Webb and the owner of the home he lived in gathered what guns they had and posted a guard ready to sound the alarm should any danger approach. Fortunately, the night remained quiet. The next morning, Webb cautiously ventured into

Detroit to see what damage had been done. He noted that "the colored people were very scarce in the places I had been used to see them, and I found that some had run over into Canada, and some of them had run into the woods." When Webb heard a number of white residents remark that it was a pity the riot had occurred, he bravely asked if there was no law in town to prevent such a mob. The only reply he received was that there was no law *for* a mob.[41]

Detroit's elite white citizens were shocked by the unrest and by how close the flames had come to destroying valuable *white-owned* property. In addition to destroying black homes and businesses, the rioters had threatened arriving firefighters with violence and cutting their hoses if they attempted to put out the third ward inferno. When it appeared, however, that the fire might spread to the valuable business district, the fire companies started to work frantically to douse the nearby flames while citizens who had been standing by merely watching also rushed forward to help.[42]

For days, the great riot was the talk of the town. In her diary entry for March 6, Fannie Wright mentioned the "dreadful riot" and how it had stirred "great excitement" throughout the city. Meanwhile, Henry Billings Brown had apparently been out on those very streets, later noting the "awful riot" in his diary and how he had been "kicked around all the evening and got knocked around."[43]

In the days to follow, many whites chose to do what they could for the newly homeless blacks within Detroit. Writing to her husband from her home in Grosse Ile, twenty miles south of Detroit, Elizabeth Campbell Douglass even saw a perverse benefit for the now-homeless blacks in Detroit: "*Abstractly* considered, the burning of those houses was something to be thankful for. They must build better ones if they build any." The city's Democratic-controlled Common Council, however, was another story. A special committee was created to determine just how much private property had been destroyed and what, if any, the city would be responsible for. It reported back within several weeks to the full council that, in the committee's opinion, "the city is not legally liable for property destroyed, or for injuries to persons by the mob in the riot referred to in the communication of the acting Mayor, and in the petitions and bills of the sufferers." When it was therefore suggested by the legislature that some type of assistance should be offered to the third ward's homeless blacks, the council declined to offer any measure of city-sponsored support or restitution.[44]

With the vote, jury duty, militia service, and so many other civil privileges and responsibilities not granted to them, Detroit's "free" blacks must now have surely realized the truth of what historian Jean Baker has called all Northern blacks' one permissible public function from the white perspective: as victims of white, anti-black rioters. Such attacks by whites against blacks had been so common and accepted in the antebellum and Civil War–era North, and police intervention so rare, that blacks became the natural scapegoats for all societal ills that had befallen the country despite their relatively small numbers in the North. Undeniably, when Supreme Court Chief Justice Roger Taney opined in the 1857 *Dred Scott* decision that a black man had no rights that a white man was bound to respect, he hardly exaggerated the black man's low station in life. This dynamic has been explained by David Roediger, who postulated that blacks were viewed not only as noncitizens but also as *anticitizens*, as "enemies rather than members of the social compact." As discussed in chapter 1, that compact dictated that blacks were at the bottom of the social pecking order, with the great white fear being that any collective improvement for free blacks would surely come at white expense by showing their working freedom to be illusory—in essence, a zero-sum scenario. Whites rioted in Detroit in 1863 not because a black man purportedly raped two girls, nor because an innocent white man was shot by white troops, but rather as a socially acceptable means (in some quarters) for working-class whites to reinforce what they saw as the established racial order or, as Matthew Jacobson described it, as "a racial ritual of civic differentiation."[45]

The shock that such a horrific event had occurred in Detroit extended, via newspapers, to the town's soldiers out on the battle lines. First Division general Alpheus Williams of the Army of the Potomac's Twelfth Corps was a native Detroiter and veteran military man. In a March 20 letter to his daughter, he decried the actions of Detroit authorities. "These mobs are generally composed of nine-tenths spectators, whose presence serves to encourage the rioters. . . . This Detroit riot was about as absurd an affair as I have read of, only equaled by the weakness and want of action on the part of somebody in power." Realizing the huge mistake that the green Provost Guard had made in firing into the mob and then quickly abandoning the scene, Williams concluded, "The provost guard rather inflamed than quelled" the riot.[46]

The saddest fact of what became known as the 1863 Detroit Riot is that the trial of William Faulkner and the subsequent disturbance should never have occurred. Just over six and a half years later, during which time William Faulkner had languished in jail, then sixteen-year-old Mary Brown came forward and admitted that she had perjured herself on the witness stand. She had fabricated the entire story and persuaded Ellen Hoover to go along with it solely as a means of avoiding trouble at home because she was late finishing her errands. Brown and Hoover had, in fact, been in Faulkner's tavern that fateful February day, but only briefly to warm their feet from the winter cold outside. William Faulkner was pardoned on December 30, 1869, due to "the severity of the sentence, of strong proof tending to show that the prisoner was guiltless of the offense, and because the girl upon whose testimony he was convicted was at the time utterly depraved." Once freed, Faulkner was set up in the produce business by several wealthy Detroiters whose conscience demanded some type of beneficent action on the man's behalf. Faulkner continued to work in his new business until he passed away in 1877, leaving behind a wife and two children. In its small mention of his passing, the *Free Press* described Faulkner in his final years as an "exemplary citizen," a far cry from only fourteen years earlier, when that same newspaper callously referred to him as "the black fiend, the monster Faulkner."[47]

The riot in Detroit was not a completely isolated affair. Race-related strife had occurred the previous July only fifty miles to the south at Toledo, Ohio, when Irish stevedores attacked blacks who had agreed to accept lower wages than the Irish dockworkers had previously demanded. That same month, Irish boat hands in Cincinnati rioted against blacks for similar wage-related reasons and ended up burning or otherwise destroying a significant part of Cincinnati's black neighborhood. Still, the Detroit disturbance was the largest race-related riot to occur in the Midwest during the Civil War years. Such racial tension was building in other Northern cities as well, including Boston and Philadelphia. But far and away the most infamous disturbances occurred in New York City four months after the Detroit riot. For four days, from July 13 to July 16, 1863, New York City was brought to a standstill by thousands of rioters from New York's Irish Catholic underclass, many of whom greatly resented how they were expected to partake in a war whose causes, particularly black emancipation, meant little to them. What became known as the New York City Draft Riots occurred initially as a protest against national conscription and its seemingly class-based provisions that allowed wealthier men to avoid service by hiring a substitute or paying the $300 commutation fee. In short order, the rioters began taking out their anger against the well-to-do and any symbol of Republicanism. But as in the Detroit riot four months earlier, their most vicious rage was soon directed against blacks, whom they viewed as the unwelcome reason for the draft in the first place as well as their working-class labor competition.[48]

Even while the New York disturbances were still unfolding, they were causing consternation and angst in Detroit as to whether its draft should proceed, and if Union troops should be sent in to control the peace. Captain John S. Newberry, provost marshal for Detroit's first congressional district, met with some of Detroit's leading citizens to gauge the mood of the city and anticipate potential mob violence. All were in agreement that an organized and armed body of anti-draft men existed in Detroit, but just how many were involved no one was sure of. Though Newberry believed their numbers were no more than fifteen hundred at most, he acknowledged to Major Hill on July 14 that "there is doubtless a large number of disaffected persons who have threatened violence, and who would instantly join any attempted outbreak having for an object the obstruction or prevention of the draft." Unlike Hill, who had arrived in Detroit only a few months before, the thirty-six-year-old Newberry was practically a native Detroiter. Though not a military man, he was a successful maritime attorney and growing industrialist who had a keen pulse for what was happening on Detroit's streets. He further advised Hill, "This feeling has become intensified to an alarming degree by the successful violence in the city of New York, compelling the draft to be deferred. A spark here would explode the whole and bring it into the most violent action." From Newberry's perspective, "it would be the height of folly to attempt the drawing or the enforcement of the draft without a strong military force to protect the office and papers." Concurrent with Newberry's private memo to Hill was the *Advertiser and Tribune*'s similar public remarks that "rebel-sympathizing copperheads seem to have become more desperate and determined to create Riot and Revolution in the loyal states, to Aid the Treason of Rebels in Arms." Meanwhile, Newberry's opinion was quickly echoed by Hill, who asserted in a dispatch to Washington, "There is no doubt

John S. Newberry (Silas Farmer,
*History of Detroit and Wayne
County and Early Michigan*, 3rd ed.
[Detroit: Silas Farmer, 1890]).

but that there is among a portion of the population of this city a most bitter opposition to the Government, and it extends to other portions of the State." Unfortunately for Detroit's law-abiding citizens, Hill affirmed there was only a single company of provost guards and a few invalid soldiers to keep the peace. Fortunately, some assistance was on its way.[49]

Hill was able to report to Washington on July 21 that the six small companies of the First Michigan Sharpshooters were now on their way back to the Detroit area following Governor Blair's request for immediate home-front assistance. The First had been stationed in nearby Dearborn, but on July 8 had quickly left for Indiana by train in an attempt to help stop General John Morgan's ongoing Confederate cavalry raid into the North. Though Morgan's command had been disrupting Union communications in Tennessee and Kentucky since June 11, his Northern raid began in earnest on July 8 when Morgan and his eighteen hundred experienced troopers crossed the Ohio River into Indiana in a desire to bring the horrors of war to the Yankee populace. After nearly engaging elements of the Rebel horsemen at Vernon, Indiana, on July 11, the Michigan Sharpshooters were hastily ordered back to Dearborn following Blair's plea. The cover story for the press was that they were returning home for the purpose of completing the regiment's organization, because no one in authority was going to admit that another riot was feared in Detroit. Two Parrott guns were also made ready and attached to the Provost Guard at the Detroit barracks. For additional firepower, about four dozen cavalry recruits now at Coldwater were also ordered to the Detroit Barracks.[50]

The concern that public violence would erupt over the upcoming draft was still high, though the imminent arrival of these Union soldiers helped Hill breathe easier. "There has been a very excited state of feeling in the community for some days," he reported. "Prominent distinguished supporters of the Government have apprehended attacks on their dwelling-houses and have made preparation for their defense, but I do not think there is ground for further apprehension."[51]

Helping Hill protect Federal interests at Detroit as well as other Great Lakes port cities was the USS *Michigan*, a powerful, steam-powered paddle frigate built in 1842 that held the distinction of being the navy's first-ever iron-hulled warship. At 176 feet long, it was a vessel that also employed the then revolutionary propulsion and weapons systems. This new class of warship was fast, heavily armed, and designed to operate independently from the central battle fleet.[52]

Despite its military prowess, it seemed the *Michigan*'s primary role on the lakes in the years prior to the war had been that of rescue vessel, which over time gave the ship an unwarranted reputation within naval circles as that of a tug. Certainly, such a mission was understandable considering the lack of an enemy on the nation's inland seas. Once war came, the *Michigan*'s initial task was to steam from port to port and recruit men for the U.S. Navy. In fact, over four thousand men from the Great Lakes region were recruited by the *Michigan*'s crew into the Federal navy. Such work continued with little fanfare; however, by the early summer of 1863, the growing resentment and anger toward the newly created draft in the North prompted a change in the *Michigan*'s mission. Hostility toward what many viewed as a conscription law that favored the rich had caused the *Michigan* to cruise to various Great Lakes cities that spring to help suppress potential riots. Detroit had already experienced civil unrest back in March, but by midsummer, draft-related tensions in Detroit were again rising as quickly as the temperature, making the *Michigan*'s appearance in Detroit's harbor a welcome sight to the

USS *Michigan* (Historical Collections of the Great Lakes, Bowling Green State University, Bowling Green, Ohio).

town leaders. On July 28, the ship's commander wrote to Secretary of the Navy Gideon Welles explaining that the *Michigan's* arrival at Detroit was "most opportune" because "I found the people suffering under serious apprehensions of a riot in consequence of excitement in reference to the draft, probably brought about by unscrupulous sensational newspapers predicting such riots. The presence of the ship perhaps did something toward overawing the refractory, and certainly did much to allay the apprehensions of an excited, doubting people. All fears in reference to the riot had subsided before I left."[53]

Much of the tension in Detroit and elsewhere regarding the draft was due to the Democrats' undying and ever-growing conviction that the Lincoln administration's primary war goal had dramatically changed from the preservation of the Union to the emancipation of the black slave, which then led to the fear that abolitionists wanted to make the black man the social and political equal of the white. Simply put, many Northern white men who were willing to lay their life on the line for the Union had no desire whatsoever of risking life and limb for the slave. Such sentiments were painfully apparent in the dismal enlistment numbers as 1863 dragged on. An Englishman taking the train from Ann Arbor to Chicago discovered this when he found himself seated next to a "dyspeptic looking" officer from the

First Michigan Cavalry who had been in the state seeking recruits. Finding only slim pickings, the officer sadly complained to the Englishman that "people have lost their interest in the war," fully realizing that the 1861 public clamoring for glory had long since dissipated.[54]

From the perspective of many Northerners, especially Democrats, the black race was now the chief cause of the national troubles. Race relations in Detroit had certainly hit a low point with the March 1863 riot, and tensions continued throughout that summer.

By the late summer of 1863, Detroit had been and still was a Democratic island surrounded by a sea of Michigan Republicanism. Democratic mayors had been elected in 1861 and 1863. Of the seats on the Common Council, a majority were held by Democrats in 1861 and 1862. By 1863 each party held half the seats; however, the council's stubborn refusal to compensate black riot victims was indicative that Democratic influence continued to dominate. With Republicans holding the advantage at the state and national levels, Detroit Democrats found themselves on the defensive, especially when it came to enforcing the draft, an act that many if not most Democrats abhorred. Towns and counties in general also hated the idea of having to hold the draft in their community, as it was perceived by others as a lack of patriotism indicated by the area's collective unwillingness to voluntarily send enough men to the front. It was certainly a point of pride for a town if it was not subject to the draft because its quota had been met via the volunteer system.[55]

Administering the draft was not easy in all locales. The events in New York in mid-July 1863 proved the danger that draft-related tensions could create. Enrolling officers were particularly despised. These men were to visit every residence within their jurisdiction and record the name, address, age, race, and occupation of every able-bodied male. Sensing potential problems, Provost Marshal Newberry had been direct in his June 10, 1863, instructions to his Detroit enrolling officers: "Be firm, but conciliatory; if threatened, remonstrate kindly." Nevertheless, many officers often came away with fictitious information, while some residents simply refused to give their names or even fled from their homes when they knew the enrolling officer was coming. Worse still, the enrolling officers soon learned to fear for their safety as they made their rounds in isolated, rural areas. This was especially the case after word was received that several had been beaten up and even murdered in other parts of the country. Detroit was hardly different, for Newberry was compelled to report to Washington that his officers were "threatened with violent obstruction."[56]

By late summer, Republican concerns in Detroit regarding Democratic intentions and even loyalties were increased by the news that Clement L. Vallandigham, a onetime Ohio congressman and the North's most famous antiwar Copperhead, had now taken up residence in Windsor, just across the river from Detroit. Earlier that summer, Vallandigham had been convicted of "declaring sympathy for the enemy" in a courtroom overseen by Union major general Ambrose Burnside. Certainly not wanting to make a martyr of Vallandigham with a death sentence or even a jail sentence, President Lincoln shrewdly had the congressman exiled into the Confederacy, where he could be considered "to be amongst friends." If he returned to the North, he was to be arrested and tossed into jail. While Southern newspapers did their best to present Vallandigham's presence in a positive light, it became clear that all would prefer that he leave the South as soon as possible, for as Vallandigham had often stated, his loyalty was still to the United States as his goals were peace *and* reunion. On June 17, Vallandigham left Wilmington, North Carolina, on a blockade runner headed to Bermuda, then from there to various stops in Canada, with every movement dutifully reported by the American consul to Secretary of State Seward. Vallandigham arrived in Windsor on August 24, 1863. Major Hill and Vallandigham both knew that the congressman's presence just across the river would give Democrats and Vallandigham loyalists easy access to the famous politician. In this highly charged environment, where rumors and reports of Rebel operatives in Windsor were a constant, the controversial Copperhead's presence only added to Hill's worries, for it was not a stretch for Republicans or Lincolnites to believe that Vallandigham was meeting with such men. Three days after Vallandigham's arrival in Windsor, Hill telegraphed Washington, asking what should be done if the congressman attempted to cross the river. One superior replied that he should be immediately arrested and sent under heavy guard to Fort Warren in Boston harbor. Meanwhile, Vallandigham had rented an upper-floor, two-room suite at the Hirons House, a waterfront hotel that offered a beautiful vista of Detroit and the river. Included in that picturesque view was the USS *Michigan*, serenely lying at anchor in the Detroit River, its heavy guns seemingly pointed at Vallandigham's window.[57]

❀ ❀ ❀

In late October 1863, four companies of a different type of Union soldier arrived at Fort Wayne from Kentucky for added help in enforcing the upcoming draft. These men were part of the recently created Invalid Corps, which was intended as a "Corps of Honor" that would serve under the auspices of the Provost Marshal Bureau. Essentially a reserve service, the Invalid Corps was created by the U.S. government in April 1863 as a means of providing military duties to those honorable soldiers who had been too disabled by wounds, disease, or accident to continue serving on the front lines. The army's assumption was that if these men could no longer wage war, some were indeed healthy enough to carry out other, less stressful duties, thereby freeing their more vigorous comrades for duty at the front. As Provost Marshal General Fry later pointed out, "The drain caused by the war on the able-bodied men of the country had been so severe that an intelligent economy of the public strength demanded that some portion of the vast numbers of soldiers unfit for field service should be utilized for military purposes." Other typical tasks for these men included working in the hospitals or, for those well enough to bear arms, performing garrison duty, which in Detroit would mean Fort Wayne or the Detroit Barracks, provost duty, or serving as guards at Northern prisoner of war camps. Men who were too feeble for even that level of work or who had lost limbs were often employed as cooks or orderlies.[58]

Bennett Hill, promoted to lieutenant colonel as of August 1, had reported to Washington back in mid-June that "everything is being done possible by me to hasten the enrollment and creation of the Invalid Corps," but that none of his district provost marshals had yet sent him any applicant, whose admission into the corps had to be medically approved. When they did start to arrive in October, the appearance of "those invalid soldiers" in Detroit, regardless of their stated role, caused considerable apprehension, for other than the Provost Guard, almost no Union soldiers were actually stationed in Detroit. Considering the riot that had occurred in March coupled with the ongoing racial and conscription tensions, local Democrats no doubt wondered if martial law or a police state was about to be imposed.[59]

Detroit's Democrats need not have worried, however. These newly arrived men were in no condition to enforce anything. The ladies from Detroit's Soldiers' Aid Society hosted a three-day fund-raiser in October and invited sixty members of the corps to a dinner as part of that event. They were surely surprised at the physical condition of these men; one woman noted that some were missing limbs while others appeared utterly exhausted. "There were few who were more than mere fragments of what they were when they entered the service."[60]

Despite the honorable intentions of the national government, many would come to view the Invalid Corps with a skewed eye. They were derisively referred to by some as the "cripple brigade" or as "Condemned Yanks" when it was noticed that the initials of the Invalid Corps were the same as those used to designate worthless government equipment as "Inspected—Condemned." Still others viewed the Invalid Corps as simply a haven for shirkers and cowards. In fact, Michigan's adjutant general felt compelled to note in 1864 that there were men "who are always taken a little lame just before the fight, and drift back from the rear of the army to the hospitals. This fact has become so patent, that a dread of being thus assigned to [Invalid Corps] duty is nearly universal with our soldiers." The government meant well by initially issuing the corps a distinct sky blue field jacket rather than its regular dark blue; however, that uniform was resisted from the beginning by many in the corps as a form of separation from the regular service. These men, who had given their health and even their limbs in support of the Federal government, resented what they viewed as being deemed unworthy of the army's standard uniform. The corps was renamed the Veteran Reserve Corps in March 1864.[61]

The men of the Veteran Reserve Corps stationed in Detroit did little more than provide provost duty and watch over the draft. The rioting that Hill feared never materialized, allowing the first draft in Wayne County to occur on November 5, 1863. Though there was an ample armed presence and an even larger crowd, First District Provost Marshal John Newberry conducted the affair without incident in front of his offices on Larned Street. Another draft occurred in September 1864 after Lincoln's call for another 500,000 men on July 18, 1864. Michigan's quota was set at 12,098, though the state was ultimately credited with furnishing 12,532 men, including another 23 who paid the $300 commutation fee to avoid the draft. By this stage, any volunteers acquired were more likely to come from the Republican-controlled outstate areas rather than Democratic Detroit. "From the interior of the state we have the most gratifying assurances relative to volunteering," noted the *Advertiser and Tribune* on September 19, one day before the draft was scheduled, "but in this city it seems to be dead. During the past two weeks there have not been five men credited to the city." As the city's ethnically diverse population was far more antiwar and Democratic than Michigan as a whole, such results were not surprising.[62]

Through the newspapers as well as via letters from home, Michigan soldiers in the field were certainly aware of the "skedaddling" and the other means some men used to avoid service. Not surprisingly, there was little sympathy for such men. "We hear that there is another draft a coming off," wrote one Michigan soldier to his friends in early 1865, and "that will make some more running for some of them down there in Michigan, but I hope that [the draft] will catch some of them that ran before." After the war ended four months later, one congressman reported to Secretary of War Stanton that many draft evaders were starting to filter back across the border. He suggested to the secretary that a guard be placed along the border to arrest these "deserters" and prosecute them, as such an action would deliver justice to the skedaddlers while giving significant satisfaction to the brave soldiers returning home. Unfortunately for the congressman and like-minded boys in blue, no such policy was ever enacted by the Federal government, thereby allowing draft evaders to return home and continue their lives without consequence.[63]

For years, the small Canadian town of Windsor in what was then known as Canada West had been the freedom gateway for runaway slaves crossing the Detroit River. Now, with the advent of the draft, Windsor also became an easy point of refuge for midwestern Union men seeking to avoid conscription. At one point, the number of draft-eligible Michigan men seeking such sanctuary exceeded 20 percent. While a few were honorable men of conscience who objected to drawing the sword against their own countrymen, most were considered skulkers and idlers who did little more than bemoan their present fate. Most Northern citizens loyal to the Lincoln administration were somewhat ambivalent about these skedaddlers—the original "draft dodgers"—seeking to flee conscription. The Lincoln administration had even anticipated such a northward exodus, to the point that on August 8, 1862, the president signed an executive order stating that "no citizen liable to be drafted into the militia shall be allowed to go to a foreign country." In public, many citizens bid good riddance to such "cowards," but internally, many wished they were still around to help lessen their own odds of being drafted. This "fight versus flight" ambivalence was illustrated by one Michigan farmer who admitted to his brother after learning he had been drafted, "I don't want to go, especially as a drafted man, neither do I wish to be considered a deserter." Such uncertainty was especially the case for those men of means who, while quietly opposed to the draft philosophically, nevertheless paid the $300 commutation fee rather than risk their high standing in the community. Poorer men often had no such options.[64]

Although Great Britain had delivered a Proclamation of Neutrality on May 13, 1861, Windsor and its twenty-five hundred residents constantly feared what an angry United States might do if it believed that Canada in general and Windsor in particular were aggressively providing haven to American deserters and draft evaders. The townsfolk were painfully aware that while British troops had once been garrisoned at nearby Fort Malden, those troops had been withdrawn over a decade earlier in 1851. Nor had Canadians forgotten the long-standing desire on the part of some Americans that Canada should somehow be acquired by the United States. That craving had gone as far back as Canada's 1838 Patriot War and had not diminished by the start of America's Civil War. After England had loosely threatened military action in November 1861 against the United States for a clear violation against its flag on the high seas in what became known as the Mason and Slidell Affair, Zachariah Chandler had confided to a friend, "I hope she will attempt to bite as well as bark, by the first day of March next we can spare 200,000 troops for the conquest of Canada and I trust in God we shall have an opportunity to use them for that purpose." Soon enough, rumors were rife of Detroit's plans for capturing the small Canadian town just across the river, prompting Windsor's mayor, James Dougall, to appeal in late 1861 that two companies of regulars and an artillery battery be sent to the town to provide some semblance of defense and to act as a "discouragement to the inhabitants of Detroit." Concurrently, Sarnia and other Canadian towns that bordered Michigan begged "for protection against invasion."[65]

Matters were not helped any when it was learned in October 1863 that two drunken Canadian sergeants had forcibly attempted to haul down the Stars and Stripes from an American steamer at anchor in Windsor. The two rowdy soldiers were quickly dealt with by their superiors, who publicly condemned their actions, but this "outrage" upon the American flag was duly noted with a stern warning from the Detroit press.[66]

Despite the ongoing Canadian fears, a Detroit reporter visiting Windsor came away with the conviction that Windsor, for the most part, aligned its sympathies with the Union cause. Though it was acknowledged that Windsor tolerated a healthy number of "Secession runaways," the reporter noted that "the great majority of intelligent citizens there feel that they have a common interest with us in the suppression of the rebellion, and entertain but little sympathy with the rebel strangers who have sought refuge among them."[67]

With the advent of the Union's draft and bounty system in 1863, authorities in Detroit and Windsor came to realize that the traffic ran both ways. While the military commanders in Detroit did their best to prevent deserters or draft resisters from escaping into Canada, Canadian and British authorities quickly became aware of the possibility, and likelihood, of their own troops abandoning their posts in order to make their way across the river into Detroit, where they then enlisted in the Union army. These men were often persuaded to enlist by substitute brokers stationed in Detroit, who were derisively known as "crimps." Like many young American men, Her Majesty's soldiers found American bounties handsome enticements indeed, for British army pay was low, living conditions were often dismal, and discipline was frequently callous. Of the 22,261 foreign-born troops who served in Michigan's various regiments, 19,341 were born in either Great Britain or Canada. Further, many of the Canadian troops serving the British crown were young, illiterate Irishmen, most barely over eighteen years of age. The chance for an American adventure, all the while making extra money, was more than many British troops stationed in Windsor could resist. An 1864 British military dispatch in Canada acknowledged the severity of the problem: "The inducements to desert are too much for the 'virtue' of any British soldier. I should be glad to have authority to remove from Windsor men who are evidently meditating a trip across the [Detroit] river. . . . Any detachment near Detroit will melt away; the facilities will be nearly as great at Sandwich [part of modern-day Windsor] for there is also direct communications across." The exodus was so great that the Canadian government felt compelled to station at Sandwich a squad of soldiers known to all as the Lookout Party. Its sole responsibility was to prevent desertion from the ranks with orders to arrest any soldier found over one mile from camp and to apprehend any civilian with him. At the same time, British officers urged their most loyal soldiers to act as if they were looking to desert as a ruse to attract crimps, whom they could then arrest and deliver to the authorities.[68]

The quantity of Americans fleeing the draft quickly became an onerous problem for Canadian authorities in the Windsor area. Jobs were all but impossible to find; nevertheless, these newly arrived men still needed to eat and have some type of roof over their heads. In fact, by 1863 and into 1864 Canadian farmers were reporting they could find all the workers they needed in their fields by offering nothing but food and shelter. Meanwhile, many Canadians who were unable to find work in the Windsor area due to the huge influx were now crossing the Detroit River on a daily basis to fill the labor shortages created by so many of Detroit's men having gone off to war. "The only thing to be regretted," opined Canada's *Weekly Globe* regarding this cross-border movement, "is that we have received skedaddling Americans, while the States are taking from us a great many solid and sturdy Britons, who are not liable to the draft, and consequently the most eligible employees in Yankeeland." In an effort to stem the tide and to show the United States that Canada was serious about not being a haven for shirkers, military authorities in Windsor posted a general order on September 21, 1864, stating that anyone from the Federal States of America who had taken refuge in Canada in the past month and was fit for military duty was to report immediately to the local military headquarters for immediate service in Her Majesty's government. Anyone failing to comply with the order was subject to arrest and imprisonment. After all, the order reasoned, "Refugees and exiles seeking the protection of this government must lend their aid to strengthen the power that gives them protection." According to the *Free Press*'s reporter, draft evaders throughout Windsor "gobbled down the contents of the order, which appeared to sit upon their stomachs about as agreeable as an emetic, and then turned away, pale and subdued."[69]

With Detroit's streets seemingly secured against internal unrest, though with skedaddlers still a problem, the provost marshal for the Detroit district, John S. Newberry, resigned his position on November

PROVOST MARSHAL'S OFFICE
1st CONGRESSIONAL DISTRICT MICHIGAN.
Detroit, December 1st, 1863.

Notice

Is hereby given, that any person whose name is enrolled below, may appear before the Board of Enrollment any time previous to *December, 20th,* 1863, and claim to have it stricken from the list, if he can show to the satisfaction of the Board that he is not and will not be, at the time fixed for the next Draft, liable to Military Duty on account of 1st, *Alienage,* 2d, *Non-Residence,* 3d *Unsuitableness of Age,* 4th, *Manifest permanent Physical Disability.*

☞ Persons who may know of any other persons liable to military duty, whose names do not appear on these Lists, or is incorrectly enrolled are requested to notify the Board or the Enrolling Officer of their District, giving the names and residences of such persons.

68d Sub. District,   Dover, Lenawee Co.

First Class.

Allen, John B; Allen, Edward K; Abbott, Ezra; Abbott, Oscar; Briggs, George D L; Bayles, Andrew J; Beal, Elias; Bryant, William; Bryant, Wallace; Bryant, Samuel; Bovee, Henry; Berduse, Jacob; Bovee, David; Bailey, George W; Baker, Lucius P; Baker, Amos M; Baker, Levi W; Baker, John B; Bawl, Stephen J; Bovee, Arthur; Bovee, Hiram; Brown, Charles G; Chittenden, Seymour; Chaffee, Oscar; Carners, James O; Carpenter, Andrew J; Collins, James F; Carll, Patrick; Cerrow, Ransom; Collins, Peter; Combs, James S; Cleveland, Josiah; Curtis, Farcus; Cross, Samuel; Carpenter, Frederick F; Dition, Robert; Dedline, Alanzo; Dye, John; Dye, Vincent; Downer, Jerome C; Deline, George; Deline, Edwin; Deline, Ira W; Finch, Isaac C; Fullerton, Henry H; Foster, Marien F; Foster, Daniel C; Fisk, Lyman C; Fisk, Amos; Ferman, William; Ferman, Dusenberry, J; Ferman, Ava T; Forbes, Timothy C; Fisk, Elisha; Gale, Isaac R; Griffin, Blake; Graves, Barritt B; Hulett, Frederick A; Herring, Daniel D; Hamlin, Heman; Hathaway, Jacob; Hathaway, Wilson J; How, Henry P; Howard, Daniel D; Howard, Almond; Howard, Darius M; Hunt, John L; Jordan, Judson L; Knapp, Henry F; Lingle, John; Langford, Edwin O; Lowth, John P; Lowth, Thomas F; Lowth, Nathan; Long, John; Lerock, Alexander; Latham, Edwin O; Lord, Jerome D; Lenox, John M; Lawrence, Chas R; Lord, Allen S; McLouth, Francis; McLouth, Orville; Mickley, George P; Millins, Francis; Middleton, Philip; Middleton, Charles; Maynerd, Hayden B; McLouth, Cyrus; Myers, Benjamin F; Moore, John M; Moore, Lewis P Jr; Moore, Charles F; Norton, Rily B; Nixon, John B; Nichols, Daniel D; Phillip, William H; Phillips, Saron P; Persiva, David; Pawling, Holbert; Pawling, Leonard; Porter, Charles C; Pratt, Hiram; Payne, John M; Porter, Charles B; Rickard, Samuel; Read, Enoch; Roberts, William; Roberts, Edward; Roberts, William H; Shay, Asahel H; Shepherd, James H; Salusbury, Levi O

Second Class.

Strong, Joseph T; Shaw, Charles J; Soper, George; Smith, John B; Small, Henry; Small, George; Small, James; Smith, William Z; Thompson, Jeremiah; Tolford, Joshua P; Tyler, Almeron; Torbron, Gilbert; Vaughn, Samuel D; Van ostrand, Theron; Van Sickle, Jacob M; Volder, Aaron; Voorhes, William H; Warren, Austin A; Wert, William B; Warren, Johnathan W; Allen, Thomas P; Ashby, William; Bayley, Hiram S; Bardier, David; Fennett, Louis R; Benanson, Joseph; Bailey, Benson E; Beala, Edward; Colgrove, Veader; Cooley, Austin; Commet, Elisha O; Colvin, Asa W; Collins, John J; Deline, Hiram; Fuller, Justus W; Foot, James M; Furguson, Reuben; Foot, Elbery P; Grant, John C; Hirrling, John O; Hayward, Charles R; Hutchins, Norman M; Howard, George L; Ireland, David; Johnson, Jacob C; Johnson, Paris; Kerr, Mathew H; McLouth, Alva; Milliken, Shurburn; McNight, John; McLouth, Wm W; McLouth, Peter; Phillips, Aaron M; Perkins, Newman; Palmer, Killwell N; Read, Jacob; Read, William P; Roberts, Phillips; Rowley, David T; Sweet, George; Sorley, James; Smalley, William C; Spooner, Amos B; Schooley, Hamilton; Soper, Carlisle B; Shanger, John H; Smith, John; Thompson, George; Taber, Daniel H; Thompson, Walter; Telford, John W; Tobias, Charles M; Vreeland, Sylvester

By order of the Board of Enrollment,

MARK FLANIGAN, Provost Marshal.
HENRY F. KELLOGG, Commissioner.
GEORGE LANDON, Surgeon.

Draft notice for Detroit, December 1, 1863 (Archives of Michigan, Lansing).

12, 1863, to return to his private career in business and industry. He was formally replaced two weeks later by thirty-eight-year-old Lieutenant Colonel Mark Flanigan, the longtime Detroiter who had served as town sheriff and then enlisted with the Twenty-fourth Michigan Infantry in August 1862. Flanigan lost a leg at Gettysburg in July 1863, and after his active-duty discharge was awarded Detroit's provost marshal position when Newberry resigned. As noted earlier, such positions were usually awarded to honorable military men who had suffered debilitating injury or illness in the line of duty and were therefore no longer fit for front-line service. Inevitably, though, political loyalties often played into such decisions. In such times, it was no surprise that Flanigan was considered a loyal Republican and Lincoln man.[70]

It did not take the Democratic *Free Press* long to take note of this fact and to accuse Flanigan of "commencing to apply the screws" when it learned that the provost marshal had arrested a convalescing

New Jersey soldier staying at one of Detroit's hotels for allegedly doing nothing more than publicly proposing a toast to the health of General George B. McClellan during a dinner party. McClellan had held command of the Union's Army of the Potomac from mid-1861 through late 1862, at which point he had been summarily dismissed by Lincoln. Now still technically "awaiting orders," McClellan was a vocal critic of the Lincoln administration's war policies and had subsequently become the Democratic Party's 1864 presidential nominee in the soon-to-be-held election. Moreover, this was apparently not Flanigan's first such act of "petty tyranny," as the *Free Press* phrased it. Just a few weeks earlier, one of the paper's reporters claimed to have been an eyewitness to Flanigan arresting a recuperating soldier from the Fourteenth Michigan Infantry who had been quietly talking on the street in favor of McClellan. The *Free Press* was well aware of Flanigan's past honorable services to Detroit, Wayne County, and the Union, so it stressed that it had nothing to say against him as an individual, "but he holds an office under an Administration which requires him to do this dirty work and he evinces a remarkable promptness in doing it." By this point in the war, many Republicans in Congress and the administration equated opposition to their policies or voicing pro-Democrat sympathies to simple treason. As the man charged with maintaining loyalty to the Union within Detroit, Provost Marshal Flanigan was going to make sure the city's streets were safe for all right-thinking citizens.[71]

Despite the fears of disturbances in Detroit's streets throughout 1863 and much of 1864 due to the conscription act, no such riots ever occurred. President Abraham Lincoln's reelection in early November 1864 all but ended any violent opposition to the war and effectively silenced Copperhead voices in the North. Not only did Lincoln win by a wide margin in Michigan, Republicans overall scored huge victories in both the state and national November 8, 1864, elections. All six newly elected members in the U.S. House were Republicans, which meant the Democrats had lost the lone seat they had picked up in 1862. In the state legislature the results were similar. Republicans handily controlled the state Senate, with twenty-one members compared to eleven Democrats, and at the same time maintained overwhelming control of the state House of Representatives by a margin of seventy-eight to twenty-seven. To be a Democrat in Detroit after the 1864 election was to feel a sense of political isolation.

Though the threat of social unrest and fears of street riots faded in Detroit throughout 1864, culminating in Lincoln's reelection, the city had other worries. Ongoing threats and rumors of invasion and sabotage by Rebels hiding in Canada first manifested themselves in November 1863 and would continue through early 1865. These feared attacks against Detroit will be discussed fully in chapter 7.

"In all the shops . . . everything has become so expensive"

Gender Issues, Labor Strife,
and Economic Ills Confront
Wartime Detroit

Detroit was a city rapidly on the rise as the 1860s began. For the first time ever, the total yearly value of Detroit's manufactured products surpassed the $5 million mark. Despite that growing number, Detroit could hardly be considered a fully industrial city; nevertheless, at the start of the new decade the Detroit area was home to several blast iron furnaces, two plants that manufactured railroad cars, seven copper smelters, a brass foundry, and a dry dock used for shipbuilding, all of which had been constructed in the 1850s. In fact, copper smelting was the most valuable manufacturing industry in the Detroit-Wayne County area in 1860, with a value of $1.5 million dollars, due in large measure to the discovery of vast tracts of iron ore and copper ore in Michigan's Upper Peninsula over the previous fifteen years. This dollar value of $1.5 million for copper ore more than doubled that of sawed lumber, which was second, with $619,000 produced. The city also featured a few dozen breweries, fifteen tanneries, and six flour mills; all of which were directly connected to agriculture which, despite the industrial development in Detroit, was still the prevailing force in Michigan's economy. More and more, it was becoming apparent that the men of industry who owned these businesses were also making their way into the ranks of Detroit's wealthy elite.[1]

Perhaps the single most important industrial presence in Detroit at the start of the new decade was the massive, twenty-two-hundred-acre Eureka Iron and Steel Works, located on the river nine miles below Detroit in what is now the city of Wyandotte. Started in 1854, the company was owned by Eber Brock Ward, pioneering industrialist, ardent Republican capitalist, and Detroit's first millionaire. It employed close to 250 men when the war started, making it the Detroit area's single largest employer. Located as it was on the Detroit River, it was perfectly positioned to receive via ship those vast new quantities of iron ore discovered in Michigan's Upper Peninsula. Much of the time, those raw materials arrived in vessels also owned by Ward. In 1864, Ward's plant, which was the largest in Wayne County, became the first in the United States to produce steel commercially through the Bessemer method, which was the first cost-effective manufacturing method for the mass production of steel from molten pig iron.

As the 1860s began, the quality of life in Detroit was accelerating at a pace previously unseen in this frontier town. Stoves were a common feature in most homes, and by 1860 coal had replaced wood as the primary fuel for heating. Natural gas was common for street and home lighting, and for those who could afford one, the home sewing machine had been recently introduced. Running water in homes was also available, prompting indoor bathtubs to become a popular feature in upscale Detroit homes.[2]

Yet, to add context for the modern reader, practically no one lived more than a mile and a half from the city center at Campus Martius. During the Civil War, most residences were no more than a ten-minute walk from the Jefferson-Woodward business district, though there was only the slightest amount of business activity on Woodward north of Larned. Woodward Avenue, in fact, ended at Grand Circus Park, which was mostly swampland. Beyond that point were great forests and wide open spaces.[3]

Detroit's rapid growth throughout the 1850s contributed greatly to improvements in travel to the city, making it far easier to get there than it had been a decade or so earlier. When the Civil War started, Michigan had over eight hundred miles of railroad track laid, much of it leading to Detroit. The town could also boast of the Detroit & Milwaukee line, which ran from Detroit across the middle of the state to Lake Michigan. A bit farther south the Michigan Central line ran from Detroit to Chicago. The railways were necessitated by Detroit's key position on the Great Lakes, which helped make it a valuable port for goods being shipped to and from the Wolverine State.

Transportation on the city's roads was changing as well. Throughout the 1840s and 1850s, the sole form of "public transportation" was horse-drawn coaches—forerunners of the modern taxi—that shuttled passengers between Detroit's downtown hotels and the railroad stations or boat docks. By the start of the Civil War, however, Detroit's exploding population and the resulting slow-moving traffic on its streets prompted city leaders to explore other options. Furthermore, the seasonal impact of mud and dust often made the rough ride over cobblestone streets only more aggravating. The solution was horse-drawn streetcars on rails, which began to appear in 1863 under the auspices of the newly created Detroit City Railway Company. Its charter dictated that speeds were not to exceed six miles per hour and the company was not required to run the cars more than every twenty minutes, fifteen hours a day, between April 15 and October 15. Twelve hours a day was the maximum for the remainder of the year.

The fare was a nickel, or frequent riders could purchase a "trip ticket" at the discounted price of twenty-five for $1. For that fee, the passenger was treated to a ride in an unheated car, though straw was placed on the floor in winter to warm the passengers' feet. By the end of the year, these horse-drawn, sixteen-foot-long streetcars with their metal wheels turning on steel rails were transporting citizens along Jefferson, Woodward, Gratiot, and Michigan avenues.[4]

Travelers visiting Detroit in 1861 who needed overnight accommodations could choose from among several fine hotels. According to *Appleton's Illustrated Hand-book of American Travel*, the Michigan Exchange and the Biddle House were two of the better establishments, though for many visitors, the Russell House located on the Campus Martius was Detroit's premier hotel. In the case of the Biddle House, located at the corner of Randolph Street and Jefferson Avenue, guests could stay for $2.50 per night.[5]

For over two decades, in fact, Detroit's hotels had been the center of the city's nightlife and social scene. Like most burgeoning cities, Detroit had an "upper-crust" society in which everybody knew everyone else. For the most part, these people lived along Jefferson or Woodward avenues or in large homes in the downtown area. Helped by their many domestic servants, members of Detroit's gentry entertained the many distinguished guests and visitors who came to Detroit and stayed at places like the National Hotel or the Michigan Exchange. The military town often hosted gala balls graced by soldiers in full-dress uniforms.[6]

France's Prince Napoleon and his aide-de-camp visited Detroit in August 1861 and were charmed by the old French town's appearance, later commenting favorably that the city reminded them of the Canebière in Marseilles. Clearly, Detroit was rapidly transforming from frontier town to modern city, though the growing pains were evident everywhere. Three years later, in 1864, another visiting Frenchman wrote somewhat less approvingly. He was initially transfixed by the sight of the moonlit city from a Windsor ferry. The next morning, however, "The charm was broken. Detroit, which the night before I had seen as it were transfigured by the luminous vapor of the moon, now showed itself as it really is, a half-built town, where wooden sheds are near neighbors to gigantic stone and brick stores, where immense avenues, marked out for a capital, are bordered everywhere by waste and unoccupied lands."[7]

Despite Detroit's population and commercial growth, much of that economic opportunity was deemed off limits to women by the social mores and values of mid-nineteenth-century society. For the most part, by midcentury women were considered the natural keepers of hearth and home, but acceptable roles in the public sphere were few and far between. Few vocational pursuits were deemed "ladylike," for women were viewed by the dominant patriarchal society as being too delicate in mind and body to stand up to the rigorous daily demands of the marketplace or public life.[8]

It had not always been this way for women in the American workplace. During colonial times, the "Puritan work ethic" had dictated that all members of society, male and female, contribute to the economic benefit of the community at large, to the point that work outside of the home for single or widowed women was not only socially acceptable but was even regarded as a public duty.[9]

As the country prospered in the first several decades of the nineteenth century, such thinking about the role of women changed. Class distinctions began to flourish, which led to the idea that the genteel lady of fashion should represent the perfect model of American femininity. Of course, wealthy women who did not need to work had always been a romanticized part of American society; however, by 1830, the formation of "the lady" as cult and status symbol had come to dominate public perceptions of idyllic womanhood. This bourgeois ideal was beyond the reach of most American women, however, for this lady was a cultural myth and hardly fit the day-to-day realities for most women. Moreover, the Irish immigrant woman in Detroit and elsewhere certainly rejected this American myth, for her Irish culture and its societal values had always dictated that she was a self-reliant being who was expected to foster an economic role within her family and community. Many had permanently migrated to America simply because there was such an abundance of work available, especially as domestic servants. Though much of mid-nineteenth century America looked down its nose at the uneducated Irish, the Irish immigrant woman knew she could always find honest, relatively well-paying work in that field.[10]

Despite their inner feelings of frustration with male-dominated society, most women publicly aligned themselves with their husbands' beliefs and values. Most Northern women and almost all Southern women viewed suffrage issues with indifference or apathy. This was certainly the case in Michigan. For example, a petition had been put forth to the state legislature in 1846 addressing "the need and right of women to the elective franchise," but it met with little interest. The matter was raised again three more times over the next nine years with similar results, and the issue was tabled for the next ten years.[11]

Few vocations open to women offered any type of viable career path. If they were able to obtain outside work, it was often because they were willing to work longer hours and for less pay than their male brethren. Any complaints they brought forward about such inequities resulted in little to no change.[12]

Teaching was one of the two principal mid-nineteenth-century vocations open to women, though by the start of the Civil War, most communities still preferred a man over a woman if one was available. In fact, Detroit's school board had stipulated for a number of years that while women were suitable educators for primary schools, men must direct all middle and junior schools. The edict is illustrated by Detroit's 1861 city directory, which shows that all but one of the city's forty-six first- and second-grade teachers were unmarried females earning approximately $300 per year. The one male exception taught first grade at Detroit's lone primary school for "colored" children and was paid $400 per year. Meanwhile, all school principals were men. As men headed off to war, however, more opportunities in the field became available for women. School boards that had previously refused to consider female teachers were now obliged to do so as the supply of male educators dried up. As in other fields, however, tolerance for women teachers was often driven in large measure by the fact that they demanded less pay and did not view teaching as a mere stepping-stone to more lucrative employment. Additionally, the war had forced a wage cut for Detroit's schoolteachers, making women educators even more desirable to teach the 7,986 children in Detroit's public schools in 1863. For example, such circumstances allowed one Michigan woman the opportunity to choose among four positions offered to her, ultimately selecting the one that paid the highest wage, $4 a week.[13]

Whether male or female, teachers in Detroit at the start of the Civil War now also had an opportunity to teach older children, as the first high school in Detroit offering free public education opened in 1858 with twenty-three students in a building on Miami Avenue. No girls were admitted, however, until 1860, making the class of 1863 the first to include young female graduates.[14]

Other jobs existed in which women could utilize teaching skills. One young teacher from Illinois named Mary Davis secured a position as matron at the then new Detroit House of Corrections. This facility opened in 1861 on the city's east side to address what its first superintendent described as Detroit's "frequency of crimes, pernicious police practice, insufficient jail accommodations, and pestilential influence of jail imprisonments." The correctional center housed young men from the ages of sixteen to twenty-one who were first-time offenders convicted of any felony other than murder or treason. It also housed women of all ages for similar convictions. Teaching a sense of morality and some rudimentary academics was an integral part of the facility's routine. In 1864, Davis noted that she was working with about one hundred women and between sixty or seventy men. "The regularity and precision of our habits here are so much like those of any school life that I sometimes feel as if I were back again," she wrote. "Yet any such illusion is quickly dispelled I assure you. The many sources of enjoyment to be had there are wanting here."[15]

The other primary vocation deemed appropriate for women was that of sewing, and many Northern women found work sewing shirts and uniforms for the Union army as well as clothing for local citizens. Nine-tenths of these women were white, and in a textbook case of "classism" typical of the era, they chose to perform this type of work, which paid "starvation wages," rather than hire themselves out as better-paying domestic help, which, as mentioned in chapter 1, would have placed them on a social level commensurate with black or Irish women. Furthermore, in the words of the famous black activist W. E. B. DuBois, this avoidance of domestic "blackness" paid these white sewing women a sort of additional "public and psychological wage" that was every bit as important as real money. This was especially the case when the near-starvation wages they did earn almost became a literal rather than figurative description. Such needlework had always meant low wages and long hours, but now the Civil War's casualty rates added unintended competition in the field in the form of what became known as "war widows." These newly widowed women, for the most part, had little if any experience of earning a living on their own, and many turned to needlework as the least doubtful and most respectable field for unskilled females. As each year of the war went by, the number of such workers swelled all across the country. This was especially the case in the larger urban areas, and soon the supply far exceeded demand, prompting an inevitable downward spiral in wages. In fact, one New York newspaper's investigations showed that in 1863, the income of these women had declined 25 percent to 50 percent since 1860, while in the same time frame, the cost of living had risen over 50 percent.[16]

As the dwindling supply of male breadwinners at home stretched fragile family finances to the breaking point, many women had no choice but to enter the workplace. Moreover, soldiers' paychecks were often disgracefully unreliable and insufficient to support their families, especially once wartime inflation was factored in. In these cases, women often took up work in the needle trades or sometimes stepped into the very jobs vacated by their husbands. Making up for the lack of male-generated wages in this manner was consistent with working-class respectability; nevertheless, these women risked their social reputations by working in traditionally male-dominated fields, such as filling cartridges at arsenals. These working-class women who felt the need to publicly justify their employment against those in high society who looked down their noses at them often did so by defending their actions in the most patriotic, war-related manner they could conjure.[17]

The struggling needlewomen in Detroit certainly had an ally in the highly Democratic *Free Press*, which had always positioned itself as a friend of the working-class white man. The paper highlighted in August 1864 that a public meeting of the sewing women had "brought to light a condition of suffering, oppression and wrong which the people of Detroit little think exists in their midst." Most of these needle workers, regardless of where they lived, worked for government subcontractors who sought to maximize their profits by habitually ignoring the Federal government's suggested pay scales while crowding their workers into inadequately sized working areas. The *Free Press* noted that their wages were so low that it was literally impossible to make a living, and further warned that "the distress and suffering existing among the needle women must soon very much enlarge the area of pauperism and demoralization, unless measures are adopted to alleviate the evil."[18]

Another gathering on November 21 was deemed "the largest public meeting of workingmen and women that ever occurred in Detroit." The speaker was Richard Trevellick, president of the local Detroit Trades Assembly, who had also served in the Ship Caulkers' International Union. His eloquent speech on the current relationship between labor and capital, as well as plight of Detroit's sewing women, was so vivid and moving that the *Detroit Tribune* reported that "the audience [was] frequently moved to tears." Trevellick pointed out with pride that one year earlier, workingmen in Detroit were paid only $1 per day—now they were getting $2. Why? His answer was simple: because of the power and benefits of union, and if the sewing women wanted better wages, they needed to follow that lead. The *Free Press* built upon the growing sentiment for the needle workers with another appeal in early December 1864. It noted that there were now more than five hundred such workers in Detroit, often toiling from dawn into the night. In the name of justice, the paper demanded an immediate 50 percent to 100 percent increase in their piecemeal wages so that they and their children would literally not starve or freeze with winter at hand. The appeal noted the "domineering superciliousness" of one Detroit employer who coldheartedly denied a request from some of his sewing women for higher wages. The employer apparently felt their plea was a firing offense, for he then cruelly asked the women if they "expected to walk the streets" as prostitutes if he ended their employment. In that same vein, other well-off employers within the city had callously responded to similar wage requests with the answer that the women "may starve or do that which is worse for a living." "Worse for a living" meant prostitution and such sentiment was certainly not limited to Detroit. Only five years earlier, Caroline H. Dall, an early champion of women's rights, had bitterly commented that it seemed to her that "the command of society to the uneducated class is, 'Marry, stitch, die, or do worse.'" While sewing was deemed somewhat respectable for a woman if she was unmarried or widowed, society apparently considered death socially preferable to sexual solicitation.[19]

Richard Trevellick (University of Michigan Library, Ann Arbor).

Richard Trevellick was the right man at the right time to better wages and conditions for Detroit's Civil War–era working class. Born in Britain around 1830, he had traveled and worked in Australia, New Zealand, South America, and along the Gulf of Mexico. In each instance, and in addition to performing his trade as a ship's carpenter, Trevellick had fought for the rights of workers, with his signature concern being the implementation of the eight-hour workday as an industry norm. At the start of the Civil War, Trevellick and his new wife left the South to stay briefly with his brother in New York City, but by 1862 he headed to Detroit where, according to his biographer, Trevellick was determined "to put his talents of memory and oratory to the education of the toiling masses." Soon after his arrival, Trevellick began to rise in influence to the point that he became the city's most vocal labor leader. By the spring of 1864, he was organizing Detroit's first trades' assembly, a loose-knit gathering of all of Detroit's workingmen. The assembly's primary tools were persuasion and propaganda.[20]

In an ongoing attempt to aid Detroit seamstresses, who found themselves in such a dismal financial plight, the Detroit Sewing Women's Protective Association was formed in early 1865 with ample assistance from Trevellick and his male-dominated Trades Assembly of Detroit. The local Trades Assembly had taken an interest in the women's plight as far back as August, and some weeks after the Protective Association's formation, the Trades Assembly even purchased eight new sewing machines and rented a hall for the women. Thus customers who needed tailoring or other sewing work done could bypass the usual middlemen, taking their cloth straight to the hall and the seamstresses, knowing that their money went straight into the purses of these hard-working women rather than to what the assembly termed the "capacious pocket of the capitalist."[21]

The Trades Assembly of Detroit went even further to help these struggling women. Richard Trevellick publicly declared that the seamstresses had the full backing of Detroit's various trades and that if a case of "oppression" was brought to his attention, a committee from the Trades Assembly would pay a visit to the alleged offender to discuss the matter. If the issue was not settled to the assembly's satisfaction, "every trade is notified, and all the members cease trading at the obnoxious establishment. Sentinels are placed around notifying people of the facts, and in every case the offender is brought to terms." Such aggressive action was a very unusual tactic for the time, but apparently an effective one, as the power of labor unions and boycott threats was brought to bear to help workingmen and women in Civil War–era Detroit. One of the key successes of the Trades Assembly and the Detroit Sewing Women's Protective Association was the implementation of a set price scale for each particular type of sewing work.[22]

The labor strife between the sewing women and their employers was hardly the only such conflict in Detroit during the Civil War years. Almost from the day Michigan's volunteers began streaming to the front, Michigan and Detroit employers began feeling the pinch in finding a sufficient supply of male labor, especially in those industries where women clearly could not participate as the job required a high degree of physical strength. Michigan's lumber industry, for example, quickly suffered for want of men. As early as March 1862, Michigan lumberman and future governor Henry Crapo expressed concern over his difficulty in hiring men at the old prices, lamenting that he would be compelled to pay a "moderate advance" to secure the men he needed. A year later Crapo described the wages he was paying as "enormous"; he was shocked "that common labor is now $1.50 per day." These labor shortages prompted the industry to turn to Canada to help fill its labor force. There was one obstacle, however. Daniel Munger, the American consul in Windsor, wrote to Secretary of State William Seward that although there was an abundance of men in Canada "who would readily make engagements to work" in the United States, they feared "being pressed into the war." Munger asked Seward to send him assurances that would allay Canadian fears.[23]

Detroit industry's mounting demand for labor throughout the war, along with rising prices, had a direct impact on the formation of trade unions. Unlike in the East, where wages had risen slowly, labor in the West had become so scarce that organized workers held the whip hand in just about any dispute. Still, trade unionism was somewhat of a new concept when the Civil War began. The first such organizations had begun to form in the Northeast in the mid part of the nineteenth century, motivated primarily by social reasons, with economic concerns taking a back seat. National economic recessions in the 1850s and their resultant negative impact on labor provided new impetus to organize.[24]

One of the most notable organizations was the Iron Molders' Union, initially formed in Philadelphia in 1855, which by 1860 had expanded into Detroit through the efforts of William Sylvis, who was the face and voice of that union. Sylvis was one the leading champions of his era for the fair treatment of workingmen, and he had seen how markets had greatly expanded from a local to a national scale throughout the 1850s. The miles of railroad track laid had quadrupled during the decade, while at the same time the cost of other means of conveyance had been lowered. Industrialists now had access to a much larger market than merely the local, and it was available to them at a cost-effective rate. The sense of security that prohibitive transportation costs had provided to local manufacturers had essentially melted away throughout that decade. A case in point involved key iron foundry owners, who attempted to dominate the national market by lowering their profits to the least possible margin while employing the latest mass-production techniques. The effect this had on wages is self-evident and led to a rise in the union movement.

During the 1850s Detroit saw its first notable rise in organized labor as a small handful of local shops became affiliated with national unions, including the city's printers, who became Local 18 of the International Typographers Union in 1852. Detroit historians Frank and Arthur Woodford surmised that much of this new interest in the labor movement within Detroit can be credited to the city's then rapidly increasing German immigrant community; many of the new arrivals were skilled workers who had brought their homeland's notions of union or guild organization with them.[25]

Driven by a fear of layoffs and unemployment when the war ultimately ended, the number of labor unions formed within Detroit increased from four to nine between December 1863 and December 1864. The success of the Iron Molders' Union helped make that one-year time frame the greatest expansion in Detroit labor unionization, though such organization occurred throughout the war. After the Molders', the Machinists' and Blacksmiths' Union was created in 1861. That union began agitating for better wages and conditions in 1862, pointing out that the average daily wage for its members was only $1.68. This was important because after the Civil War commenced, retail prices began rising in Detroit considerably faster than wages. In light of the rampant price inflation, the union asked for an across-the-board increase of 15 percent, which equaled 25¢ a day for all its workers, which was promptly denied by the employers. This led to a strike against six employers in early 1863, who responded by hiring strikebreakers and blacklisting any worker who refused to return to work. In July 1863, workers for the Michigan Central Railroad also went on strike in Detroit, protesting that management's insistence on paying them by the run, regardless of how long it took, amounted to an unfair working condition compared to the previous practice of paying a set monthly wage. Such labor unrest only added to the tension in Detroit's streets in 1863, already high because of the March 6 riot and the ongoing resentment toward conscription and the draft.[26]

Despite an apparent shortage of labor, local employers were certainly not going to give in to the new unions without a fight. Toward the end of the war, what were called "large and heavy capitalists" were banding together to check the power of the growing union movement. On July 25, 1864, Detroit's newly formed Employers' General Association of Michigan announced its purpose and objectives via the Republican-leaning *Advertiser and Tribune*. While the employers acknowledged the "laudable" intentions that Detroit's new trade unions may have started out with, they asserted that the unions had now "come to assume a dangerous attitude, and to act a disorganizing and ruinous part." Detroit's large employers were outraged that these unions, in the middle of a war, "assume to dictate to employers, and the employed, the rates of wages to be demanded and paid; what men may be employed, and what number of apprentices; who shall be discharged, and who retained" as well as other terms on which the businesses could operate. The employers were adamant that such rigid rules would not allow them to respond properly to the vagaries of a constantly changing marketplace. From their perspective, such work rules resulted in predictable negative consequences: "Discriminations in favor of skill and efficiency are, in great measure, excluded. The bungler and laggard is placed on the same footing as the skillful and efficient. Merit receives no recognition or reward; indeed it is ignored. As a natural result, the motive for exertion is taken away," which inevitably resulted in skillful and motivated workers sinking to the level of the slacker. In particular, foundry owners decided to act in unison on all labor matters where they held a joint interest. They attempted to "classify labor" and to assign "maximum wages," but in the end were overcome by a successful strike by the Molders' Union. The strike emptied the union's coffers by $650, but William Sylvis considered it a bargain.[27]

Such a public proclamation by Detroit's employers against workingmen could not go unanswered as far as the city's new unions were concerned. A week after the employers published their position in the *Advertiser and Tribune*, the unionists published their retort in the Democratic-leaning *Free Press*. In it, the unions ridiculed the employers' association for what the unions saw as the employers' attempt to martyr themselves and enlist public sympathy. From the workingman's vantage point, the real design of Detroit's employers was "to bring down the working classes to a condition little above the level of Russian serfs." The union men also accused the employers of threatening workers who had left their employ by making sure they did not get jobs anywhere else in town, "merely to gratify a malignant spirit of revenge." It appeared that an adversarial relationship was developing, though the union men assured readers and Detroit's employers that they were always ready to sit down and discuss differences, but in so doing, the workers of Detroit demanded "to be met as men, and not with haughty arrogance so commonly assumed by employers when treating with their hands."[28]

※　　※　　※

DESPITE societal pressures to limit female involvement in certain vocations, the lack of available male labor prompted an easing of previous "standards." In August 1862, the army's growing manpower shortage at the front prompted the *Free Press* to print a letter signed by "Manufacturer" suggesting that Detroit women should now be "allowed" to work behind the counters at retail establishments. Women shopkeepers and clerks were not uncommon in the colonial era; however, changing societal mores at the turn of the nineteenth century resulted in there being fewer female shopkeepers in the 1830s than there had been only a half century earlier. Some of these women were merely taking over the jobs their husbands, now fighting at the front, had left. Manufacturer argued that such a change would result in no fewer customers and increase the pool of military volunteers, "for no one supposes that the young men who are now occupied behind the counter would hold back their aid to the government, if their places could only be supplied by females." Manufacturer admitted a personal motive, pointing out that many mills and workshops were facing work stoppages or slowdowns due to a want of mechanical laborers. A similar plea appeared within the *Free Press* only nine days later on September 1 in a letter signed by "Mulier." Again, the letter's author cited the economic and social justice of recruiting local women to work in retail shops since the government had sent their men off to battle, thus depriving women of their normal means of support. Mulier also argued that while women may be inexperienced in matters of trade, "there can be no doubt that they are natural judges of the articles usually sold in dry goods stores." Of course, such employment dictated that a woman had to have a certain level of education and be good with numbers; nevertheless, Mulier asserted that with only a little training, they could be transformed into efficient saleswomen in less time than it would take "to transform an effeminate clerk into a robust, well-drilled soldier." The author offered a final warning: if the open retail jobs were not given to Detroit women, they would probably be filled by out-of-work Canadians "who were subjects of a government which has never cared to see us prosper."[29]

Earlier, in July, Frederick Law Olmsted, the executive director of the U.S. Sanitary Commission, had expressed similar thoughts. Olmsted wrote to a friend explaining his belief that if more women were able to take jobs in retail shops, it would generate more enlistments from the male clerks. As the war progressed, more and more shopkeepers came to accept female workers because not only was their work of an acceptable quality but, like women teachers, they were often willing to accept a lower wage than their male counterparts. Nevertheless, working in a Detroit store offered a wage of around $9 a week to women at midcentury, an income significantly higher than either teaching or needlework offered. The fact that businessmen felt compelled to make such forceful pleas for female workers illustrates the degree to which women were viewed as inappropriate workers in the public marketplace during the war's first year.[30]

Though employed on a smaller scale than in retail operations, women also replaced their husbands in manufacturing shops due to their need for income coupled with the town's constant labor shortage. This was not an entirely new phenomenon, as the 1860 census had shown that 1,046 women worked in the state's 3,448 manufacturing shops at the time. Farm labor was not immune to the influx of women either. In May 1863, the *Free Press* noticed, "The war has effectually thinned out a large proportion of the laboring population, leaving many places so destitute of help that even women have been compelled to labor in the fields. . . . When the harvest season arrives, this scarcity will even be more severely felt." Nothing had changed in that regard as the war's end neared. "The spectacle so often dwelt upon with astonishment and indignation by American tourists, of women toiling with the spade and hoe in the fields of Germany and France, has already ceased to be unknown in our rural districts," remarked the *Free Press*. This overall shortage of home-front labor during the war opened the door for scores of women who wished to enter the workplace. Indeed, Valeria Campbell, the secretary of Detroit's Ladies' Soldiers' Aid Society, explained to a Sanitary Commission worker in July 1864 that Detroit's demand for labor in practically every field had been consistently greater than the supply ever since the war began, thus impacting the "new" acceptability of female workers. This new tolerance of women in the Detroit workplace was not viewed by all as something to be celebrated. As previously discussed, in an era when the domesticated lady was put on a pedestal, women being forced to work in the "man's world" was viewed with sadness by some. As the *Free Press* opined, "Our women may as well prepare themselves to play a sterner and less ornamental part in the general economy than has heretofore been their lot."[31]

The effect of this new pattern was predictable. Where women had replaced men in the past, the wage standard in that occupation tended to lower itself to the level of women's wages in other occupations. As more women obtained work as clerks in retail, this trend became apparent. Compared to the long hours of needlework or domestic positions, however, working in a storefront became so attractive that the sheer pressure of numbers reduced wages even further. Ironically, the competition from free black labor that white workingmen had feared was instead coming from white working women.[32]

❀　❀　❀

THOUGH Detroit was far from Southern battlefields, the consequences of the war hit home in a myriad of ways that went well beyond the return of wounded men or pine coffins. Increased taxes, a shortage of labor, the draft, and especially price inflation all conspired to constantly remind Detroiters that they were not immune to the war's side effects. Price inflation for all manner of goods and services was a particularly insidious public enemy.

The Lincoln administration's initial plan to pay for the war was to finance it through the sale of government bonds and keep the gold standard intact. That system soon fell apart with the introduction of the first non-gold-backed paper money into circulation. On February 25, 1862, Lincoln approved the Treasury Note or Legal Tender Act, which ultimately resulted in over $450 million of what were pejoratively called "greenbacks" coming into use; so called because the backs of the notes were printed in green ink. In a classic case of Gresham's Law, which states that bad money will drive good money out of circulation, the new greenbacks quickly replaced gold-backed dollars as the primary circulating medium of exchange. By July 1864, the value of a greenback had fallen to only 35¢ worth of gold. Of particular controversy was the fact that this now cheaper dollar could be used to repay debts that had been contracted under the earlier gold standard. Using 1860 wages and prices at a baseline of 100, Detroit's consumer prices had spiked to 216.8 by 1865, though monetary wages had only increased to 143.1, while *real* wages had actually fallen to 66. Therefore, the city's residents faced a rising price inflation that more than doubled the price of goods between 1860 and 1865.[33]

As the war progressed, Detroit's populace became painfully aware of how such economic statistics played out in reality. In May 1863, German immigrant and Detroit resident Johann Look wrote to his children complaining, "In all the shops, there is not much to buy and everything has become so expensive all of sudden." Look was grateful for one thing, however: "At least here there are higher wages for the working folks." Only a few months later, in September, the *Free Press* was reporting how local lumbermen were refusing to contract next season's shipments at current market prices. A month and a half later, the paper explained why: prices had gone up 100 percent due to the higher wages that had to be paid to a scarce workforce as well as a scarcity of capital. Furthermore, lumber prices were expected to double again before the arrival of spring. It was a good thing, the paper facetiously noted, that people did not live to the extreme ages that they did in the days of Methuselah because, at current prices, few could afford it. There was, however, little humor in the inflationary reporting by the following spring. Many poor and struggling workers were indeed in danger of going without the essentials. In a sober March 1864 article and editorial, the Democratic *Free Press* pointed out that the price of coffee had more than doubled since the beginning of the war, rising from 20¢ to 45¢ cents a pound. Concurrently, potatoes that had sold for 25¢ a bushel in 1861 were now commanding that price for a peck, while eggs had doubled from 10¢ to 20¢ a dozen. Meanwhile, Detroit's citizens could no longer smirk at the constant reports of skyrocketing prices throughout Dixie. "We have little cause to congratulate ourselves in preference to the people of Richmond," the *Free Press* opined, noting that the prices of just about any food staple, as well as rents and housing costs, had at least doubled over the past year and a half. Rather, "any schoolboy good in figures can tell just how long before we in Detroit reach the fabulous Richmond prices." Of course, such inflationary pressures hit the working poor the hardest and these people, for the most part, most likely identified with the Democratic Party.[34]

In addition to inflation, the switch from gold to paper also had important side effects. The corresponding price inflation resulted in an illusory increase in property values, which oftentimes led to an increase in luxury-good purchases and general extravagance for those with money. On the other side of the coin, working-class men and women fought to maintain hearth and home through rising prices coupled with a decrease in real wages.[35]

Despite the economic hardships felt by many of Detroit's working-class men and women, the Civil War helped transform Detroit into an industrial city. In the ten years between 1860 and 1870, the amount of capital invested in Michigan and Detroit increased by 201 percent while the number of manufacturing facilities increased by 174 percent. In Detroit alone, the Michigan Car Company, the Detroit Bridge and Iron Works, the Detroit Safe Company, and the E. T. Barnum Wire and Iron Works were all among the factories started during the Civil War.[36]

Detroit, of course, served as the state's largest supplier of the tools of war. Two clothing firms, Samuel Sykes and Co. and E. S. Heineman and Co., supplied uniforms and blankets to the Union army, with sales totaling $180,000. Concurrently, Trowbridge, Wilcox & Co., which was an outfitter for Great Lakes shipping, sold the state some $24,000 worth of tents since they were made from the same type of canvas used for ships' sails.[37]

A rampant increase in crime and illicit behavior was another important though unwelcome presence in Detroit as the Civil War progressed. Noisy dance halls, brothels, and rowdy saloons had always been present in Detroit which, as discussed in chapter 1, culminated in German residents in Detroit's east-side tenth ward taking matters into their own hands in 1857 to destroy a number of suspected brothels.[38]

The onset of the Civil War only amplified such issues. The construction of barracks and vast training camps on the city's east side for thousands of soldiers meant that these young men, many away from parents, preachers, and even wives for the first time in their lives, would flood into Detroit when off duty to seek out the city's various taverns and brothels, which were more politely known then as "houses of ill fame." Such eagerness prompted the Second Michigan Infantry's Charles Haydon to predict during his training at Detroit's Fort Wayne in May 1861, "If the men pursue the enemy as eagerly as they do the whores, they will make very efficient soldiers." Only a few weeks later, Haydon was complaining in his diary that the regiment's officer of the day was, "as usual," trying to clear the camp of "lewd women," with a typical lack of success. These downtown businesses were booming by serving not only Michigan's boys in blue but also the sailors, toughs, and vagabonds that filled Detroit's boisterous waterfront. This scenario was certainly not unique to Detroit, as it occurred in every Northern city where soldiers congregated. Meanwhile, Union officers seemed to tolerate these "temptations to evil" but were more concerned about the debilitating effects of venereal disease. In addition to the huge influx of soldiers in 1861, the surge in Detroit's population throughout the 1850s had spurred the growth of downtown boardinghouses, which in turn led to more illicit entertainment in the central business district. Such a huge uptick in "demand" by both soldier and civilian prompted a greater "supply" in the form of even more such businesses opening in the downtown area. Many of these new businesses were disturbingly close to some of the more fashionable residential areas. The fact that such drinking and whoring was now within a short walk from the homes and business of Detroit's elite prompted renewed calls for formal police protection.[39]

Prostitution affected the men not only when they were off duty but apparently when they were on duty as well. For instance, William Nesbitt of the Fifth Michigan Infantry was ordered to escort two draft substitutes from Detroit all the way to Washington, D.C., the first leg of trip via the steamer *City of Cleveland*, which was waiting at the Detroit docks. Nesbitt was instructed to take the two men to the Cass Hotel for dinner and then hurry back to board the ship for an early departure. Instead, though, after dinner Nesbitt and his two charges went to a house of ill fame at the corner of St. Catherine's and Russell streets. Apparently Nesbitt went into one room while the other two men went into another. When Nesbitt later came down into the parlor, his two recruits were nowhere to be found, having slipped out a back door. For his efforts, Nesbitt was sentenced to three months at hard labor.[40]

Then there was Private James Collins of the Detroit Provost Guard, who was on sentry duty at "Post Number 9" on May 1, 1863, when, according to his court-martial records, Collins "abandoned his post and knowingly permitted a public prostitute to enter the camp and pass his beat on post and hold conversation with her and then and there have illicit intercourse with such prostitute at Detroit Barracks." Collins was convicted and sentenced to ten days' rations of bread and water. The prostitute received a one-year jail sentence. The prostitution problem was so great *everywhere* where soldiers were stationed that it has been estimated that at the close of the Civil War, one in four Union soldiers was infected with some kind of venereal disease. That the prostitute in the Collins matter received such a stern sentence is indicative of just how aggressively Detroit tried to eliminate, or at least lessen, what it saw as a moral hazard.[41]

On a more serious note was the death of Isaac Webb of the Veteran Reserve Corps. Webb was shot down in front of a Detroit "house of ill fame" on Waterloo Street when the owner apparently thought that Webb and his comrades had come seeking vengeance for a falling-out the owner had displayed with one of his girls earlier in the day.[42]

Clearly, something had to be done in Detroit to gain a measure of control over the city's streets. In every year from 1863 through 1866, the number of persons sent to the state prison in Jackson increased, including the number convicted of murder. Part-time night watchmen or few marshals were no longer adequate. The idea of a permanent professional police force had been discussed in Detroit several times over the years but in the end was always rejected due to perceived costs and the fear that taxes would have to be increased. Moreover, it appeared to some that the supposed need was usually for the benefit of the wealthy elite who ran Detroit's business district. The onset of the Civil War changed much of that perception. Corruption in general and female crime in particular soared in Detroit during the Civil War years, with most of the offenses committed by women being transgressions against the public order such as drunkenness, prostitution, or vagrancy. So great was the vagrant problem that by 1863, one in every eleven Detroit vagrants was incarcerated in the city's jail, a huge surge from 1848 when the number was a mere one in 450. In such circumstances, the matter of a police force was again taken up by the Common Council in early 1863. On February 10, two reports were submitted to the council, one favoring and one opposing the creation of a professional, salaried police force. One of the reports admitted that "within the last three months almost every crime in the catalogue of crimes has been committed in Detroit." The March 6 riot only a few weeks later seemed to put the matter beyond debate, yet nothing was done until August 5, when the anticipated draft and the almost constant fear of Rebel raids from Canada (to be discussed in chapter 7) prompted the council to establish a temporary police force of twenty-five men.[43]

The lack of nighttime safety on Detroit's streets only worsened with the dawn of 1864. On February 4, the *Free Press* reported that the previous evening had been "one of considerable activity among the thieving fraternity" and that it was now unsafe for peaceable citizens to walk even the most frequented streets after sundown. Four men on various downtown streets had been knocked down, beaten, and robbed that prior evening, including a soldier from the Third Michigan Infantry. Like many others, even the *Free Press* was now admitting that "an effective police would obviate this to a considerable extent."[44]

Crime and vagrancy reached such a high level that by March 1864, the Common Council passed an ordinance for "the Punishment of Vagrants" that asserted that any able-bodied person wandering the streets without gainful employment or apparent means of supporting himself faced a charge of vagrancy, which carried a potential fine of anywhere from $5 to $100. The matter peaked with Mayor Kirkland Barker's address to the council on January 10, 1865, urging the creation of a permanent, professional police force. A purely volunteer force would no longer do for, as Barker noted, after a while, most volunteers failed to respond when called for night-watch duty. He admitted that taxes were a key reason such a force had never been created in the past, but now there was no choice: "Our city is and has been for months past infested by itinerant thieves, highway-men, pickpockets and incendiaries," declared Barker, "and there is no way to reach such characters except through an efficiently organized police." Opposition to the idea remained, but council members in favor of the force refused to let the question die, ultimately resulting in the establishment of Detroit's first formal police department in February 1865. In what was a partnership between the moneyed downtown interests and the Republican Party, Detroit's Metropolitan Police Department was, from the beginning, beholden to the city's business community.[45]

Despite the numerous social and economic concerns that plagued Detroiters during the Civil War years, most rested easily in knowing that the war's bloody battlefields were far away in distant Southern states. That comfort would be seriously shaken in late 1863 and 1864.

CHAPTER SIX

"There is no department of our work that has afforded more satisfaction"

Detroit Responds to Its Soldiers' Needs

For those fortunate Detroit women who did not have to worry about earning a living but still wanted to contribute to the war effort, nothing took them closer to the front lines than working in the North's hospitals or camps set up to care for wounded or ill soldiers. Securing such a position was often easier said than done, for while all admitted the natural tendencies of women to provide tender care, many men still felt that the horrors of the military hospital were no place for a woman. In fact, hospitals in general were a bit unusual before the Civil War, as most middle- and upper-class individuals received any needed nursing care in their homes. Hospitals were generally considered asylums for the destitute or terminal patient; most, such as St. Mary's in Detroit, were set up and run by Catholic nuns as a charitable institution for the poor.[1]

Most of the resistance to women serving as nurses was initially expressed by male surgeons and physicians, for social mores of the era dictated that a military hospital was no place for a lady. It was firmly believed that the physical and emotional strains of such an environment would be far more than any member of the so-called weaker sex could stand. Moreover, even if a particular woman could handle the pressures, the very nature of the job was such that any prim and proper lady should want to avoid it. On this matter, one anonymous physician asked his readers in a July 1861 medical journal to "imagine a delicate, refined woman assisting a rough soldier to the close-stool, or supplying him with a bedpan, or adjusting the knots on a T-bandage employed in retaining a catheter in position."

Such routine duties as giving sponge baths or dressing wounds in sensitive areas might present numerous embarrassing scenarios, the mere thought of which was deemed appalling to "proper society." Such was the case in June 1862 when the *Free Press* printed a letter from the U.S. Sanitary Commission signed by its all-male board instructing all "male nurses volunteering their services" to register at their local office. There was no mention of female nurses. By January 1863, however, the situation had altered somewhat. The *Free Press* reported in its January 10 issue that the surgeon general had approved a measure before the Senate Military Committee to promote a careful selection of female nurses for the army; the measure was designed to "encourage ladies to enter on such duty as an honorable profession."[2]

Despite societal pressures, thousands of women across the North yearned to be nurses almost from the outset, yet in Detroit and most other Northern cities, finding out how to volunteer and then being accepted into the army nurse ranks were always a bit problematic. For the most part, the number of applications far exceeded the available positions. For instance, a September 15, 1862, letter from the Michigan Soldiers' Relief Association in Washington to an applicant, printed in the *Detroit Advertiser and Tribune,* reminded its recipient that the organization was receiving applications on a daily basis from thousands of similarly patriotic women. "We do not think it advisable for any lady to leave home for the purpose of getting thus employed, until notified that a place is ready for her, unless she can come prepared with means for her support while waiting for employment."[3]

Of course, many of the army's medical directors still held to a prejudice against female nurses, which resulted in many of the available nursing positions being filled by male soldiers from the Invalid Corps or even the use of recovering convalescent soldiers to care for their bedridden comrades. And for Detroit women, there was the matter of geography. The long distance from Detroit to the East's important military posts and large hospitals was a further detriment to the city's women who wished to serve, as the available slots for volunteers were usually filled by those who lived closer to the hospitals.[4]

Regardless of the initial doubts about the propriety of women serving as nurses, the lowly privates who received most of the Rebel bullet and artillery wounds during the war quickly came to respect their female nurses, most hoping to be cared for by a woman. As might be expected, some men fell in love with their nurses or became lifelong friends. "The superiority of females as nurses for the sick is unquestioned," opined the *Free Press* in May 1863. "However skillful and tender a man may be, he is harsh and unsympathizing in the sick room compared to women." In the end, the women's genuine feelings of patriotism and compassion—and the practical admission that they were needed—overcame concerns about the impropriety of women working in hospitals.[5]

By 1863, the lack of proper hospital care in Detroit for Michigan's returning wounded, not to mention the general civilian population, was acute. There was a fairly small marine hospital that had opened in 1857 on an eight-acre site at the corner of Jefferson and Mt. Elliott avenues, with a primary mission of treating injured or sick seamen. Fort Wayne and the Detroit Barracks on Clinton Street also had small infirmaries, but these could house only a handful of men. Beyond those undersized facilities, St. Mary's Hospital was the only major hospital in Detroit and the only public hospital in the entire state. Its predecessor was a twelve-bed facility named St. Vincent's that was originally opened in 1845 by four Catholic Sisters of Charity in a small, two-story structure at the southwest corner of Randolph and Larned streets. Five years later, the Sisters erected a larger building on Clinton Street near St. Antoine, which they christened St. Mary's. This served Detroit's poor and destitute throughout the 1850s and was pressed into wartime service with the onset of the Civil War. By 1863, however, with the war now in its third year, this 150-bed facility was so overcrowded with Union soldiers that the Sisters erected a temporary pavilion to care for 100 more. In December 1864, a hospital official reported that the facility, now known as the St. Mary's U.S. General Hospital, had 273 patients. Meanwhile, there was precious little room for Detroit's sick or poor civilians.[6]

Fortunately for Detroit and its wounded boys in blue, a significant change was about to occur. A nondescript seventy-year-old Irishman named Walter Harper, a Detroit resident for over twenty-five years yet well known by almost no one, had amassed a small fortune in Detroit-area real estate over the previous decades. A widower and apparently disdainful of his surviving children, Harper had met with town leaders on February 3, 1859, to inform them that he wished to give this land, close to a thousand acres, to the city for the express purpose of building a hospital that would serve Detroit's sick and poor. In return for this gift, Harper stipulated that the hospital was to be run by a board of trustees with lifetime tenure handpicked by him, though future candidates for board vacancies were to be selected by the pastor and congregation of Detroit's First Presbyterian Church. Harper also asked for a lifetime annuity payment of $2,000 per year, which was, of course, readily agreed to. It was one of the largest philanthropic donations ever given to the city of Detroit.[7]

The stunning though wonderful news did not stop there. Two weeks after Harper's announcement, his housekeeper, Mrs. Ann Martin, better known to all as Nancy Martin, announced to the recently selected board that she, too, wished to make a land gift. This most certainly surprised the board, for while Harper was reclusive and reticent, Martin was well known in Detroit's marketplace for her boisterous, salty, and unladylike mannerisms. Martin explained that she owned two parcels of land directly fronting Woodward Avenue: a valuable five-acre tract within the city limits and a fifteen-acre tract four miles outside the city. She was willing to give all this land to the board, gratis, with the stipulations that the forthcoming "Harper Hospital" be built on the five-acre tract and that she receive a $600 per year lifetime annuity and a small cottage to live in. Like Harper's, her offer was readily accepted.[8]

The Harper Hospital trustees knew from the beginning that they were land rich and cash poor. Tracts of Harper's land were sold over the next few years to raise funds for the hospital's construction. Though the board's coffers slowly grew due to the land sales and earned interest, no suitable plan took shape for an institution on the grand scale envisaged; by March 1864, board discussions were under way for a more modest design. Mounting Civil War casualties and illnesses soon changed the board's focus, helped in large measure by the urgings of Colonel Charles S. Tripler. A physician, Tripler was fifty-five when he entered the war as the post surgeon at Newport Barracks, Kentucky. By spring 1862, his skill had advanced him to the position of medical director for the entire Army of the Potomac. With the perceived failure of the Peninsula Campaign and the resulting political finger-pointing, Tripler was removed from that position in July 1862 and at his request sent back to his home in Detroit, where he was given the position of U.S. medical director for the army's Northern Department.[9]

Almost immediately, Tripler realized that a military "general hospital" was needed in Michigan to care for the state's wounded soldiers. Such hospitals were referred to as "general" because sick or wounded men were sent to them without regard for their military units. Prior to this, most western cities had not had such a hospital, because the Union's western armies had penetrated so far into the South that it seemed more prudent to build them in Union-held towns closer to the front, such as Memphis, Chattanooga, and Nashville. Tripler angrily noted in letters to his superiors that dozens of such hospitals had been built throughout the East and even in neighboring western states but not in Michigan. By the summer of 1863, state politicians as well as Michigan's U.S. senators Zachariah Chandler and Jacob Howard had joined in the call. Of course, where such a facility would be built and who would be in charge always involved a healthy dose of politics and special interests. The army had inquired about the possibility of taking over Detroit's marine hospital or even converting the Detroit Barracks, both of which suggestions were strongly discouraged by Dr. Tripler and his Detroit colleagues. Nevertheless, Secretary of War Edwin Stanton issued orders on November 16, 1863, to convert the Detroit Barracks to a general hospital and to construct any other buildings deemed necessary. Tripler had apparently unsuccessfully lobbied for a new structure to be built, making the case that construction would cost no more than conversion. He also put forth the idea that he and his colleagues should have had absolute control of the new hospital, which apparently ruffled some feathers back in Washington. When Dr. Joseph Tunnicliff, the state agent for Michigan at Washington, learned of Tripler's plans, he assumed the doctor had ulterior motives and informed Michigan governor Austin Blair, "The faction at Detroit, of which Drs. Tripler and [Zina] Pitcher are the head and Dr. [William] Brodie the tail—would undoubtedly have succeeded in their movement, had not the question of cost defeated them." Michigan's adjutant general, John Robertson, later wrote that soon after Stanton's orders, the whole project began to encounter "unexpected difficulties," which ultimately led to shelving the idea of converting the Detroit Barracks.[10]

With the army finally showing some interest in building a military hospital at Detroit by late 1863, the Harper trustees stepped forward in March 1864 and offered Ann Martin's previously donated five-acre lot on Woodward to the Federal government on a rent-free basis. Army negotiators were certainly interested in the offer, though it was immediately realized that five acres would be insufficient for a hospital of the size the military would need. This prompted the board to purchase the five acres that bordered its currently owned five at a price of $10,557. These combined ten acres were then offered free of charge to the government as the site for the proposed military hospital. The U.S. government would build the hospital and have control of the facility for the war's duration, and for as long thereafter as it might desire. The key stipulation in the lease was that at the end of its occupancy, the government was to give the Harper board "preferred opportunities" for purchasing whatever improvements the government might have made to the land during its usage. Captain George W. Lee, the assistant quartermaster for Detroit and a former farmer from Howell, was a man as anxious as anyone to see the hospital built. After obeying instructions to personally inspect the property, Lee reported back to the quartermaster general in Washington recommending acceptance of the offer. The Harper proposal was soon agreed to by Federal authorities with little hesitation.[11]

Construction began in late spring 1864 and was well under way by the summer. Located between John R. Street and Woodward Avenue, near the old state fairgrounds at Woodward and Canfield, the hospital consisted of eleven one-story, barrackslike buildings capable of handling over five hundred patients. Key to the design of the hospital was the great care that had been focused on matters of drainage, ventilation, and water supply. The hospital seemingly could not be completed fast enough. The Harper Hospital opened on October 12, 1864, with a full gala that featured Detroit's leading citizens, a local military band to provide musical entertainment, and a sumptuous buffet laid out by the local ladies. Most pleased of all was Nancy Martin who, according to the *Free Press*, "was apparently in a whirl of delight" that her dream and that of Walter Harper was coming to pass. Most of the hospital was still only roughly finished—in fact, the sounds of carpentry and the smell of fresh paint were still everywhere. Nevertheless, two wards had been properly completed in time to receive the 120 wounded Union soldiers who were scheduled to arrive that very day. Caring for wounded men quickly became the hospital's main charge, while sick men were sent to St. Mary's or to private facilities. When the hospital was fully finished, the final cost was close to $60,000. With its five hundred–plus beds, it was larger than any medical facility Detroit had ever seen, but by military standards it was considered rather small, for some of the larger eastern military hospitals contained as many as three thousand beds. Nevertheless, in short order, hundreds of sick and wounded Michigan soldiers were immediately sent there to be cared for.[12]

George W. Lee (Howell Area
Historical Society, Howell, Mich.).

Harper Hospital's original buildings (Silas Farmer, *History of Detroit and Wayne County and Early Michigan*, 3rd ed. [Detroit: Silas Farmer, 1890]).

While the wounded or ill soldier sent to these hospitals generally had praise and admiration for the volunteer female nurse, his opinions regarding the quality of care in general and the talents of the male doctors in particular were often less kind. Immanuel Brown of the First Michigan Sharpshooters arrived at Harper Hospital on February 6, 1865, and immediately wrote to his wife that some of the hospital's patients were suffering from an outbreak of deadly smallpox. Four days later he noted how "very nice" the new facility was, though he complained that he did not like "the way the rangements of the hospital affairs is conducted." Only a few days after Brown arrived, Frank Marsh, a male nurse at Harper's, was also expressing concern about treatments and protocols. In a February 15 letter to his mother, Marsh asked her if she had a good home remedy to fight erysipelas, a highly contagious, painful, and acute bacterial skin infection that often extends into the lymphatic system and can even lead to death. Marsh sadly informed his mother that he had already faced three such cases, losing the first man and fearful that he was going to watch his third infected patient die. "I do not like the treatment the Drs. give it here." In the Civil War era, doctors had not yet gained a thorough understanding of bacteriology, nor did they possess knowledge pertaining to antibiotics or the importance of antiseptics. Marsh was positive he had cured his second infected patient with a cranberry poultice, "but the Dr. would not let me use them on this man, and he is going to die. I have done all in my Power for him." That the new hospital was already suffering from smallpox outbreaks and serious bacterial infections indicates how far Civil War–era medical science had to go in maintaining sanitary conditions.[13]

Twenty-one-year-old Frank Gross arrived at the new Harper Hospital two months later, on April 6, 1865, and quickly formed an opinion similar to Brown's and Marsh's. "The hospital quarters are excellent," acknowledged Gross, "but I do think the doctors are very incompetent for hospital surgeons, especially the one in this ward. I guess they come in the service to keep from starving. It is a disgrace to the state of Michigan to employ such doctors." Gross's opinion regarding hospital surgeons was not isolated; it even became fairly widespread in the North. While most hospital doctors had obtained some measure of professional training, it was later discovered that many had not. As George W. Adams noted in his medical history of the Union army, those army hospital doctors who did have some training were often the "lame ducks" of the medical profession, having often failed in private practice due to incompetence or even drunkenness. With so many qualified doctors away from their practices serving at the front, the result was a "golden harvest" of patients for private-practice physicians who stayed behind. Therefore, a medical man had to either have an outstanding level of patriotism to enter the government's employ at home or suffer from an absolute inability to build up his own practice. Luther Willard, Michigan's state agent in Nashville and the man responsible for aiding wounded Michigan men with paperwork and assisting their relatives within his territory, noted in his 1864 year-end report that some army surgeons were considered by the men to be little more than money-grubbing army sutlers. "There are too many professional men in the army," Willard complained, "who, by reason of incompetency, cannot earn a living at home, seek and obtain a position in a General Military Hospital, where they can 'play off.' A shameful and criminal neglect of their patients—the brave sons of our land—is the result." Although these men sometimes wore an officer's uniform within their hospitals and had the title of "acting assistant surgeons," in reality they held no official military commission and were engaged under contract for wages that were noticeably less than a commissioned doctor in the Union army. Highlighting the low station that these medical men held was a March 28, 1864, letter from the surgeon general's office in Washington to Lieutenant Colonel Joseph R. Smith in Detroit explicitly stating that these surgeons had no authority whatsoever to sign the final statements and discharges of any soldier. Instead, that responsibility lay with the military commander. To prevent any type of embarrassment that might arise, the surgeon general's office urged Smith to place commissioned medical officers in charge of general hospitals in his territory as soon as possible.[14]

Rumors also abounded in Detroit that the quantity and quality of the food and supplies administered to the Harper patients were substandard. The hospital administrators knew such gossip was false; nevertheless, the negative stories reached such a level that Harper's management felt compelled to invite a special committee to visit the hospital at its convenience to determine the facts for itself. Showing up announced on June 5, 1865, the committee toured the hospital's kitchen, dining room, cellar, patient wards, and outdoor areas. In all areas, the hospital's operations passed with flying colors, which allowed the *Free Press* to declare the hospital fully vindicated of the malicious charges.[15]

The rules at Harper and other army hospitals also riled some patients. When men who tried to slip out of the ward after dark and go on a fling were caught, they quickly realized that the cozy relationship of doctor and patient could change in an instant to that of stern

Harper Hospital building (National Archives, College Park, Md.).

officer and enlisted man. Frank Gross complained, "Men here are put in the guard house for the least thing out of the way. . . . A private soldier is little better than a dog in some of these Doctors' eyes. I expected to get a furlough when I got here but found myself mistaken. A person here can hardly get away after he is there." Harper Hospital was, after all, in essence a military base, not a pleasure spa.[16]

Matters of efficiency were apparently not much better downtown at St. Mary's Hospital. Joseph Tuttle wrote to his sister that he was feeling better and hoped to be home in time to help plant the corn and potatoes; however, the wheels of government were grinding painfully slowly. They are "beginning to muster out men here as fast as they can get their descriptive lists from Washington . . . but I can't tell how soon [as] it takes a good deal of writing to muster the men out of the service."[17]

As has been discussed, opportunities for Detroit's Civil War–era women to earn a paycheck for their families were often few and far between. If Northern society in general was willing to accept women in the workplace, such tolerance was often granted with a touch of pity, especially for those who had no other means of income in a man's world. For those fortunate women who did not have to work, volunteer work was viewed as a socially acceptable and valuable way to assist in the struggle. In fact, almost from the day the Civil War began, Detroit women, like those all across the North, yearned to contribute in any way possible. When the war began and as long as their soldier husbands or sons were stationed at one of Detroit's training camps, these women could visit their men, bring them home-cooked food, and even nurse them if they fell ill. Circumstances obviously changed once these men departed for the front, for then it was difficult if not impossible to determine how women could aid the war effort. With so many options considered "unladylike," Detroit's females floundered for close to six months before finding their collective answer.[18]

Throughout the initial months of the war, Mrs. George Duffield, wife of the First Presbyterian Church's pastor, and her daughter, Mrs. Morse Stewart, had considered it their duty to solicit food and clothing donations for Michigan soldiers from the public through newspaper appeals. From May through November 1861, these two Detroit women received several dozen boxes of supplies, which were distributed to Michigan regiments both in state and in and around Washington, D.C. Eventually, the successful operation began to grow too large for the two women to handle, prompting them to seek official assistance. As in any other Northern town, the solution for these patriotic women was to consolidate their individual efforts into formal organizations that would solicit, gather, and then ship all manner of food, clothing, and medical supplies to the soldiers at the front. By far the most valuable volunteer home-front groups these Northern women created were what became known as the "Ladies' Aid Societies." In fact, women's roles within these volunteer groups were generally so dominant that the word "Ladies' " was often used by the public to describe any given group even when it was not a formal part of that group's name. They generally met in churches, private homes, or wherever the necessary items were collected. Initially, at least, and perhaps not surprisingly considering the gender biases of the era, men often looked down at these gatherings, believing that the women were more interested in gossiping than in performing actual aid work.[19]

In order to create economies of scale and to avoid duplication of efforts, most of these city- or statewide societies eventually became official branches of the U.S. Sanitary Commission, a national civilian organization whose duties and activities during the Civil War were strikingly similar to the American Red Cross of later years. Created in June 1861 and authorized by President Lincoln and Simon Cameron, then secretary of war, the commission's mission was to help minister to the supply and service needs of Union soldiers alongside the more formal branches of the military, such as the Quartermaster, Commissary, and Army Medical departments. Rather than duplicate the duties of these military departments, the Sanitary Commission, through its smaller branches, solicited the public for donations of food, clothing, bandages, sheets, and so on, gathering those supplies in central locations and then shipping them to the Union armies in the field as needed.[20]

The patriotic desire of the women of Detroit to assist the war effort in some way led to the creation of the Detroit Soldiers' Aid Society. With the exception of Dr. Zina Pitcher, a highly respected surgeon and former mayor of Detroit who acted as counselor to the society and served as the Sanitary Commission's official representative in Detroit from 1861 to 1863, the establishment and subsequent operation of the Detroit Soldiers' Aid Society was entirely the work of women. Led by the aforementioned Mrs. Duffield, and her daughter, Mrs. Stewart, a considerable number of Detroit women met in the basement of the Woodward Avenue Methodist Church on November 6, 1861, to take the necessary steps in the formation of such a society. Many of these upper- and upper-middle-class women were the wives, sisters, and daughters of some of Detroit's most prominent businessmen, politicians, and clergy, which gave them and their new society immediate recognition and credibility. A benefactor immediately stepped forward to donate a vacant storefront at the corner of Woodward and East Jefferson avenues, which the society could use for warehousing its donations. With its organization and storage needs fundamentally completed, Detroit's Soldiers' Aid Society could now begin its mission of providing for Michigan troops in the field. Though not yet a formal branch of the Sanitary Commission, the society intended from its inception to cooperate with the larger entity, after which it had modeled its organizational procedures. From its creation until July 1863, the Detroit Soldiers' Aid Society often used Sanitary Commission facilities.[21]

Therefore it was not a complete surprise when in the summer of 1863, the Detroit Soldiers' Aid Society became the official Michigan branch of the U.S. Sanitary Commission. To reflect its new geographic responsibilities, the society changed its name to The Michigan Soldiers' Aid Society and, in concert with the smaller Ladies' Aid Societies from around the state, industriously continued its work of collecting an increasing amount of supplies gathered from all parts of the state. As the donations arrived in Detroit, they were properly boxed or crated and sent to the commission's depots at Louisville or New York, or even directly to the front when necessary.[22]

While the city's women did an admirable job collecting supplies for their men at the front, by the middle of 1863 the Michigan Soldiers' Aid Society realized that soldiers also needed help at home: healthy soldiers temporarily returning to Detroit on furlough or passing through to other parts of the state should have a clean, reliable place to stay. Up to that point, such men had been directed to the Detroit Barracks or some other building, with their care and provisions being handled on an ad hoc basis. Some stayed at hotels, others at saloons, while still others decided simply to bed down outdoors as if they were still on campaign. Michigan men started to complain, asking why the care they had received at Nashville, Cincinnati, or other places was better than what they were finding in Detroit. Thus began the creation of the Detroit Soldiers' Home, a hostel-like operation where Michigan's fighting men could stay for a night or two, get a hot meal and, for a brief while anyway, enjoy the comforts of home.[23]

After examining several properties that were deemed unsuitable, the old arsenal building at the corner of Jefferson Avenue and Wayne Street was selected for the new home. Provisions were made for thirty men when the home first opened in January 1864, though the establishment could accommodate up to double that number in an emergency. The carpenters and plasterers had barely finished their repairs before men from the Eighth Michigan Infantry arrived on their way home from the miserable conditions they had endured in the just-concluded Knoxville campaign. According to a Sanitary Commission official, "After sleeping in half-frozen mud, and living on a few ounces of bread made from corn and cobs ground together, warmth and shelter and a sufficiency of wholesome food were luxuries." From that day on, the Detroit Soldiers' Home was a welcome relief station for Michigan's tired boys in blue. By April 1864, the home was being run under the auspices of the Ladies' Army Committee, a branch of the U.S. Sanitary Commission. In March of 1864 alone, the Detroit Soldiers' Home provided over 1,000 lodgings and 2,163 hot meals.[24]

In her 1864 year-end report to Michigan's adjutant general, Valeria Campbell, the corresponding secretary for the Michigan Soldiers' Aid Society, described the Detroit Soldiers' Home as the organization's most important work of the year. Though it was initially thought that the rented space was larger than necessary, it was quickly realized that it was in fact too small for the comfort of those admitted. The unfortunate result was that many soldiers were unable to secure a bed when they needed one. "Imperfectly, however, as it has answered our expectations," noted Miss Campbell, "there is no department of our work that has afforded more satisfaction."[25]

The home-front challenges faced by "war widows" and households whose husbands and fathers were off fighting at the front were not the only social problems in Detroit during the conflict. The Civil War also dealt Detroit a growing population of orphaned and homeless children. It was not an entirely new challenge, for Catholic and Protestant charities had cared for orphans in Detroit for at least two decades. Cholera epidemics in 1849 and 1854, coupled with the 1857 financial crisis, had all conspired to create an unusual number of orphans in Detroit. Adult casualties of the Civil War along with a rapidly increasing population only worsened matters. To help alleviate the growing crisis, women from the Ladies' Christian Union organized the Society for the Home of the Friendless in the spring of 1862, with the intent of building a permanent home "for the temporary protection of homeless women and helpless children." Throughout the war, these women were able to provide shelter for homeless children, successfully placing some for adoption and sending older children to school.[26]

Such children's societies were born all across the North during the war. In New York alone, over eight thousand homeless children were given new starts by the city's various children's aid societies.

Most of these children were placed on what was known as "the orphan train" and sent to new homes in the agricultural sections of western states such as Michigan, where the war had made farm labor difficult to find and newcomers of almost any age were happily welcomed.[27]

With various societies seeing to the physical needs of the Union troops, it was not long before organizations were formed to tend to the soldiers' spiritual needs as well. Various chapters and branches of the Young Men's Christian Association had, from the beginning of the war, worked to gather and hand out Bibles and other devotional materials to soldiers. Such independent attempts soon proved haphazard, however, and by November 1861, representatives from across the North met to form what became the United States Christian Commission, whose mission was to enhance "the spiritual good of the soldiers in the army, and incidentally their intellectual improvement and social and physical comfort." The soldiers were considered "absent members of Christian homes and communities," with the commission aspiring to take the place, as far as possible, of those family members and friends back home who would normally "cheer and sustain them in their hardships, toils, and perils, temptations and privations."[28]

The Michigan branch of the Christian Commission was created in Detroit at a public meeting held on June 15, 1863. Besides gathering religious supplies for Michigan's men in the field, the local commission provided ample support to the wounded and sick in Detroit at St. Mary's Hospital and at the infirmary at the Detroit Barracks. Here were found wounded Michigan men from the November 23–25, 1863, battle of Chattanooga who yearned for conversation or a sympathetic ear, in addition to whatever else Christian kindness could do. On December 7, 1863, a Ladies' Committee of the Christian Commission was also formed in Detroit; this, like the male-dominated Christian Commission, performed spiritual and charitable work for Detroit's ill and wounded soldiers. In its first public circular, the Ladies' Committee announced "work of the first importance": the erection of a small chapel, reading room, and library at the Detroit Barracks. In its first year alone, Detroit's Christian Commission sent nine delegates to the army in the field, collected $2,300 in cash for general commission work within the army, and furnished 239 boxes of hospital supplies for the benefit of the soldiers.[29]

By early 1864, it had already become quite apparent just how important the role of women had been and still was to the Union war effort. In his speech at the closing of the Sanitary Fair in March, President Abraham Lincoln remarked, "I have never studied the art of paying compliments to women; but I must say that if all that has been said by orators and poets since the creation of the world in praise of woman were applied to the women of America, it would not do them justice for their conduct during this war. I will close by saying God bless the women of America!"[30]

"Our people are now fully warned"

The War Almost Hits Home

Within a year of the war commencing, Confederate authorities yearned to take the fight into the North and, from their vantage, give the Yankee invader a taste of his own medicine. After all, from the very beginning practically the entire conflict had been waged within Southern states, thereby sparing the Northern citizenry the hardships and terrors that had been visited upon Confederate women and children. After the September 1862 and July 1863 strategic defeats at Antietam and Gettysburg respectively, such plans had taken on a renewed sense of urgency within the Confederacy. General Jubal Early would lead the last of three Rebel ground invasions of the North in the fall of 1864, but it, like the two aforementioned campaigns, failed to achieve the results Confederate leaders had hoped for.

In spite of such battlefield failures, Confederate authorities still desired to wage war on Northern soil and as part of their strategy, they devised a series of clandestine missions in the North that would emanate from Canada, clearly a violation of that country's stated neutrality. The mounting public dissension in the North throughout 1863 regarding the draft, the use of black soldiers, and changing war aims helped generate these new Confederate plans. Before the war ended, the South's covert activities in Canada would involve the commitment of over $1 million in Confederate gold. The overarching strategic goal of such plans was to generate support for the growing peace movement in the North, with the ultimate hope of seeing Abraham Lincoln defeated in the November 1864 presidential election. The Confederate government in Richmond was banking on its conviction that a new, peace-oriented Democratic administration would immediately push for a cessation of hostilities with an eye toward a negotiated settlement, thereby preserving the Confederacy as well as slavery. Tactical disinformation campaigns would be used to help bring about that end. In addition, as the war dragged on, the lack of experienced officers in the Confederate army due to death or capture, coupled with an overall manpower shortage, began to show itself. From a tactical perspective, this problem would be dealt with by designs that included planned paramilitary raids that would hopefully free Confederate prisoners from Union prisoner-of-war camps.[1]

Specifically, Confederate operatives laid plans to surprise and capture the USS *Michigan* which, due to the 1842 Webster-Ashburton Treaty with Great Britain, was the sole Union warship allowed on Lake Erie. Once the warship was in Rebel hands, the Confederates could free their prisoners of war at Northern prison camps situated on or near the Great Lakes. With no other Union gunboat to stop them, lakefront cities such as Buffalo, Cleveland, and Detroit could be shelled and sacked. Despite the fact that these men would be considered nothing more than pirates in the eyes of Union authorities, guilty of inflicting terror upon innocent noncombatants, Acting Master John Yates Beall, Rebel leader of what became the ill-fated 1864 Johnson's Island raid, later put forth the Confederate justification in a Canadian newspaper: "The United States is carrying on war on Lake Erie against the Confederate States, by transportation of men and supplies on its waters; by confining Confederate prisoners on its islands, and lastly, by the presence of a 14-gun steamer patrolling its waters. The Confederates clearly have the right to retaliate."[2]

Lieutenant William H. Murdaugh of the Confederate navy formally proposed the first such plan to Confederate government leaders in early February 1863. Murdaugh presented his scheme to Stephen Mallory, secretary of the Confederate navy, who immediately endorsed the idea. However, lack of funds initially stalled the plan. Eventually Murdaugh and his conspirators were granted $25,000 and told to prepare themselves for the mission, but at the last minute the plan was vetoed by Confederate president Jefferson Davis, who feared that such an operation on the Great Lakes might hinder Southern relations with England.[3]

The key to Murdaugh's scheme, as well as all subsequent plans, was the successful capture of the *Michigan* and the ensuing release of the Rebel prisoners of war on Johnson's Island. That island, named after its owner, Leonard B. Johnson, was a perfect spot for a prison camp as it was located on the south side of Lake Erie just at the mouth of Sandusky Bay on Ohio's northern coast. Sandusky itself was a small, nondescript town of approximately eighty-five hundred residents, whom Charles Dickens had described as "morose, sullen, clownish, and repulsive" during a brief 1842 visit. The U.S. Army had leased forty cleared acres of the island from Johnson in the fall of 1861 to establish a prisoner-of-war depot that (it was naively believed at the time) would be sufficient to house all captured Rebels. The depot commenced operations in April 1862, and from its inception had been a prison camp primarily for Confederate officers. By 1864, however, the camp was woefully overcrowded, and many of its twenty-five hundred prisoners suffered from a lack of food to the point of near starvation. One prisoner later recalled that "the parade ground was dotted with gaunt, cadaverous men, with a far-away look in their eyes and hunger and privation showing in every line of their emaciated bodies." Though forbidden to do so, many men took to catching and eating rats. Major Edward Stakes of the Fortieth Virginia Infantry wrote that he had happily eaten the fried hindquarters of one, "which was as tender and good as a young squirrel." Stakes concluded that he would never suffer hunger again as long as he could catch and eat a rat. For prisoner James Caldwell, however, "Nothing short of absolute starvation could induce me to overcome my repugnance to those creatures who feed on the most loathsome garbage."[4]

Almost from the day the prisoner-of-war camp on Johnson's Island opened, Union spies and informants were reporting purported Rebel plans to attack Northern towns and cities along the Great Lakes. As early as June 1862, a Union spy with the nom de guerre "Canadian" was reporting that a plan was afoot near the river towns of Sandwich, Canada, and Detroit to liberate the Johnson's Island prisoners. Describing what would become the standard method of operation, Canadian reported that Southern sympathizers were scheming to commandeer a vessel, sneak into Sandusky Bay, surprise the Yankee guards, and then free their Confederate brethren.[5]

Lieutenant Colonel Hill, acting assistant provost marshal general of Michigan, was the Detroit man primarily responsible for ferreting out fact from fiction, at least as far as such matters could impact Michigan. He now had to ascertain the truthfulness of the reports crossing his desk. Having heard all the stories, Hill telegraphed his superiors in Washington on November 9, 1863, that "a good many rumors [have] reached my ears recently" regarding Rebel plots against Johnson's Island and elsewhere. He considered most reports "so wild that I have not attached any importance to them," but "in the last few days disclosures have been made to myself that I place some reliance on." In this particular case, Hill knew from his operatives that a Rebel agent had arrived in Windsor with certificates of deposit worth over $100,000—a huge sum that, according to Hill, was destined to purchase steamers at Montreal for the planned raid. Hill estimated there were about two thousand Rebel refugees and sympathizers in Canada, including several Confederate naval officers. "That some project of magnitude is in contemplation I feel very certain," Hill stressed, "and I have communicated with the U.S. consul-general at Montreal." That U.S. diplomat in Montreal essentially dismissed Hill's warnings, thinking the stories and rumors to be merely the grandiloquence of Confederate agents in Canada. General Jacob Cox, however, who was running the District of Ohio's Cincinnati headquarters for General Ambrose Burnside, took Hill's admonitions far more seriously and immediately ordered five hundred new recruits and a battery of three-inch rifled cannon to proceed immediately to Sandusky.[6]

Hill's suspicions were well founded, for such a plan was indeed in the works. Confederate Lieutenant Robert Minor had essentially taken Murdaugh's original plan and repackaged it in August 1863 to the Confederate authorities in Richmond. As before, Mallory agreed to the plan, but this time Confederate president Jefferson Davis approved it as well, admitting that "it was better to fail than not to make the attempt." Minor had carefully developed a revised plan to capture a civilian steamer on the lakes, crash it into the *Michigan* as if by accident, and then overpower the Yankee crew. Meanwhile, the prisoners on the island were to be ready and awaiting their opportunity to overwhelm the prison guard, thanks to surreptitious coded messages placed in the personal columns of the *New York Herald* that advised the prisoners of the plan's timing. Once captured, the *Michigan* with its new Rebel crew could terrorize the Great Lakes unimpeded. Fate intervened at the last moment, however. The plot was betrayed by one of Minor's band to a member of the Canadian provincial cabinet, who immediately notified Lord Charles Monck, the governor-general of Canada.[7]

On November 11, only two days after Hill had notified Washington of the rumored impending attack, Washington was formally notified by Lord Richard Lyons, the British minister to the United States, who had received the report from Monck, of "a serious and mischievous plot" among Southern sympathizers in Canada to take possession of some of the steamers on Lake Erie, surprise the guard at Johnson's Island, free the Southern prisoners there, and then proceed to attack and burn Buffalo. The warning was immediately telegraphed by Secretary of War Edwin Stanton to all the governors of the Great Lakes states and lakefront city mayors, including Detroit's. Detroit mayor William Duncan then immediately forwarded it to the city's Common Council with his urging that the council members give it their immediate attention. Duncan feared that if the information was well founded, it could "result in great disaster to our frontier and city." With their plot utterly exposed, the Rebels were forced to abandon their plan and disperse as swiftly as possible.[8]

All the same, the Detroit *Free Press* reported the very next day of two suspicious ships hovering near Sandusky Bay, purported to be the privateers intent on rescuing the prisoners at Johnson's Island. These renewed rumors of an imminent Rebel attack, coupled with the fact that the highest levels of the Canadian and American governments had acted on them, sent new waves of panic through Detroit. On the day the rumors hit the city, one thousand laborers were ordered to cut trees on the then privately owned Belle Isle in the middle of the Detroit River and to use the wood to build barricades. Adding fuel to the fire was a lead article in the November 12 *Free Press*, "Is Detroit in Danger!" which brazenly put forth the fantastical and mind-boggling story that not fewer than one hundred thousand able-bodied, well-drilled Rebels were sequestered in neighboring Canadian provinces. Their purported plan was to seize Detroit during the winter and then launch an invasion of neighboring states come spring. Despite the ridiculousness of the story, military officers in Detroit quickly met with John Robertson, Michigan's adjutant general, Senator Zachariah Chandler, and the city's leading citizens to brief them on the situation and to allay fears. Chandler, in fact, wasted no time in looking out for his hometown's interests. On November 12, he wired Secretary Stanton informing him that there were only four small artillery pieces posted on the Great Lakes and that Stanton should order heavy guns sent from Pittsburgh immediately. That evening, the Detroit Common Council held a special session and passed a resolution stating that Mayor William C. Duncan would be given "full power to take and enforce all such action as to his judgment shall seem proper under now existing circumstances."[9]

Such stories in the local press and the building of barricades hardly calmed the public's nerves. "Our whole lake region has been thrown into a violent commotion in consequence of a rumor of a contemplated raid by the rebs," reported Detroiter Nathan Brooks to his brother less than a week after the story first broke. From Brooks's perspective, the plot appeared to be at least as plausible as Morgan's raid through Ohio and Indiana the previous spring. "Nevertheless," wrote Brooks, "the scare has had the good effect of putting government and the people on the lookout." Meanwhile, Lieutenant Colonel Joseph Smith had wired Washington on November 13 that his city "was in a state of wild excitement at all the rumors," but that he had somewhat succeeded in calming fears by sending the steamer *Forest Queen*, newly armed with an artillery battery, up and down the river on a showy reconnaissance.[10]

While Detroit's populace was abuzz with news of the failed raid, the city's newspaper war continued unabated, as the Republican *Advertiser and Tribune* was hardly impressed with the concern put forth by the Democratic *Free Press* over the preceding two days. In a November 13 front-page editorial riddled with vitriol, it accused the *Free Press* of being "jubilant" about the planned "Copperhead-Rebel expedition" against Great Lakes cities. With the discovery of the fiendish plot, the Democratic paper was, according to the *Advertiser and Tribune*, obviously "disappointed" and in order to screen itself and its Copperhead friends on either side of the Detroit River, the paper had resorted to its usual tactic of "*seeming* to be greatly alarmed about a particular thing." As mentioned earlier, such journalistic contempt for one's political opponents was standard fare during the antebellum and Civil War eras.[11]

By now, such rumors and reports were so widespread that they had even reached the ears of General William T. Sherman, five hundred miles to the south at Nashville, Tennessee. "I have a series of papers from General [Henry] Halleck which go to show a conspiracy on the part of mischievous men residing in Kentucky, Indiana, Ohio, and Canada for the purpose of destroying steam-boats and even cities," reported Sherman to General Stephen Burbridge in Louisville. "We cannot operate by military force against such devils, but we can shelter and protect steamboat captains who resort to extraordinary measures to guard the property and lives in their charge against such villains." The feisty Sherman had no tolerance for men who waged war in such a manner and instructed Burbridge to inform the steamboat captains that if they detected such persons among the crew or passengers, they "should be disposed of summarily, viz, drowned or killed on the spot." Of course, Sherman stressed the need for clear proof, then justified his orders by declaring, "It is not war for individuals to burn steamboats or supply them with coal or wood charged with gunpowder, and the laws of war do not apply to such people; therefore, I don't care to have our military prisons or courts encumbered with such cases."[12]

❀   ❀   ❀

As 1864 dawned, Lieutenant Colonel Hill surely found himself with the weight of responsibility pressing down on his shoulders: charged with overseeing the new conscription law throughout Michigan, beset by concerns of civil disturbance in Detroit as well as elsewhere, and disturbed by the ongoing fear of Rebel attack against Detroit from Canada. A career military man and former West Pointer, Hill certainly approached his duties with every ounce of training and skill learned from his thirty-six years as a professional soldier. The military education he had acquired at West Point and its attendant caste system had instilled a level of elitism in its officers' corps that resulted in low regard for politicians and the arts of compromise and favoritism they practiced. It is likely that many civilians and politicians came to his office seeking favors, privilege, or outright exemption from possible conscription. Hill was a busy man who took his responsibilities seriously and no doubt quickly showed these people the door. Unfortunately for Hill, such actions over the past eight months had rubbed a number of state legislators the wrong way.[13]

The payback came on January 21, 1864, when state legislator Richard Winsor put forth a resolution in Michigan's House of Representatives censuring Hill and urging that Michigan's Federal congressmen and senators use whatever influence they had to remove him from his position as acting assistant provost marshal general. In his resolution Winsor expressed dismay that the position had not been filled by a Michigan man in the first place; considering the state's unquestionable loyalty and patriotism during the crisis. According to Winsor, Michigan's residents should not be "tyrannized over by a stranger who exhibits no sympathy except by availing himself of every opportunity to insult her citizens." When it came time to vote, the resolution was referred to the chamber's committee on Federal relations.[14]

Five days later, on January 26, the committee reported to the state House of Representatives that it was "convinced" that Hill, based on the testimony of "several gentlemen," had on numerous occasions been "insolent, overbearing and arbitrary, to an intolerable degree, toward citizens of this State" who had come calling on him requesting information pertaining to recruitment and the draft in their particular localities. In somewhat rewording Winsor's original resolution, the committee opined that Hill's "arbitrary and insolent deportment" had rendered him so "odious" to the people of Michigan that his removal from office was recommended, with the issue then passing on to the state Senate for concurrence.[15]

After receiving the House resolution the next day, the state Senate referred the matter to its Federal relations committee, which reported back a week later, on February 4. From the evidence it had obtained, the three-man committee reported that while Hill may have been "hasty and imprudent" in several instances, he was "a capable, faithful and efficient officer—fair and impartial in his decisions, and performs his duties with fidelity to the Government." The committee's formal recommendation was that the resolution not pass. Unfortunately for Hill, he had apparently made too many enemies. A motion to discard the resolution failed, with the Republican-held Senate then voting fifteen to eight to pass the resolution. The censure against Hill stood, but that was as far as the matter went. Neither James Fry nor any of Michigan's Federal delegation ever attempted again to remove Hill.[16]

The rumors and rumblings of planned Rebel attacks against Great Lakes cities persisted well into the spring of 1864. Major General Samuel Heintzelman, newly appointed to head the army's Northern Department, traveled from his headquarters in Columbus to Sandusky, Ohio, in April to meet with Brigadier General Henry Terry in an attempt to get to the bottom of the matter. Terry was in command of the prisoner-of-war camp at Johnson's Island and had heard repeated warnings of an armed vessel controlled by the Rebels that was purportedly lying in Canadian waters awaiting an opportunity to attack after the ice fully melted. With Canadian authorities, he had personally visited the ship in question and come away convinced

Samuel Heintzelman (Library of Congress, Washington, D.C.).

that it was engaged in legitimate business, presenting no threat. Despite Terry's newfound belief that there was nothing to the armed-vessel report, he stressed to Heintzelman, "I beg leave to add that there are many rebel refugees in Upper Canada, and that their headquarters are at Windsor, opposite Detroit; that they have some organization there is no doubt." Heintzelman concurred with Terry to a degree, though he doubted there was any danger of a large-scale coordinated attack. "I am satisfied, however, that there is an organized band in Canada watching for an opportunity to do us some damage should a favorable occasion offer," wrote Heintzelman. "It will probably be turned into burning steamboats and warehouses of stores."[17]

Meanwhile, back in Detroit, Lieutenant Colonel Smith was acting on suggestions that a small, fast ship be immediately procured for purposes of patrolling the Detroit River. Smith wrote to Heintzelman at Northern Department headquarters seeking authorization, explaining that the tug would be manned by twenty-five to thirty men and armed with a small cannon. The cost would be not more than $50 per day, and the ship should be procured for a few weeks "while this thing is threatened." No doubt to Smith's surprise, he was advised that although he could use any of the men under his command as he saw fit, the general commanding "cannot at present" approve the expenditure for the ship Smith had requested. If the Rebels were coming, Smith would be forced to deal with them on the Detroit side of the river.[18]

While Union authorities continued to concern themselves in the spring of 1864 with rumors of Rebel attacks along the Great Lakes, a far smaller and different type of hostility was now starting to show itself in Detroit. Having had to deal with an attempted censure by the Michigan state legislature in January along with the attempt by some of those politicians to have him replaced, Bennett Hill was now facing a military turf war between himself and Lieutenant Colonel Smith, a battle that appeared to be of his own making. Smith had been appointed the U.S. military commander for the District of Michigan back in October 1862, but had also served as the state's mustering and dispersing officer since January 3, 1862, after the promotion of Colonel Erastus Backus. It was Smith who had formally mustered in all of the Michigan regiments since that earlier date. He believed through his orders that an important role of his office was the tracking and arresting of deserters. When Hill arrived in Detroit in May 1863 as the acting assistant provost marshal general for Michigan, he well knew that dealing with deserters was also in his domain. Despite what appeared on the surface to be overlapping responsibilities, the men had maintained a cordial relationship, though cracks started to appear by early 1864.[19]

The conflict was essentially over whose office had the right to utilize special agents to arrest, interrogate, and even discharge men who were picked up as deserters. The matter boiled over when Smith learned that Hill had written to Major General Heintzelman, the commanding general for the army's Northern Department, stating his belief that the Detroit Barracks and its garrison should be under his control rather than Smith's, as it was at the time. In a March 31 letter to the department's assistant adjutant general, Smith cited previous 1862 orders in an attempt to point out why Hill was grossly mistaken. Moreover, Smith declared that the "Provost Guard" quartered at the barracks had merely adopted that name when it was formed in late 1862 and was "no more a force for Provost purposes than any company of invalids." After Hill wrote directly to Smith on April 4 alleging that Smith had appointed special agents to arrest deserters, a Provost Bureau prerogative, Smith fired back to Hill the next day denying the accusation and defending his office. He pointed out that he had been "especially careful, not knowingly, to interfere with any duty, or department under your control." But within his own command, "I claim, also, the right of discharging my own duties without interference from any other officer." If loyal men came to him claiming to know where deserters were hiding, Smith reserved the right to authorize them to arrest the suspects. Smith then accused Hill's provost marshal for Detroit, Captain Mark Flanigan, of foolishly releasing men charged with desertion after asking only a few simple questions—men who had been picked up by Smith's loyalists, who were convinced of the suspects' guilt.[20]

Flanigan, previously Detroit's sheriff and a member of the Twenty-fourth Michigan Infantry who had lost a leg at Gettysburg, was not a man to take such an insult without a retort. Furthermore, Smith had written directly to Flanigan on April 13 with allegations about Flanigan's Detroit operations that the captain considered "an attack on my ability and integrity." In an angry April 18 reply, Flanigan likewise accused Smith of releasing men he had arrested as deserters and maintained that Smith had practically slandered the Detroit provost marshal's office by publicly stating that "it was a fact patent throughout the community that poor soldiers were picked up and treated as deserters by the Provost Marshal whether they were so or not." Continuing the tit for tat, Flanigan also accused Smith of "assuming the duties of the Provost Marshal by assigning special agents to arrest deserters and then trying them after they have been examined and discharged at this office."[21]

It was a nasty turf battle that Hill ultimately won. Joseph R. Smith's time as Michigan's military commander ended in mid-May 1864. On June 11, 1864, he was transferred to Northern Department headquarters at Columbus, Ohio, to fill the role of assistant commissary of musters. With Smith gone, Hill assumed the roles of military commander for Detroit and chief mustering officer in addition to his provost marshal position, thereby making him the sole military authority in Michigan. The change had taken Smith completely by surprise, as he admitted to his wife, but he also fervently believed that holding both positions was what Hill had been surreptitiously seeking all along. "I cannot but feel that Col. Hill has shown himself to be small potatoes, *exceedingly*," wrote Smith. Hill, however, believed the issue to be all about military effectiveness. As he later wrote in his final report regarding Michigan's Provost Bureau operations, "The union of all these different offices under the control of one person added very much to the efficiency of them all." For the remaining ten months of the war, Lieutenant Colonel Hill would be a very busy man.[22]

Despite declining health, Smith held his new administrative position until the end of the war, at which time he was given the honorary rank of brevet brigadier general for "long and faithful services" rendered to his country. He died of stomach cancer in Monroe, Michigan, on September 3, 1868, at the age of sixty-seven.[23]

❀ ❀ ❀

FOR close to two years, most of the reports and rumors of Rebel attacks along the Great Lakes had turned out to have no basis in fact. They would, however, gain an undeniable level of credence with the arrival of September 1864. For months, Confederate naval officer John Yates Beall had been working on yet another plan to bring the war onto the Great Lakes and to free the Rebel prisoners on Johnson's Island. Beall was a good choice for the secret mission, for he had garnered some previous success as a privateer on Chesapeake Bay. Like Murdaugh before him, Beall also surmised that a privateer, secretly manned and properly armed, could sweep the Great Lakes and lay waste to Northern towns from Chicago to Detroit and beyond. In lieu of destruction, Beall reasoned he could demand heavy ransom from these cities as the price for their survival. His general idea was the same as the ones before; he and several dozen men would commandeer a Great Lakes steamer and then set off for Johnson's Island. Armed with ample handguns, knives, and cutlasses, the raiders would surprise and overwhelm the sailors on board the USS *Michigan*. Ever since October 24, 1863, the *Michigan* had been anchored in Sandusky Bay to provide additional protection to Johnson's Island due to the ever-increasing number of rumored plots against the prison camp. At a predetermined signal, the prisoners in the camp would rise up in revolt and overwhelm the guard. Not an unreasonable assumption, for as one prisoner later noted in his diary, "If we had somebody to attend to the gunboat, *we* could soon overpower the guard."[24]

The man Beall was reporting directly to and who was also intimately involved in the plot was Charles H. Cole, a Confederate who claimed to have had previously served as a captain under cavalry general Nathan Bedford Forrest. After earlier meeting with Beall to finalize their scheme, Cole positioned himself in Sandusky, where he posed as a free-spending Pennsylvania oilman. The key objective of

John Yates Beall (author's collection).

his new character was gaining the confidence of the *Michigan*'s officers. Before long, Cole had befriended the ship's officers, wining and dining them whenever possible. Cole's plan was to drug the officers' wine during dinner on the night of the raid, thereby making it far easier for Beall and his men to capture the *Michigan*. Once that objective was completed and the ship's fourteen guns were trained on the camp, the newest commandant of Johnson's Island, Lieutenant Colonel Charles Hill, would be forced to release the prisoners. Sailing ships in Sandusky harbor would be seized and used to remove the prisoners from Johnson's Island.[25]

The plan commenced in Detroit on September 18 when one of Beall's lieutenants, a thick-set Scotchman named Bennett G. Burley, walked to the Detroit harbor and approached the clerk representing the *Philo Parsons*, a 222-ton side-wheel steamer built in 1861 that was named after one of Detroit's most prominent businessmen. The *Parsons* was primarily a passenger transport, with trips regularly

Philo Parsons (Historical Collections of the Great Lakes, Bowling Green State University, Bowling Green, Ohio).

scheduled between Detroit and Sandusky, Ohio, on Lake Erie. The ship would leave Detroit at 8:00 a.m. on Mondays, Wednesdays, and Fridays, returning from Sandusky at the same time on Tuesdays, Thursdays, and Saturdays. There would be stops at the Canadian port towns of Amherstburg (aka Malden) and Sandwich, but only if the ship was signaled in advance. In addition were regularly scheduled stops at North, Middle, and South Bass islands and Kelley's Island, all within twenty miles of Sandusky. Burley's initial objective was to gain assurance that the ship would indeed stop the next day about three miles down the river at Sandwich, Canada, to pick up Beall and two other colleagues waiting there. Burley stated that they all wished to go on to Sandusky, but that one of his friends was lame and therefore could not cross the river.[26]

At 8:00 on the morning of September 19, Burley boarded the *Philo Parsons* along with about forty other passengers at Detroit. The ship actually had no formal authority to stop at Sandwich, so instead it gradually coasted to within inches of the dock, allowing Beall and his two compatriots to jump easily from the wharf onto the slowly passing ship. Fourteen miles to the south lay Amherstburg, where sixteen more of Beall's men boarded the ship. All were dressed in nondescript civilian clothes, and the only baggage they brought on board at Amherstburg was a large trunk tied shut with rope. The

Parsons continued on its southward course, making its normal stops at the three Bass islands and then continuing on to Kelley's Island, arriving there at around 4:00 p.m.[27]

Shortly after the ship left Kelley's Island, Beall and his men opened their trunk, which turned out to be well stocked with navy revolvers and hand axes. They announced they were Confederate soldiers and seized control of the *Philo Parsons*. All the passengers quickly realized that discretion was the better part of valor and surrendered; they were ordered belowdecks. After about an hour of circuitous sailing, Beall ordered the ship to turn back toward Middle Bass Island to gather fuel after he learned from the mate and engineer that wood supplies were running low. Most of the passengers were ordered off the ship at the island. The *Parsons* had barely left the dock when it was approached by the *Island Queen*, another passenger ferry on its way from Sandusky. Beall and about fifteen of his men jumped onto the *Island Queen* as it pulled alongside, and again they announced their identity and their intentions. The shocked passengers included a number of soldiers from the 130th Ohio Infantry who were on their way to Toledo, Ohio, to be mustered out of service. Some scuffling occurred and a few shots were fired, resulting in one crew member being seriously injured. Nevertheless, Beall wanted nothing from these travelers so they, too, were all left on Middle Bass Island. Upon setting sail again, Beall had his men lash the *Island Queen* to the *Parsons*, but after sailing about five miles, they decided to simply scuttle the *Island Queen*.[28]

As part of the plan, Beall had expected to find a messenger from Cole waiting for him on Middle Bass Island with word of Cole's success in his end of the plot. No one was there, which meant that Beall and his men now had no knowledge of what lay before them. They also feared that the lack of a messenger meant that the scheme had been somehow uncovered. Still, they sailed on toward the mouth of Sandusky Bay, arriving there in the early evening. Beall and his men anxiously looked toward Johnson's Island and the Ohio shore, hoping to see the signal lights or rockets that Cole had promised, which were to indicate success on his end. None were spotted—however, what they could clearly see in the moonlit night was the *Michigan*, jealously guarding Johnson's Island.[29]

Other than Burley, John Beall did not really know any of the twenty men accompanying him. Their personal loyalty to him was nil and, after weighing the situation, seventeen of the twenty in-

Island Queen (Historical Collections of the Great Lakes, Bowling Green State University, Bowling Green, Ohio).

formed Beall they would go no further. From their perspective, the lack of a messenger at Middle Bass Island coupled with no signal rockets from the Sandusky shore clearly indicated that something had gone horribly awry, which meant the ruse had been uncovered. To Beall, however, their refusal was a simple case of mutiny. He pleaded with them to no avail, finally demanding that they put their position in writing, which they agreed to do. Beall had no choice but to turn the *Parsons* around. The ship retreated up the Detroit River, a Confederate flag flying defiantly from its masthead, and docked at Sandwich after releasing the few remaining prisoners at Fighting Island on the Canadian side of the river. Beall had his crew remove everything of value from the ship and then scuttled it, after which the men disbanded.[30]

Unfortunately for Beall and his men, what would later be revealed was that Lieutenant Colonel Hill had learned of Beall and Cole's plans through a mole in the Confederate ranks who had sought out Hill at his Detroit hotel on the night of September 17. In retrospect, Beall's men were right to surmise that an attack on the *Michigan* would have been suicide, for immediately after his meeting with the informant, Hill telegraphed the *Michigan*'s commander, Captain John C. Carter, that an attack on his ship was imminent. Early on the morning of September 19, at 6:00, two hours before Burley boarded the ship, Hill had gone down to the Detroit docks to personally look

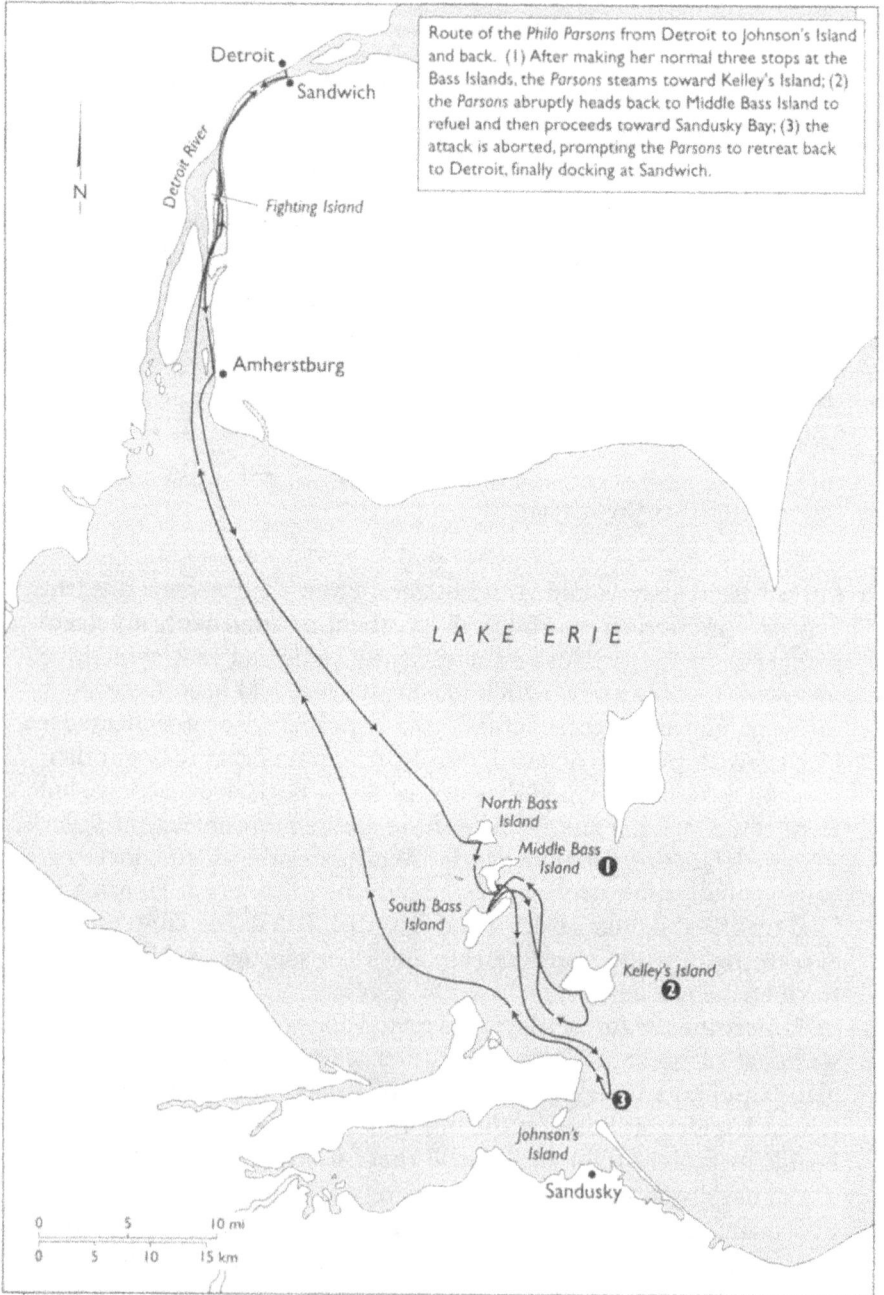

Map of Lake Erie from Detroit to Johnson's Island showing route of the *Philo Parsons* (Bill Nelson Cartography).

over the *Philo Parsons*. Concluding that the ship was too small to be of any real danger to Union forces if seized by the Rebels, and after some deliberation, he decided it would be wiser to let the raiders' plan proceed. Since Captain Carter and his sailors would be on full alert, the whole raiding party could be bagged if the Rebels were allowed to follow through. What concerns, if any, Hill had for the innocent civilians that would be on board the *Philo Parsons* are unknown. He was convinced, however, that had he hindered the departure of the *Parsons* for any reason, Rebel suspicions would have been aroused, raising the possibility of the Confederates delaying the plot to a time when Hill would have no knowledge of it. Meanwhile, Captain Carter, who was later described by General Jacob Cox as "a bluff and hearty seaman of the old school," had arrested Cole and had his ship ready at general quarters.[31]

After his arrest, Charles Cole was taken to District of Ohio headquarters in Cincinnati, where he was tried and convicted as a spy. He was sentenced to hang on Johnson's Island on February 16, 1865. Up to the very day of his expected execution, Cole remained the entertaining, charming gentleman who had endeared himself to many of the Union officers; despite his deceptions, many Union officers on the island were sincerely distraught at his fate. At the last moment, though, President Lincoln commuted his sentence to life imprisonment. Cole was taken to Fort Lafayette in New York harbor, where he remained imprisoned until released by President Andrew Johnson in 1867. John Yates Beall was not so fortunate. He was arrested by local police at the town of Niagara, New York, on December 16, 1864 (the police did not initially recognize him, arresting him as merely an escaped Confederate prisoner of war). He was later clearly identified by Sylvester Atwood, the captain of the *Philo Parsons*. In a show trial whose outcome was politically preordained, Beall was tried and convicted on February 8, 1865, as a Rebel spy and "guerrillero." Despite a vociferous argument that he was a legitimate Confederate soldier engaged in a lawful military operation and therefore deserving of prisoner-of-war rights, Beall was sentenced to hang for his "crimes." Although numerous appeals for leniency were submitted, including those from eight dozen congressmen and six U.S. senators, the young Confederate met his fate on the gallows at Governor's Island, New York, on February 24, 1865.[32]

Considering the steady stream of threats and rumors over the past year, the ill-fated raid created quite a stir in Detroit, almost to the point of disbelief. "Great excitement on account of raid on Lake Erie," recorded Detroit attorney Henry Billings Brown in his September 20 diary entry. As a specialist in admiralty law and wanting to do his part, Billings noted that he had gone over to Windsor that very afternoon "and got out a warrant for piracy" against the Confederate "scoundrels." The *Free Press* described the aborted attack as "reckless" and "impudent," further opining, "No one with reasonable sagacity could have been involved in such a raid, and the whole affair bears the marks of being projected and executed by crazy fanatics." That the Confederacy would officially sanction such actions was indicative of their last-ditch desperation. Furthermore, the last thing the *Free Press* wanted to do was give the raid any type of legitimacy, which would have played straight to local Republican fears and possibly brought about the imposition of martial law. Meanwhile, Detroit's *Advertiser and Tribune* sternly noted, "Our people are now fully warned and it will be their fault, and the fault of the authorities, if they are caught napping."[33]

The failed attack also caused consternation among British authorities. Lord Monck in Canada was notified of the planned Rebel attack by coded telegram from the British diplomatic office in Washington. Obviously concerned that the Americans might accuse the British of duplicity with the Confederates, Monck immediately ordered the Canadian Rifles stationed at Windsor to offer all possible assistance to U.S. authorities in Detroit.[34]

❀ ❀ ❀

ON the American side of the Detroit River, a high-level change in command of the Northern Department had garnered significant attention. On October 1, 1864, less than two weeks after the failed Johnson's Island raid, Major General Joseph Hooker, who had led the Army of the Potomac during the May 1863 Chancellorsville campaign, became the man now ultimately responsible for defending the Great Lakes region. After Hooker's inglorious resignation during the Atlanta campaign in July 1864, Lincoln ultimately assigned him two months later to command the U.S. military's Northern Department, which comprised the states of Michigan, Ohio, Indiana, and Illinois. He replaced fifty-nine-year-old General Samuel Heintzelman, another star-crossed officer whose fall from grace two years earlier had resulted in similar banishment to remote commands. In his first formal communication to the men in his new command, Hooker put

Joseph Hooker (Library of Congress, Washington, D.C.).

on the proper martial face and announced that "the commanding general requires energy, earnestness, and fidelity in the performance of duty on the part of every officer and soldier in the department. The trust and responsibility reposed in each will be carefully and fully executed. No one will consider the day as ended until the duties it brings have been discharged." Nevertheless, to now be responsible for little more than supervising the draft, maintaining the security of prisoner-of-war camps, and guarding the frigid Northern frontier was quite a comedown for a man who at one time held field command of the entire Army of the Potomac.[35]

Less than three weeks into his new position, Hooker and the rest of the Union army learned that on October 19, Confederate agents sequestered in Canada had launched a surprise raid on the small border town of St. Albans in northern Vermont, in what would become the northernmost engagement of the Civil War. Clad in civilian clothes but giving ample "Rebel yells," the twenty-one armed and mounted raiders rounded up all of the town's residents who happened to be outside and placed them under guard in the town park. Some of the Confederates then robbed three banks of over $200,000 while others attempted to torch the town, though this latter action ultimately failed. Before the raiders beat a hasty retreat back across the border with their loot, two men had been wounded and one killed. Coupled with the failed Johnson's Island raid, the small affair at St. Albans caused considerable anger and angst all along the Great Lakes frontier, including Detroit. Thirteen of the raiders were eventually captured and arrested by Canadian authorities, who promised the Americans to handle the matter legally and promptly.[36]

Though the Confederates were disheartened by the failure of both raids, their desires to take the war to the Northern lake cities did not cease, though their methodology was about to change. Confederate operatives now realized that any opportunity to capture the *Michigan* and attack from the water was gone, as was any likelihood of freeing the prisoners on Johnson's Island. Considering that these men were no doubt aware of General William T. Sherman's destruction in Georgia and General Phil Sheridan's total devastation of farms and mills in Virginia's Shenandoah Valley, new tactics for revenge were called for. Indeed, Bennett Young, the leader of the captured St. Albans raiders, later testified during their Canadian trial that retaliation for such "barbarous atrocities" was the primary rationale for attempting to raze that Vermont town in the first place. That Southerners might adopt such a mindset was not a surprise to many Northerners, including the editors of the *Free Press*; that paper grimly predicted, "The depopulation of Atlanta, and the laying waste of the Shenandoah Valley will undoubtedly call out acts in retaliation equally terrible." Decrying what it described as "the vandalism of the [Lincoln] administration," the newspaper denounced such warfare against noncombatants and asserted that the burning of every farm and house in the South only sent several more able-bodied and revenge-seeking men into the Rebel army. What the *Free Press* did not know was that relatively speaking, in the late fall of 1864 there were virtually no more able-bodied men for the South to call upon.[37]

The final Confederate plan to bring the horrors of war to the North centered on torching Northern cities with what was known as "Greek fire," a highly incendiary compound that dated back to the Byzantine Empire and was said to be inextinguishable by water. The underlying purpose of Confederate plans to burn Northern cities was to create chaos on the North's November 8, 1864, Election Day, along with a desire for vengeance. Indeed, an October 15 editorial in the *Richmond Whig* urged the burning of Northern cities, declaring, "New York is worth twenty Richmonds." Detroit, in fact, was said to be high on the Confederates' hit list. Confronting this threat would be "Fighting Joe" Hooker's biggest challenge.[38]

The Rebel attempt to free the prisoners at Johnson's Island and the St. Albans affair proved to Detroit's citizens once and for all that there were indeed Confederate agents among them and that rumors of the daring plots to carry the war into the Great Lakes region that they had read about for months were true. Therefore, why shouldn't these latest warnings of Detroit and other lake cities being incinerated also have some basis in fact? In the late fall of 1864 and early winter of 1865, the fear in Detroit that such an assault would occur was quite palpable, possibly akin to what modern New Yorkers felt in the days after the 9/11 attacks. The result of such angst was that residents in Great Lakes towns and villages began viewing all strangers or newcomers with suspicion. One upstate New York woman perhaps spoke for the entire region when she advised her neighbors not to open their doors to anyone they did not know and to make sure their homes were locked and secure at night. For months on end, her greatest fear was that her "Southern brethren from over the [Canadian] border" would come galloping into town, guns ablaze. The Confederacy may have been losing the battlefield war in the fall of 1864, but its agents positioned in Canada were winning the war of nerves against Northern civilians.[39]

The rumor mill again picked up steam in Detroit throughout late October 1864. On October 30, Detroit mayor Kirkland C. Barker received a telegram from the U.S. consular agent at Toronto urgently warning of an imminent plot to burn Detroit. Barker immediately went to the Firemen's Hall, where he organized a special police force of anyone he could find from Detroit's militia companies, provost guards, or Veteran Reserve Corps men stationed at the Detroit Barracks. The men of the Veteran Reserve Corps (VRC) were from the Second Regiment VRC, which had been organized in Detroit the previous October. They numbered approximately 275 and had been commanded since early October 1864 by Lieutenant Colonel Fabian Brydolf, a forty-four-year-old, hard-charging Swedish immigrant who had lost his right arm at the April 6, 1862, battle of Shiloh as part of

Fabian Brydolf (Shawn West Collection).

the Sixth Iowa Infantry. This hastily assembled, somewhat ragtag force was divided into squads and ordered to patrol the portion of Detroit lying between Jefferson Avenue and the river, and then from Third Street to Brush. Concurrently, a detail of fifty men from the Michigan Central Railroad was organized to protect the railroad's extensive property, while a similar sized force was engaged by the Detroit and Milwaukee Railroad Company to guard its assets above Brush Street. Lastly, Barker secured a small steamer and placed a small number of men on it; their sole mission was to patrol up and down the Detroit River in an attempt to prevent the landing of suspicious boats coming from the Canadian shore. Barker reported to Detroit's Common Council two days later that no arrests were made that night and nothing was seen from the steamer to lead anyone to believe that "enemy" ships were on the river with incendiary purposes. The mayor did note the next day, October 31, however, that "a number of persons who were here without visible employment, and who seemed to be here for no good purpose, have left the city."[40]

Another report held that an anti-draft riot was imminent in Detroit and that it would occur before the November election unless it was publicly guaranteed that there would be no further conscription. When Henry Walker, the editor of the *Free Press*, voiced these concerns to Eber B. Ward, the leading Republican industrialist in Detroit as well as its wealthiest citizen, Ward purportedly assured Walker that if the "Copperhead riot" occurred, he and his men would make sure that the *Free Press* plant was burned to the ground. Such animosity and loathing between Detroit's Republican and Democratic factions was as intense as ever, despite the feared Confederate threats emanating from across the river. Even Michigan soldiers on faraway battlefields wrote of their thoughts on their hometown papers when they were able to get and read copies. In an October 29, 1864 letter to a friend, Michigan's famous "boy general," George A. Custer, wrote that he saw little difference between the editorial policies of the Rebel papers of the South and the *Free Press*, other than "the rantings of the former have a little truth among them, while those of the latter are base fabrications from beginning to end." The general decried what he saw as the "malice" of the *Free Press*, concluding his missive, "I hung a rebel spy a few weeks ago who I believe was a more loyal man than the Editor of the *Free Press*."[41]

To ensure preparedness just in case an external attack or internal riot did occur, the city's board of trade passed a resolution urging the mayor to appoint a committee of five men in each ward who would be responsible for calling on the citizens in their area to, in essence, form a city militia. Meanwhile, Lieutenant Colonel Hill contacted the Michigan branch of the Union League, a national "popular front" society dedicated to promoting Republican Party war policies and, indirectly, to crushing the so-called Knights of the Golden Circle. Though the league had initially promoted itself as nonpartisan, by 1864 it readily admitted that it was an important adjunct of the Republican Party, combating what it saw as the treasonous propaganda of the Peace Democrats by properly "educating" the public. Yet to many poor immigrants, especially Catholics, the league signified the resurrection of the Know-Nothing movement, what with its midnight gatherings, its ceremonial secret oaths and, in some cases, its brutal imposition of loyalty oaths upon immigrants. At Hill's suggestion, each Michigan Union League lodge was organized into a company with the lodge officers reporting directly to Hill. "In [Detroit] alone," Hill later wrote, "four thousand loyal men could have been called together in half an hour." To outfit those men, Hill explained, the state had a thousand stands of arms with ten rounds in every cartridge box, all under constant guard at a central locale and in a constant state of readiness.[42]

By November 1, Detroit was being patrolled at night by a large, well-armed force of civilians and police, which prompted a public measure of confidence from the *Advertiser and Tribune:* "Ample preparations have been made to thwart any designs the Rebels may have." Despite its own approval of the security measures, the *Free Press* was starting to grow a bit suspicious of the depth and breadth of the rumors and the attendant alarm they were creating. It pointed out that even if several hundred Rebels, armed to the teeth, were to cross the river and attack the city, they would be met by several thousand well-armed and organized citizens and three companies of trained Union soldiers, not to mention the men of the Veteran Reserve Corps as well as the soldiers under the command of the provost marshal. The paper feared that the whole affair was being orchestrated for political purposes, as "it is currently reported that more than one radical republican is loud-mouthed in demanding martial law." As discussed earlier, the paper was no great ally of the Lincoln administration, believing as it did that enough individual civil liberties had already been trampled on.[43]

The reports from Union spies and detectives regarding perceived threats against Detroit were now so frequent and detailed that Joseph Hooker wrote to Secretary of War Edwin Stanton on November 3 suggesting that a new, thousand-man Michigan infantry regiment be raised for the sole purpose of guarding the state along the Detroit and St. Clair rivers. "No lesser force can render the frontier of Michigan secure from the incursions of the disaffected in Canada," wrote the general, who also urged that the regiment should be mustered, drilled, and in place before the Detroit River was frozen over. Stanton issued his approval the next day, allowing recruiting to begin almost immediately for what would become the Thirtieth Michigan Volunteer Infantry, a twelve-month regiment that would perform only home-guard service within the state.[44]

Hooker wrote to Governor Austin Blair the same day he received Stanton's approval to inform him of the plan, stressing that he was "deeply anxious" to have the new regiment staffed by experienced and capable officers. Concurrently, the government chartered the towing steamer *Prinderville* to act as a patrol ship on the Detroit River.[45]

Hooker's concerns about Rebel incursions from Canada merited nothing but outrage from the *Free Press*, which made the ridiculous assertion that the general was hoarding one hundred thousand men in the Northern Department for the express purpose of looking for

"Copperheads." What that paper was likely not aware of was that only seven months earlier, every post in the Northern Department, including Detroit, had received orders straight from Lieutenant General Ulysses S. Grant, supreme commander of all Union armies, stressing that every available man not absolutely necessary for safeguarding his post was to be made ready and shipped out for service at the front. Such an absurd allegation earned yet another return broadside from the *Advertiser and Tribune:* "In mendacity and downright lying, we think there is not a journal in the United States that can excel the Secesh organ in this city, the *Free Press.*"[46]

At the same time that it was skewering Hooker, the *Free Press* took a somewhat mocking view of Michigan's new "home-guard" regiment, noting that the new regiment "presents many attractions for those having a fancy for the milder experience of military life," especially since regular pay and bounties would be offered to the recruits. Such ridicule toward "home guard" units was not unusual throughout the North, even considering that the Thirtieth was to be an official regiment mustered into service by the Federal government. From the time the war started, home guard units had often been depicted as cowardly or even feminine for their reluctance to march off to the seat of war. As one historian noted, "Northerners readily concluded that avoidance of service was explained by selfishness."Certainly, no one imagined there would be recruitment problems, yet within a few weeks, officers were reporting that potential recruits simply refused to believe that the unit would be kept in Michigan. In Hillsdale, recruiting officer George Douglas complained on November 26, "I exhaust my powers of eloquence every day in this direction and still they are not convinced, thinking it is an underhanded game to get them to the front." Only a few days later, Captain William Atwood wrote from Ypsilanti of similar frustrations: "I have found some difficulty in enlisting men, from the fact that it is difficult to convince them that the regiment is for service in the state." Such concerns ultimately worked their way to Grover S. Wormer, former colonel of the Eighth Michigan Cavalry and now the new colonel of the Thirtieth Infantry who, on December 1 formally replied to his officers in an attempt to allay such fears: "You can give my assurance to those who make inquiries of you that this organization will not leave the state." Wormer then warned his men that in his opinion, another draft was "almost certain." The colonel urged that this fact be firmly impressed upon any prospective home-guard recruits, as "this opportunity will soon be closed and they will be deprived the privilege of enlisting in the service for state duty." From Wormer's perspective, this was a subtle yet clear hint that soldier duty in Michigan was a far better choice than rolling the dice with the draft and possibly ending up in a Southern trench facing Rebel shot and shell.[47]

The hesitation on the part of many to enlist at this point and the reasons for it were no secrets to anyone. By this late stage of the war, the visions of gallantry and glory that had animated so many young men in April 1861 were well dissipated, supplanted by the realities of warfare. As in all wars, many of the killed had been hastily buried where they fell, though in some cases, the relatives of those who had died in battle or later in army hospitals were able to arrange for their loved ones to be sent home in pine boxes. Many of the returning wounded had sustained injuries that would impair them for the rest of their lives. The worsening lack of sufficient volunteers to meet the North's ongoing manpower needs had, according to the Lincoln administration, necessitated the need for the draft in the first place. So whether a man chose to stay home because he was his family's sole breadwinner or because he wished to protect a promising career in business or politics, by late 1864 many of the North's able-bodied men of soldier age were those who had no desire to go anywhere near Confederate minié balls or cannon shot.

Illustrative of that mindset were the thoughts of Detroit attorney Henry Billings Brown. Twenty-eight years old in August 1864, Brown had confided to his diary that he had done "some hard thinking about this confounded draft," working out "a calculation of chances." Brown was certainly well aware that the opportunity to merely pay the $300 commutation fee to the Federal government was now gone, for the public uproar against that option, which seemingly favored the affluent, had been so great that Congress had repealed it only one month earlier. After sleeping on it overnight, Brown decided that he would avoid the chance of being drafted by offering $800 directly to a substitute if one could be had; it was a staggering sum—almost three times the average annual factory wage only four years earlier in 1860. Nonetheless, he immediately discovered that willing and able-bodied Detroit men were scarce; by the end of the day, Brown was "getting anxious" about the whole matter. Anxiety turned to disgust when he was forced to up the ante and pay the exorbitant sum of $850 for a ready substitute, but from Brown's perspective, it was obviously money well spent to avoid the front lines. As some in both the North and the South had described it, it was indeed "a rich man's war but a poor man's fight."[48]

Despite the initial recruiting difficulties, the new Thirtieth Michigan Infantry was filled to the maximum by early January 1865. Many if not most of the recruits were eighteen or nineteen years old, far too young for service when the war had started almost four years earlier. In fact, several hundred men who had finally enlisted in the expectation that they would now formally avoid the draft could not be mustered in due to the regiment's size restrictions. Good pay for staying near Detroit and family coupled with an attractive bounty apparently overcame any initial fear about the unit's ultimate destination. Such a reality was not lost on the *Free Press*, which could not contain its sarcasm: "Since these men have volunteered for service, it is hoped they will not be particular about the regiment, but, having been refused permission to drill and stand guard in a home regiment, will show their pluck and spirit by going into the field." In short order, the Thirtieth Volunteer Infantry was mustered in, with its headquarters in Detroit on Larned Street, between Woodward Avenue and Bates Street.[49]

Meanwhile, Lieutenant Colonel Hill's detectives were giving him intelligence that he felt warranted the highest level of alert in Detroit. Of great concern was the large number of strangers moving around the town. Hill was no doubt aware that on November 25 Confederate agents, again operating out of Canada, had unsuccessfully attempted to burn down New York City using Greek fire. The men had succeeded in firing twelve buildings, but the city's volunteer fire departments had ultimately extinguished all the flames before more than minor damage could be sustained. Only two of the eight Rebels involved were ever caught. One of those two was Captain Robert Cobb Kennedy, who was ultimately captured in Detroit by New York detectives while waiting on a train to escape back into the South. He admitted after his trial and conviction, "We wanted to let the people of the North understand that there are two sides to this war, and that they can't be rolling in wealth and comfort while we in the South are bearing all the hardships and privations." Like John Beall, Kennedy was hanged for his crimes, though he and his conspirators had certainly gotten the North's attention. The fact that they had reached New York and attempted such a desperate deed in the first place only added to the anxiety in Detroit.[50]

To patrol the border upriver, Hill had two armed tugs cruising the St. Clair River watching everything that passed up or down. As far as the perceived problem that strangers posed, Hill issued a general order on November 30 for the city that, while not a declaration of martial law, was close to it. All deputy provost marshals and their assistants were ordered to arrest "all strangers who may be regarded in any degree suspicious, and who cannot give a good account of themselves." Four days later, on December 3, Hill informed Northern Department headquarters that "very extensive preparations are being made in Canada for burning not only cities on the lakes, but others; and it is very necessary that great precaution and vigilance should be observed everywhere." He was more confident than ever that Greek fire was being manufactured right across the river in Windsor and that Detroit was the key target. In addition, reports warned of armed men who would attempt to cross the river to rob and plunder. And not merely a few men, for other intelligence that he deemed reliable reported that large numbers of Rebel soldiers had made their way through the lines in civilian clothes and were now regrouping for an attack. Because of this rumor, Hill reported that he had "called the attention of the hotel keepers to the necessity of observing great vigilance in regard to their guests, and the hotels are daily visited by a secret agent in my employ."[51]

Two days later, Hill telegraphed his immediate superior, Brigadier General James B. Fry, the army's provost marshal general, with essentially the same information. He informed Fry that he had learned that "a regiment of Kentucky rebel troops had been disbanded in Kentucky, with directions to make their way through the lines and report in Canada, and that they had done so in large numbers." Hill stressed that his intelligence was "derived partly from persons who are looked upon as being thoroughly in the confidence of the rebel agents in Canada, and is confirmed by information through other sources." One of those sources was an east Tennessee man now living in Canada whom Hill had interviewed and believed loyal to the Stars and Stripes. Despite his confidence in his spies and the aforementioned confidence exhibited by the *Free Press* in the town's ability to resist attack, Hill knew the forces at his command were woefully inadequate to counter any sizeable organized assault. "I have but a small military force here, not more than enough to guard prisoners." He feared that "unless a military force is maintained by the Canadian authorities on the frontier to keep in check the rebels congregated there, there will be frequent raids from Canada at exposed points, which will lead to retaliation by our citizens whose property may be destroyed, and lead to trouble between the two Governments."[52]

The *Free Press* itself was now ringing the alarm bells as well, urging all able-bodied citizens who had not made themselves available to local authorities to do so at once. "There is not an hour to be lost," it urged on December 7, warning that no one who went to sleep at night wanted to "awake to find warehouses which line the river front . . . a mass of smoldering ruin." The paper then revealed to its readers that Hill had sent a message to Mayor Kirkland Barker on December 5 urging that a regiment of local militia be organized as he was confident that a Rebel raid from Canada was imminent.[53]

Meanwhile, Joseph Hooker was forwarding on to Washington the information that Hill had sent his headquarters, assuring General Edward Townsend, the army's assistant adjutant general, that "the information has been furnished by one of our most reliable detectives, and unusual confidence may be placed in it."[54]

As the New Year neared, Hooker felt compelled to ask Governor Blair for more men even as the new regiment was still being recruited. He informed Blair that his reports "relating to the activities and designs of the Confederates with their sympathizing friends make me solicitous for the property of your citizens in the vicinity of the border." Unlike Hill, Hooker had no fear that any type of large, concerted attack was likely; the general was far more uneasy about a raid like that on St. Albans, wherein a small band of three or four men could terrorize Detroit or any town along the Detroit River with fire or explosives. The frozen river "would afford these miscreants unusual facilities for carrying their designs into execution," warned the general. As Michigan was the most exposed state within Hooker's command, he urged Blair to send his new recruits to the border as soon as possible.[55]

The "trouble between the two governments" that Hill feared and had warned of was certainly not lost on the Canadians in Windsor. Ever since the Johnson's Island and St. Albans raids, American port towns all along the Great Lakes had demanded that the allegedly neutral Canada be rebuked for allowing such schemes to originate from its soil in the first place. Michigan senator Zachariah Chandler was especially livid over recent events and what he saw as British complicity in Confederate plots. From the Senate floor on December 14, Chandler delivered a blistering resolution accusing British and

Canadian authorities of being "disposed to protect these thieves, robbers, incendiaries, pirates, and murderers, not only in their individual capacities, but by the quibbles of the law." Only one day before, a Canadian court had released the St. Albans raiders after determining that they were legitimate belligerents and therefore could not be extradited to the United States. In the United States, this stunning decision was angrily interpreted as an implied recognition by Britain of the Confederate States, prompting the fiery senator's outburst. Since, according to Chandler, Canada could or would do nothing, his resolution demanded "that the Committee on Military Affairs be directed to inquire into the expediency of immediately enlisting an army corps to watch and defend our territory bordering on the lakes and Canadian line from all hostile demonstrations and incursions." Nothing came of Chandler's resolution, but British diplomats made sure that Governor-General Monck was well aware of the deteriorating American sentiment.[56]

The anger in Chandler's hometown of Detroit was every bit the equal of its famous son's. "The old enmity against the British government and everything connected with it is revived in all its bitterness," declared the *Free Press*, noting that the freeing of the raiders had become the principal topic on Detroit's streets. The general feeling was that if Canada was unwilling to punish those who committed depredations against the United States from across its borders, then diplomatic relations were going to deteriorate rapidly.[57]

Obviously well aware of Detroit's outcry, Windsor's mayor and town council knew it was imperative to offer some type of public reassurance to their neighbor across the river. On December 16, 1864, Windsor mayor Samuel S. Macdonnell sent a letter to Detroit mayor Kirkland Barker assuring him that it was "the intention and desire of the municipal authorities of Windsor to prevent any attempt at the commission of raids from this place upon Detroit." He included a copy of a town council resolution drafted the previous evening proclaiming that body's desire to "continue the friendly feeling that has hitherto existed between this place and the city of Detroit" and at the same time, condemning and denouncing those "hostile expeditions" upon the United States. Word of the newly authorized thousand-man Thirtieth Michigan Infantry that was to be posted along the Canadian border also no doubt weighed heavily in Windsor's resolution.[58]

Despite Windsor's friendly reassurances, the American uproar over what was seen as Canadian leniency toward Rebels in Canada was so great that Canada's solicitor general asked that two companies of Her Majesty's regulars be stationed at Windsor to prevent what was believed to be a pending raid on Detroit banks by Confederates who had escaped from Northern prisons, not to mention possible retaliation from Detroit. His request must have been heard, for on December 28, 1864, not two but six companies of Canadian troops, close to four hundred men in all, arrived by train at Windsor. Two companies were to be stationed in Windsor, Sandwich, and Amherstburg respectively as a means of border defense, though the official line, as reported in the *Free Press*, was that the arrival of the soldiers "will go far to allaying the fears of an attack upon our frontier by Southern desperadoes, and assist in cementing that good feeling which exists between the people of the two countries." A British-born Canadian officer turned historian later noted that from his vantage, this action by his government "set an example of neighborly conduct which was in marked contrast to the open encouragement given in the United States to the hordes of filibusterers organized across the frontier in 1837–38," a clear reference to Detroit's support of the rebels in Canada's 1837–38 Patriot War.[59]

In spite of Hill's fears, no direct Confederate attack was ever made on Detroit, even though the Canadian and Detroit officials continued to discuss the danger of Confederates using air guns to hurl Greek fire into Detroit from some point on the frozen Detroit River. All along the Detroit and St. Clair rivers, the threat of Rebel incursion seemed to die down with the New Year and after the execution of John Beall.[60]

Meanwhile, the "soldiering" duty for Michigan's new home-guard regiment was relatively light work, even though the unit's official headquarters was moved from Detroit to Fort Gratiot on January 9. Nevertheless, the Thirtieth's adjutant tried to assure the *Advertiser and Tribune*'s readers in a February 3, 1865, letter that the regiment was "doing earnest and valiant work already for the great cause." He pointed out that the soldiers were guarding the entire line of Michigan coast from Port Huron to St. Clair and had arrested 115 suspicious men in just two days. Two weeks earlier, Captain John H. Knight of Company E had recorded from his command's downriver camp at Wyandotte that his men had likewise arrested several deserters and "passport delinquents." From the adjutant's vantage, such dangerous work illustrated that "the number of men we gobble shows that we are not at all idle in the business."[61]

Captain Knight's concern over passports was not a trifling matter. On December 17, 1864, four days after Canada released the St. Albans raiders, the U.S. State Department issued an order from President Lincoln declaring that any traveler entering the United States, other than permanent immigrants, had to have a passport. The order was intended to stop Confederate agents from passing back and forth between Canadian and American border crossings, such as Detroit, given the recent raids and unrest between the two countries. The order immediately raised a red flag in Canada due to the regulation's wording; it was "intended to apply especially to persons proposing to come to the United States from the neighboring British Provinces." The passport was to be "visaed," or signed, by a diplomatic or consular agent of the United States and applied to Americans as well as Canadians. Enforcing this directive at the border would be a key responsibility of the Thirtieth Michigan Infantry. Even those legitimately passing through Canada or those whose business took them daily between Windsor and Detroit had to have passports. Although Secretary of State William Seward approved of the order, it was immediately decried in both Detroit and Windsor. The *Free Press* correctly predicted that this "onerous system" would "seriously affect the intercourse and obstruct the business relations" between the two countries, and indeed in short order commerce between the two towns slowed to a trickle. Especially affected were the two country's railroads, which had previously worked together very harmoniously to enhance each country's commercial interests. To the economic benefit of Detroit and Windsor, the passport order was ultimately rescinded on March 8, 1865.[62]

Unfortunately, not all men arrested for desertion, Rebel sympathies, or even passport offenses were likely to be guilty, including Eli Strawbridge who, in a letter of appeal to Senator James Doolittle of Wisconsin, begged, "Don't let me lay here and die" in the Detroit Barracks. Strawbridge had been charged with being a Confederate "Raider," though he asserted he had never been anything but an abolitionist who had labored for Lincoln in the president's 1864 reelection campaign. A cold jail cell in the Detroit Barracks was a "hard place for an abolitionist," complained Strawbridge.[63]

From the average private's perspective, Michigan's home-guard duty was about as easy as military service could be. "We have good times here, plenty of rations and plenty of duty," wrote eighteen-year-old Edwin Shaw of the Thirtieth's Company H, posted in Fenton.

"Our duty is catching deserters, bounty jumpers, skedaddlers, etc. We have a good many to take care of. We arrested nine 'Johnnys' who escaped from the [Confederate POW] prison at Rock Island, Ill. They want to take the oath of allegiance, and I guess they will be allowed to take it and be liberated." In a February letter to his parents, the Thirtieth's Silas Sadler of Company D concurred with Shaw, noting that "we are having good times here skateing with the girls . . . there is lots of parties here and Jim and myself cut quite a swell with the girls." By early April, Sadler's focus had turned to the excellent hunting opportunities enjoyed by the regiment at its St. Clair camp. "We have a pleasant place here . . . we have some nice sails on the river and lots of ducks to shoot . . . all kinds of game." Farther south at the Detroit Barracks, the prospects for leisure were essentially the same for eighteen-year-old drummer Gardner White of Company I. "I am enjoying myself finely. There is lots of fun herein and I don't halve to do any duty except drum." White also bragged that he had yet to be caught by the provost patrols and put in the guardhouse due to his inclination to "take a french hors once in awhile." Clearly, for White, all thoughts of the onetime desperate need to protect Michigan's frontier or hunt Rebels had long since vanished. Eighteen-year-old George Campbell, also of Company I, seemed, however, to view matters a bit more seriously. Campbell solemnly informed his father in a January 30 letter that the ongoing political tensions meant "a man has to be careful in this city," while also complaining that "our food is not very good nor enough of it." According to Campbell, other than daily drilling, his company's only real work was to go down to Detroit's docks and perform patrol duty every other day.[64]

It was not such easy work for Michigan men in either the eastern or western theater. Wounded soldiers returning to Detroit from the front lines or even battlefield hospitals often needed additional medical care. Nearer the end of the war, Camp Backus was used as a rest camp for convalescing Union soldiers and as a discharge point. It was dismantled shortly after the war ended.

For officers who had performed their duties well and honorably, the approaching end of the war provided opportunity for one last promotion. After the successful conclusion of the *Philo Parsons* affair and the change in command of the Northern Department, Lieutenant Colonel Hill had written to Major General Henry Halleck on October 14 seeking a promotion to brevet brigadier general, tactfully pointing out that he alone was now performing the duties held by

SURRENDER OF GEN. LEE!

"The Year of Jubilee has come! Let all the People Rejoice!"

200 GUNS WILL BE FIRED
On the Campus Martius,
AT 3 O'CLOCK TO-DAY, APRIL 10,
To Celebrate the Victories of our Armies. *1865*

Every Man, Woman and Child is hereby ordered to be on hand prepared to Sing and Rejoice. The crowd are expected to join in singing Patriotic Songs.

ALL PLACES OF BUSINESS MUST BE CLOSED AT 2 O'CLOCK.

Hurrah for Grant and his noble Army.

By Order of the People.

Detroit Free Press broadside announcing Lee's surrender (Burton Historical Collection, Detroit Public Library).

two men in the neighboring state of Illinois. Moreover, he believed that his "vigilance [had] been of great service to the govt." The army agreed, and Hill was promoted for his "meritorious service" on January 31, 1865. Likewise, Mark Flanigan, who had served as lieutenant colonel of the Twenty-fourth Infantry before being wounded at Gettysburg and then served as Detroit's provost marshal, was also promoted to brevet brigadier general for "meritorious service" on March 13, 1865.[65]

❀ ❀ ❀

DETROIT exploded in celebration when word of Richmond's fall on April 3 reached Detroit. "Oh, Lord, that I should live to see this day," exclaimed Henry Billings Brown in his diary. "Great jubilee, stores and offices close. Wandered around the city till late at night like one demented. Nothing but ringing of bells, hoisting of flags, enthusiasm and cheers." There was even greater merriment when news of Robert

E. Lee's surrender at Appomattox, Virginia, reached the city. On the morning of April 10, 1865, Mayor Barker issued a proclamation calling for a suspension of all employment that afternoon, so that by 2:00, throngs of citizens were making their way toward Campus Martius. There they witnessed a thunderous two-hundred-gun salute celebrating the end of hostilities, courtesy of three companies from the Thirtieth Michigan Infantry, a company of the Veterans Reserve Corps, the Nineteenth Regular Infantry's band, and two pieces of artillery. Women screamed and children shouted as the cannons delivered the salutes. Downtown Detroit was a united scene of jubilation and joy. "Never before at any one time, has everybody, all sorts, sizes and conditions of men, women, and even the blessed baby turned out in such plentitude," noted the *Free Press*. Soldiers almost had to use the point of the bayonet to keep the celebratory throngs in check.[66]

The merriment turned to heartfelt grief a week later when the news of Lincoln's assassination on April 14 reached Detroit. The papers fanned the flames of excitement; businesses were closed, and a public meeting was called for later in the afternoon at Campus Martius. As the crowds gathered, one Southern civilian visiting Detroit later remembered, Detroit's black residents all stood on one side "in solemn array, with sorrow depicted on every face."[67]

Across the river in Windsor, Mayor Samuel S. Macdonnell issued a proclamation requesting that his town's citizens close their businesses on Tuesday, April 18, as a gesture of respect and reverence to the slain American president. Those who could attend the funeral ceremonies in Detroit were urged to do so.[68]

With the war over, Michigan's home guard was relegated to watching out for the president's assassin, as there was suspicion that the killer might try to make his way into Canada. "We have considerable guard duty to do now," explained Silas Sadler. "The whole river is guarded trying to catch the man that killed Lincoln. Our company has 24 miles of the river to guard. We go up and down on the steamboats when we want to and over the river into Canada." As history has shown, no conspirator ever made it into Michigan. It was time for the soldiers to come home, take off their blue uniforms, and reengage in civilian life.[69]

"Three cheers for the ladies!"

Celebration and Remembrance

W ith four years of arduous civil war now over, Michigan's volunteer soldiers began making plans for their way home on what would be lengthy train and boat rides. Detroit would be their first stop in their home state, and there they would be formally mustered out of service. But there was one last bit of celebratory pomp and circumstance before those trips began. On May 23 and 24, 1865, the Grand Review took place in Washington, D.C. For two full days, the Union armies paraded down Pennsylvania Avenue twenty-six abreast in front of the new president, Andrew Johnson, General Ulysses S. Grant, and dozens of other dignitaries. New Michigan governor Henry Crapo, who had been sworn in on January 4, 1865, was on hand, as was Senator Zachariah Chandler. As Lois Bryan Adams, the Washington correspondent for the *Detroit Advertiser and Tribune*, noted in her dispatch, "As far as the eye could reach on either hand, the sidewalks were densely crowded with spectators, and every window and balcony and even the roofs and the trees along the way were full."[1]

After the review, the Michigan soldiers returned to their various camps, where they met with their paymasters one last time before beginning the trek home. Once they were back in Detroit, all soldiers returning from the field reported to St. Mary's Hospital for a final checkup. Returning home immediately, however, was not the case for many of the men receiving care at the new Harper Hospital. Though the war was over, that facility was still under the control of the Federal government per the agreements previously made. Scores of wounded men were still returning home and needed proper medical care. Eight months later, though, that task was essentially completed. On December 19, 1865, the government turned the buildings back over to the Harper trustees with the additional proviso that Harper's would maintain a Soldiers' Home, which would receive and care for discharged and invalid Michigan soldiers "without calling on the Government for further aid or material." Nine days later, on December 28, the United States Sanitary Commission's Michigan Branch stepped in and agreed to pay $2,000 to the hospital upon agreement that the hospital would receive and care for the soldiers then residing in the Detroit Soldiers' Home. The very next day twenty soldiers were transferred from the Soldiers' Home to the hospital. Harper Hospital then admitted its first civilian patients in January 1866.[2]

As far as the public and Detroit's political leaders were concerned, the state's healthy soldiers should not be sent home before a proper show of respect and celebration. The Michigan regiments had all left Detroit years earlier amid public fanfare, and the city decided that their arrival back home should be equally joyous. A Committee of Reception and a Committee of Finance were assembled to oversee receptions for the returning men. Mr. R. N. Rice, the superintendent of the Michigan Central Railroad, allowed the use of the upper story of the line's freight house to serve as a dining hall which, when transformed, was capable of seating over two thousand men at a time. The Twentieth Infantry arrived first, on June 5, 1865, at around 7:00 a.m., after taking a boat from Cleveland, and the men were treated to the finest breakfast they had seen in years. All other infantry, cavalry, and artillery regiments followed over the course of the next year, with the last to arrive being the Third and Fourth infantries, which finally made it home on June 10, 1866. In the year between those two dates, more than nineteen thousand Michigan men (and thirty-five hundred Wisconsin men) returned home via Detroit, where they were welcomed as heroes.[3]

Included in the number of Michigan men was the Thirtieth Michigan home-guard regiment, which was mustered out of Federal service on June 30th, 1865, after little more than six months of duty. Of the 1,001 officers and private soldiers who served in the regiment, eighteen died of disease during their term of service. None died in battle since no such action occurred anywhere near Michigan, despite the onetime fear of Rebel attack.

General Orlando Willcox, who had led the First Michigan Infantry into battle four years earlier, was ordered to Detroit in August

1865; he then commanded the District of Michigan until he was mustered out of the service on January 15, 1866.[4]

After seeing battle in South Carolina and Florida, the 102nd U.S. Colored Regiment, better known at home as the First Michigan Colored Infantry, arrived in Detroit and was discharged on October 17, 1865. No fanfare welcomed these brave warriors, which stood in stark contrast to the tumultuous welcome that had been afforded the returning white men. Michigan's white soldiers returned home with the expectation that they would easily return to their families and previous vocations. This conviction was held with little forethought.[5]

On the other hand, how those men from the 102nd U.S. Colored Infantry and the newly emancipated black man would enter white-dominated society was a question many preferred to ignore, for though the Civil War had ended and its attendant question of slavery was now settled, the issue of blacks' proper role in society still loomed large. In a sense, it was a war still being waged. In both the North and the South, pens had replaced guns as the weapon of choice in dealing with this question. As one historian has noted, "Partisan journalism in the Reconstruction era turned out to be merely the continuation of war by other means."[6]

Certainly, in these initial postwar years, Detroit's newspapers retained their partisan perspectives. Both continued to stress the ideological purity of their respective party's positions and even went so far as to occasionally publish a prospectus that would attune their readers to the specific merits of the newspaper's positions on any given serious issue. Should any voter be confused as to the issues of the day, he could find clarification and guidance within the paper's pages.

The proper social status of freed blacks and their new political rights quickly became one of the key issues in Detroit's newspapers in the early years of Reconstruction. If one of the great debates in Detroit during the four years of war was whether black men should serve alongside whites as soldiers, no issue generated more controversy in the four years after the end of hostilities than the issue of black suffrage. Detroit's Democrats, possibly somewhat sullied by their less than stellar support of the Union cause during the Civil War, nevertheless maintained a toxic racism against blacks after the guns fell silent that bordered on mania. Only six months after the war ended, the *Free Press* was flying the "states' rights" banner, stressing that each state had the right to decide for itself whether blacks should have the vote, but clearly believing that such an act by any state would be pure folly. "Our country should be a white man's country," it argued, "to be governed by white men, and we strongly deprecate any action that may even most distantly tend to weaken or impair this state of affairs." Less than a year later the paper warned, "A race so inferior to ourselves . . . will never be recognized as our equals." As for black men engaging in politics, that Detroit daily spoke for all Democratic papers when it declared, "[We] do not believe . . . Negroes should have any part or parcel in a government for white men. . . . No Democrat . . . proposes such an idea." Such rancor continued throughout the second half of the 1860s. In fact, between June 1, 1865, and December 31, 1869, the *Free Press* devoted 124 articles to the issue of "Negro suffrage."[7]

Blacks in Detroit were not intimidated by such venom. As early as October 1843, blacks had held a convention at a Fort Street church that resulted in a petition to the state government demanding the rights of citizenship. After the passage of the Fugitive Slave Act in September 1850, whites in Wayne County had addressed the issue of black suffrage. The result was not surprising: 3,320 had voted against, with only 608 voting for the measure. A second convention was held on January 25, 1865, at Detroit's Second Baptist Church (aka Croghan Street Baptist Church), which again resulted in a petition to the state legislature urging that blacks be given the right to vote. Though this petition was again denied, it would be only five more years until all black men were granted suffrage. On March 15, 1870, the secretary of state declared the Fifteenth Amendment to the Constitution fully ratified, which made all black males full citizens and voters. Eight months later, on November 8, the voting stipulation *white* was eliminated from Michigan's Constitution by a vote of the people, allowing black citizens to cast votes in Detroit on the same day.[8]

School segregation was also technically banished in the intervening years between the end of the Civil War and the passage of the Fifteenth Amendment. On February 28, 1867, Michigan's legislature passed a bill eliminating legal school segregation in the state, although in practice, many Detroit schools as well as others in Michigan remained segregated for years to come.[9]

Women in the workplace still faced an arduous struggle, in spite of the great strides they had made during the war. Only a year after the war ended, committees from Detroit's Trades Assembly and the newly formed "Eight Hour League" had discovered that a host of girls, some as young as seven, was working in Detroit's match factories.

The girls were paid by the piece, no doubt by packing matches into boxes. If they showed up late, they were fined. Moreover, on numerous occasions they were ordered to stay in the factory, even if not on the clock, just in case work was needed.[10]

It was no different in Detroit's burgeoning tobacco and cigar factories. Those same committees were stunned to find young girls working in what were called "pigeon holes," where they were forced to "toil from morning until night, breathing constantly the poisonous odor of tobacco in an atmosphere filled with the fine particles of the plant." Here again, pay was by the piece. Most shocking to the labor committees was the poor health of many of the girls as well as the state of moral degradation many were found in. In their report, the committees expressed the opinion that "much of the prostitution which curses this city is the loathsome fruit of the depravity which dates its commencement at the tobacco factories."[11]

The *Free Press* put forth a progressive stance in the latter part of the decade on the issue of women in the workplace, as opposed to its racist view of blacks becoming engaged in white society. This was not surprising, as that organ had always positioned itself as a champion of the *white* workingman or woman. Despite ongoing limitations in opportunities for women, the paper could point with pride to the progress women had made over the past generation. But the great hurdle they must overcome, bemoaned the paper, was "the false idea entertained by men and women alike, that a woman is in some way degraded by labor that brings remuneration." This "absurd prejudice" prevented parents from giving their daughters a functional education that might provide them with the necessary training to earn an "honorable independence" if they were single. Without such training, many young Detroit women had no option but to hope for a satisfactory marriage.[12]

For Detroit's women of wealth and culture, life after the war was not much different than before it. The city's rapid growth prompted all manner of opportunities for industrious businessmen and their wives, and the city's increasing wealth spawned new retail establishments, restaurants and nightlife. Still, considering the heavy influx of poor immigrants that Detroit had experienced over the past twenty years, those stylish women must have seemed well hidden, prompting a cultured Canadian woman who was visiting Detroit in 1867 for the first time to remark in her diary, "Moving in the streets, I did not see one person whom I could recognize as a gentleman or a lady by their appearance."[13]

Detroit in 1865 was a city transformed in industry and commerce, a far cry from the town of several decades and even several years earlier. Whereas it was once little more than a fur-trading center and a way station for shippers and voyagers, Detroit was now fast becoming a major manufacturing center. Timber and copper had been the city's chief products when the Civil War started, but these were about to replaced by the manufacturing of steel, iron, and foundry products. The Michigan Car Company, the Detroit Safe Company, the Detroit Bridge and Iron Works, and the E. T. Barnum Wire and Iron Works were all thriving Detroit business in the second half of the decade that had their start during the Civil War. Tobacco products, flour milling, and meatpacking were also becoming major industries in Detroit. Throughout the 1860s, Detroit would see its number of manufacturing businesses explode, while the increase in capital invested into manufacturing skyrocketed by a huge 256 percent. The result of that outlay was a 303 percent increase in the total value of manufactured products between 1860 and 1870.[14]

Overall construction mushroomed as well. In 1869, Detroit could boast that it now held 16,152 buildings. Of that number, nearly one-fifth had been built just in the preceding two years.[15]

The rapid growth of Detroit during the Civil War coupled with an alarming increase in the crime rate dictated that a formal police department be created for the city. To some, it was apparent following the 1863 riot that a professionally trained force was needed. However, focus on the war and the presence of soldiers throughout the town pushed the matter to the back burner until hostilities ended. Once the war was over, the Detroit Police Department was finally established by a state legislative act in 1865.

❀   ❀   ❀

THOUGH the veterans had been eager to return home to their loved ones and resume their civilian lives, many had no desire to completely forget their travails of 1861–65. They knew they had made history and that the war had helped them form bonds of friendship with comrades that for many would remain intact for the rest of their lives. This desire to remember, maintain relationships, and commemorate led to the formation of numerous war-related fraternal organizations throughout the country in the years after the year. Emerging as the largest and most important of these veterans' organizations was the Grand Army of the Republic (GAR), formed in

1914 Grand Army of the Republic parade in Detroit (Library of Congress, Washington, D.C.).

1866 in Decatur, Illinois. Membership was limited to those veterans of the Union army, navy, Marine Corps, or the Revenue Cutter Service who had been honorably discharged and who had served between April 12, 1861, and April 9, 1865. The organization initially existed solely for camaraderie and charity on a localized basis, but it seemed to some Democrats to quickly take on the character of a government-sponsored "secret society" or paramilitary body. The organization quickly aroused the suspicions of the Democratic-leaning *Free Press*, which viewed it as reminiscent of the Know-Nothings and with the same unconstitutional intentions. "Professing to love the Republic more than any other class of people, [GAR] members hold themselves clearly entitled to the monopoly of the offices under it," opined that paper. With the political tensions of the Civil War only a few years passed, Democrats had no objection to a benevolent brotherhood of soldiers brought together by fraternal feelings of past comradeship, "but a drilled army, organized for political purpose and acting secretly, is an entirely different thing."[16]

Such purported secrecy and fearful intentions had vanished by the 1870s. Indeed, by the mid- to latter half of the 1880s, the Grand Army of the Republic had become an openly partisan arm of the Republican Party. More important for its members, it grew into one of the nation's first political advocacy groups, vigorously and success-

fully lobbying Congress on behalf of Union veterans for Federal pensions as well as pension rights for black Union veterans.[17]

Every Northern state that had sent men into the Union army had its own state-level "department" and community-level "posts." Detroit had five such GAR posts, comprising over several thousand members during their peak in the 1890s. Every year, the GAR held its national "encampment," an opportunity for its veterans to gather, reminisce, and commemorate. When Detroit served as the host city in 1891 for the GAR's silver anniversary national encampment, nationwide membership had peaked at just over four hundred thousand members. In fact, the arrival of thousands of Civil War veterans and their families into and around Detroit for the 1891 commemoration temporarily doubled the population of the city, with the massive gathering becoming front-page news for days. The highlight of the gathering came on August 4, 1891, when thirty thousand aging Civil War veterans marched through downtown Detroit in a cheering, flag-draped parade. It took six hours for all the participants to pass the reviewing stand. "No city in all history ever surrendered with such display of rapture and joy," wrote the *Free Press* in a front-page story far more sympathetic to the GAR than the paper had been twenty-five years earlier. By the time Detroit hosted the national encampment for the second time in 1914, natural deaths had caused membership to fall to 179,000.[18]

Detroit's Soldiers' and Sailors' monument, circa 1903 (Library of Congress, Washington, D.C.).

In 1897, Detroit's GAR members, in conjunction with the city, approved construction of a five-story, three-sided meeting hall at the corners of West Grand River and Cass Avenue to serve as a formal gathering spot as well as an archive for the city's remaining veterans. This beautiful Richardsonian Romanesque building was formally opened and dedicated with ample celebration on January 15, 1901, and proudly served Detroit's Civil War veterans for over thirty years. With membership dwindling due to the natural passage of time, Detroit's few remaining veterans deeded the building to the city in 1934.[19]

Detroit's beautiful Grand Army of the Republic building still stands to this day. Though it had fallen into disrepair in recent decades and at times appeared a likely candidate for the wrecking ball, the building was purchased by the Mindfield Company in 2011 with the intent of a full renovation.[20]

One other extremely significant Civil War monument may be found in Detroit. On April 9, 1872, seven years to the day after Confederate general Robert E. Lee surrendered his Army of Northern

Virginia at Appomattox, Virginia, over twenty-five thousand citizens from Detroit and throughout Michigan gathered at Campus Martius to pay tribute to the state's Civil War veterans by unveiling the new Soldiers' and Sailors' Monument. Plans for the memorial had begun shortly after the war ended, and construction of the final design had been ongoing for close to five years, though some of the monument's bronze statues would not finally be added until nine years later. The key inscription on the memorial read, "Erected by the people of Michigan in honor of the martyrs who fell and the heroes who fought in defence of liberty and union." This celebratory event created a scene unparalleled in Detroit or anywhere else in Michigan since the announcement of the war's end seven years earlier. Thousands of people came by train, by carriage, or even on foot. Every hotel room in the city was spoken for, prompting the larger hotels to erect rows of cots in their parlors to accommodate the throngs. The city streets had been thoroughly cleaned, and red, white, and blue bunting adorned every building along Woodward Avenue. The buildings along Jefferson Avenue were likewise covered with flags and streamers.

All veterans who made the trip to Detroit were treated to a sumptuous dinner, courtesy of Detroit's church ladies, from noon to 1:30 at the Baptist church on the corner of Fort and Griswold streets. "Three cheers for the ladies!" was a common refrain during the welcomed meals. In attendance were Generals George A. Custer, Ambrose Burnside, and Philip Sheridan. In their remarks, all three generals acknowledged the good fortune they had had in having Michigan men under their command. Though he declined to make a speech, Custer remarked to a reporter, "Had there been no Michigan cavalry, there would have been no General Custer."[21]

The guest orator for the day was Austin Blair, now fifty-two years old, who had served so ably as Michigan's governor during the great conflict. Upon the conclusion of his speech, the crowd was treated to songs by the German Singing Societies. Cheers erupted from the crowd when the singing was concluded, for all knew the long-awaited moment was at hand. A great bell tolled slowly four times and at the end of the fourth ring, the huge flags draping the monument were pulled back, revealing the grand monument. Deafening cheers erupted for the spectacular sculpture, which stands to this day in downtown Detroit's Campus Martius Park as Michigan's permanent memorial to its honored Civil War dead, who, in President Abraham Lincoln's immortal words, "gave the last full measure of devotion."[22]

Notes

Introduction

1. Bureau of the Census Library, *Population of the United States in 1860*, xxxi.

Chapter 1

1. Driscoll, *Rogue*, 8; Dain, *Every House*, 3–4.
2. Vander Hill, *Settling the Great Lakes Frontier*, 2; Dain, *Every House*, 11.
3. Dain, *Every House*, 6.
4. Fuller, *Economic and Social Beginnings*, 122–23.
5. Farmer, *History of Detroit*, 908.
6. Gray, *The Yankee West*, 4; quoted in Wilson, *Yankees in Michigan*, 2, 24.
7. Wilson, *Yankees in Michigan*, 2–3, 7; Streeter, *Political Parties in Michigan*, 31.
8. Streeter, *Political Parties in Michigan*, 31.
9. Russell, *Germanic Influence*, 57; Streeter, *Political Parties in Michigan*, 162–64; Michigan State Administrative Board, *Michigan*, 104–5.
10. Germany was not a unified nation-state until 1871. In the antebellum and Civil War years, Germany was a loosely associated confederation of thirty-nine central European states.
11. Vander Hill, *Settling the Great Lakes Frontier*, 16.
12. Formisano, *Birth of Mass Political Parties*, 300–302; Kautz, "Fodder for Cannon," 14–16; Wilson, *Yankees in Michigan*, 22; *Detroit Free Press*, June 18, 1861.
13. Quoted in Babson, *Working Detroit*, 2–3; Kenny, *The American Irish*, 105–12; Catlin, *Story of Detroit*, 464; Trowbridge, *Circular*.
14. Vinyard, *Irish on the Urban Frontier*, 53; Metress and Metress, *Irish in Michigan*, 6; Diner, *Erin's Daughters*, xiv.
15. Skavery, "A Case Study of the Irish in Detroit," 45.
16. Metress and Metress, *Irish in Michigan*, 17–18; Skavery, "A Case Study of the Irish in Detroit," 33.

17. Hubbart, *Older Middle West*, 94; Roediger, *Wages of Whiteness*, 140–44.
18. Knobel, *Paddy and the Republic*, 178–79; Jacobson, *Whiteness of a Different Color*, 11–12.
19. Schneider, "Urbanization and the Maintenance of Order," 415; quoted in Kautz, "Fodder for Cannon," 250; *Detroit Daily Advertiser*, November 3, 1858.
20. Tentler, *Seasons of Grace*, 81; quoted in Streeter, *Political Parties in Michigan*, 175–76; Hershock, *Paradox of Progress*, 106.
21. Quoted in Volo and Volo, *Daily Life in Civil War America*, 72; Wibberly, *Coming of the Green*, 23.
22. Diner, *Erin's Daughters*, 80–88; Campbell, *Prisoners of Poverty*, 221–30; Marlatt, *Stuart Letters*, 1:177, 2:792; Romero, *Maid in the U.S.A.*, 106–7.
23. Castellanos, "Black Slavery in Detroit," 42–57; Palmer, *Early Days in Detroit*, 103–4.
24. Gilpin, *Territory of Michigan*, 29; Emmer, "Civil and Political Status," 10.
25. Streeter, *Political Parties in Michigan*, 57, 59.
26. Woodford, *This Is Detroit*, 346.
27. Catlin, *Story of Detroit*, 322, 325.
28. Quoted in Pearson, *An American Railroad Builder*, 109; Baker, *Affairs of Party*, 213.
29. Middleton, *Black Laws*, 345–47; Farmer, *History of Detroit*, 345.
30. Depositions of Talbot Oldham and Benjamin Weir (slave catchers) and John M. Wilson (Wayne County Sheriff), documents 3 and 6, Thornton Blackburn Fugitive Slave Case File; Farmer, *History of Detroit*, 345–46; Winks, *Blacks in Canada*, 169; Woodson, "Century with the Negroes," 11.
31. *Detroit Courier*, June 19, 1833, quoted in Emmer, "Civil and Political Status," 18; *Detroit Journal and Advertiser*, June 19 and July 24, 1833, quoted in Schneider, "Urbanization and the Maintenance of Order," 417.
32. Grimsted, *American Mobbing*, 73, 77; Emmer, "Civil and Political Status," 15.
33. Katzman, *Before the Ghetto*, 5–6, 12–13, 25–27; Thomas, *Life for Us*, 2.
34. Emmer, "Civil and Political Status," 51; Leach, *Second Baptist Church*, 1; Katzman, *Before the Ghetto*, 18–19, 23; McRae, "Blacks in Detroit," 146.
35. Metress and Metress, *Irish in Michigan*, 16; Hyde, *Detroit*, 5.
36. Palmer, *Early Days in Detroit*, 665. Catherine Street no longer exists. It was an eastern extension of Madison that ran all the way from Hastings Street to Elmwood Cemetery, about two blocks south of Maple Street. The barracks sat in an area generally formed by modern-ay Gratiot Avenue, St. Antoine, Mullet, and the Chrysler Expressway.
37. See Coakley, *Role of Federal Military Forces*, 110–19.
38. Douglass, *Uppermost Canada*, 160, 164.
39. Ibid., 157–69.
40. Leake, *History of Detroit*, 141; Millis, "Fort Wayne," 27–28.
41. Conway and Jamroz, *Detroit's Historic Fort Wayne*, 7, 23; Millis, "Fort Wayne," 27.
42. Palmer, *Early Days in Detroit*, 879; Simon, *Papers of Ulysses S. Grant*, 1:184; Lodge, *I Remember Detroit*, 2; Brodda, "Letter to the Editor."
43. *Calhoun County Patriot*, July 6, 1838, quoted in Streeter, *Political Parties in Michigan*, 5–6; Hershock, *Paradox of Progress*, xii.

44. Streeter, *Political Parties in Michigan*, 6; Formisano, *Birth of Mass Political Parties*, 81–97; Hershock, *Paradox of Progress*, xii.

45. May, *Fugitive Slave Law*, 3–7; Streeter, *Political Parties in Michigan*, 124.

46. Holt, *Rise and Fall of the American Whig Party*, 604; Marlatt, *Stuart Letters*, 1:148–49; May, *Fugitive Slave Law*, 11; Farmer, *History of Detroit*, 346. The use of "[sic]" is presented in this one instance to inform the reader that all source quotes are spelled out in the text exactly as written by the original author.

47. Quoted in Streeter, *Political Parties in Michigan*, 131–32.

48. *Detroit Free Press*, October 8, 1850; Campbell, *Slave Catchers*, 57–58.

49. *Detroit Free Press*, October 11, 1850.

50. Thomas, *Life for Us*, 5.

51. Ferrie, *Yankeys Now*, 162; Billington, *Protestant Crusade*, 334; Jacobson, *Whiteness of a Different Color*, 69–70.

52. Granger, *Wide-Awake!* 39; Farmer, *History of Detroit*, 114.

53. Rubenstein and Ziewacz, *Michigan*, 101–2.

54. Ibid, 102.

55. Formisano, *Birth of Mass Political Parties*, 8; Foner, "Ideology of the Republican Party," 9.

56. Dilla, *Politics of Michigan*, 21.

57. George, *Zachariah Chandler*, 2–3.

58. Simon, *Papers of Ulysses S. Grant*, 1:195.

59. Palmer, *Early Days in Detroit*, 237; Farmer, *History of Detroit*, 201–2; Schneider, *Detroit*, 66; *Detroit Free Press*, June 21, 1857.

60. Marlatt, *Stuart Letters*, 2:794, 821; Scott, *Forgotten Valor*, 235; Woodford, *Detroit and Its Banks*, 83.

61. Farmer, *History of Detroit*, 670; Kaplan, *Politics and the American Press*, 1, 23; Neely, *Union Divided*, 63–64.

62. Walsh, "*To Print the News*," 46–49, 115.

63. Quinby, "Reminiscences," 508.

64. *Detroit Free Press*, April 11, 1861; Walsh, "*To Print the News*," 56–61; Sandburg, *Abraham Lincoln*, 2:128.

65. Quoted in Walsh, "*To Print the News*," 90–91.

66. Burton, *City of Detroit*, 1:803; Quinby, "Reminiscences," 510.

67. Hinton, *John Brown*, 226–27; Farmer, *History of Detroit*, 347–48; Rubenstein and Ziewacz, *Michigan*, 95.

68. Quoted in May, *Michigan and the Civil War Years*, 1–2.

69. Ibid.

70. Voegeli, *Free but Not Equal*, 4; Formisano, *Birth of Mass Political Parties*, 8, 289–90.

Chapter 2

1. Smith, "Public Life of Austin Blair," 42–43; Weddon, *Michigan Governors*, 42–46.

2. Lanman, *Red Book of Michigan*, 147–48.

3. *Detroit Free Press*, January 1, 13, and 26, 1861.

4. Basler, *Collected Works of Lincoln*, 4:332–33; McPherson, *Tried by War*, 23; Lanman, *Red Book of Michigan*, 148–49.

5. Henry Billings Brown diary, April 14, 1861; Marlatt, *Stuart Letters*, 2:934–35; Robert McClelland to "Dear Augusta," April 19, 1861, Robert McClelland Papers.

6. Moore, "Days of Fife and Drum," 440.

7. Lanman, *Red Book of Michigan*, 149; Utley and Cutcheon, *Michigan*, 3:440; Isham, *History of the Detroit Light Guard*, 24.

8. Farmer, *History of Detroit*, 136; Digest Journal of Detroit Common Council, 1856–62, April 16 and 23, 1861; Robertson, "Brief Military History of Michigan," 471–72; Long, *Wages and Earnings in the United States*, 14, 42.

9. Withington, "Michigan in the Opening of the War," 6.

10. Robertson, *Michigan in the War*, 10–11; Elderkin, *Soldier of Three Wars*, 127.

11. State of Michigan, *Annual Report of the Quarter-Master General*, 4–5; Book, "Michigan Rescues Its Boys," 20–21.

12. Curtis, *History of the Twenty-fourth Michigan*, 20.

13. *Detroit Free Press*, April 18, 1861; Isham, compiler, *History of the Detroit Light Guard*, 13, 29; Clowes, *Detroit Light Guard*, 32–33.

14. *Detroit Free Press*, April 17 and 18, 1861; Isham, *History of the Detroit Light Guard*, 29–30; Moore, editor, *Rebellion Record*, 145.

15. Isham, *History of the Detroit Light Guard*, 29–30.

16. Robertson, *Michigan in the War*, 166–67; Warner, *Generals in Blue*, 558–59; Scott, *Forgotten Valor*, 236, 239; May, *Michigan and the Civil War Years*, 95–101.

17. William H. Randall reminiscences, 9; Kidd, *Personal Recollections*, 16–17; Sears, *For Country, Cause and Leader*, 8.

18. Clowes, *Detroit Light Guard*, 37.

19. Sears, *For Country, Cause and Leader*, 4; Williams, *Michigan First Regiment*, 6; Willis C. Humphrey memoir, Humphrey Papers, 12.

20. Zachariah Chandler to Simon Cameron, U.S. War Department, *Official Records of the Union and Confederate Armies*, ser. 3, vol. 1, 78 (hereafter cited as *OR*); quoted in George, *Zachariah Chandler*, 36–37. In her endnotes (42), the author cites a Democratic broadside in the Chandler Papers at the Library of Congress as her source for Chandler's famous "blood-letting" quote, claiming that no original of this letter exists within the collection. Zachariah Chandler to Abraham Lincoln, June 15, 1861, Abraham Lincoln Papers.

21. *Detroit Free Press*, April 27, 1861.

22. Paddock, *Our Cause*, 7.

23. May, *Michigan and the Civil War Years*, 11.

24. Sears, *For Country, Cause and Leader*, 2.

25. Ibid, 18; Hodge, *Civil War Letters of Mayo*, 167.

26. Angelo, *On Guard*, 81–82.

27. Marlatt, *Stuart Letters*, 2:950; Scott, *Forgotten Valor*, 286–346. The First Michigan Infantry was authorized to reform as a three-year regiment in June 1861 and headed back to Virginia on September 16, 1861.

28. Marlatt, *Stuart Letters*, 2:952–53; *Detroit Free Press*, August 3, 1861; Randall reminiscences, 48a; Farr, "My Own Life," 28.

29. Zachariah Chandler to Henry W. Lord, November 16, 1861, Robert M. Zug Papers.

30. Marlatt, *Stuart Letters*, 2:957–58.

31. Isaac Beers to his brother, September 27, 1861, Isaac Beers letter; Mitchell, "Civil War Recruiting," 44–45; Soloman Kroll to parents, September 23, 1861, Gordon Smith Collection.

32. Lanman, *Red Book of Michigan*, 154–55.

33. City of Detroit, *Journal of the Common Council, 1863*, 256–57.

34. Streeter, *Political Parties in Michigan*, 161–77; George, *Zachariah Chandler*, 88.

35. *Detroit Free Press*, August 24 and September 3, 1861. It should be noted that 1861 Hamtramck was far larger and not in the same location as modern Hamtramck. In the Civil War era, Hamtramck Township stretched from the Detroit River to the Wayne County line, which is known today as Eight Mile Road. It also ran from Woodward Avenue in the west to the Grosse Pointes in the east. The track upon which Camp Lyon was built was located on the north side of East Jefferson Avenue, just east of Van Dyke. Parker Street, which is just east of Van Dyke and north of East Jefferson, would have been part of the racetrack. The track closed in 1893.

36. *Detroit Free Press*, August 30 and September 15, 1861.

37. Wood, *Franklin's Yesteryear*, 92; Wilbur Spalding diary, September 9, 1862; Rowe, *Camp Notes*, 14–15. Hardtack became a staple food of a Civil War army on the march. It was basic flat cracker or biscuit made from flour, water, and perhaps salt. At times the crackers were so hard that biting into one would crack teeth.

38. Kamphoefner and Helbich, *Germans in the Civil War*, 86.

39. Swanson, *Sixth United States Infantry*, 67; *Detroit Free Press*, June 15, 1862; Farmer, *History of Detroit*, 306.

40. Harris, *Personal Reminiscences*, 10; Husby and Wittenberg, *Under Custer's Command*, 10.

41. *Detroit Free Press*, November 11, 1862.

42. Montgomery, "Eleven Months Experience in a Rebel Prison"; Scott, *Forgotten Valor*, 350.

43. *Detroit Free Press*, July 27 and August 7, 1862; Woodford, *Father Abraham's Children*, 94; Curtis, *History of the Twenty-fourth Michigan*, 48; Elmer D. Wallace to parents, September 13, 1862, Elmer D. Wallace Papers.

44. Leach, *Conscription*, 154; Lassen, *Dear Sarah*, 2; *Detroit Free Press*, January 21, 1865.

Chapter 3

1. Coleman, "Use of the Term 'Copperhead,'" 263.

2. *Detroit Free Press*, September 24, 1862.

3. Voegeli, *Free but Not Equal*, 7, 14–15; Milton, *Fifth Column*, 120; Gray, *Peace Movement*, 8; Weber, *Copperheads*, 23.

4. Quoted in Wood, *Black Scare*, 17.

5. Hutter and Abrams, "Copperhead Newspapers," 144; *Detroit Free Press*, February 6, 1863, quoted in Emmer, "Civil and Political Status," 55; Webb, *History*, 66.

6. *Detroit Free Press*, June 24, 1862; quoted in Voegeli, *Free but Not Equal*, 18.

7. Parker, "From Northwest to Mid-west," 10–11.

8. Klement, *Dark Lanterns*, 1–2.

9. Milton, *Fifth Column*, 66–68; Hubbart, *Older Middle West*, 225.

10. *K.G.C.*, 16; Klement, "Civil War Politics, Nationalism, and Postwar Myths," 153.

11. *Detroit Free Press*, November 3, 1861; *OR*, ser. 2, vol. 2, 1244–45.

12. *Detroit Free Press*, December 10, 1861, quoted in *OR*, ser. 2, vol. 2, 1256; *Detroit Tribune*, December 7, 1861, quoted in *OR*, ser. 2, vol. 2, 1256.

13. Guy S. Hopkins to William Seward, *OR*, ser. 2, vol. 2, 1250.

14. See Klement, "Hopkins Hoax," for a full account and analysis of this affair.

15. Guy S. Hopkins to William Seward, *OR*, ser. 2, vol. 2, 1250.

16. William Seward to Franklin Pierce, *OR*, ser. 2, vol. 2, 1257; Franklin Pierce to William Seward, *OR*, ser. 2, vol. 2, 1257–58.

17. William Seward to Franklin Pierce, *OR*, ser. 2, vol. 2, 1260–61; Franklin Pierce to William Seward, *OR*, ser. 2, vol. 2, 1261; Martin Burke to Lorenzo Thomas, *OR*, ser. 2, vol. 2, 1263.

18. Pierce to Latham, *OR*, ser. 2, vol. 2, 1264–65; *Detroit Free Press*, April 1, 1862.

19. Klement, "Hopkins Hoax," 14; Freidel, *Union Pamphlets*, 2:1046–47.

20. Silbey, *A Respectable Minority*, 82–83; Basler, *Collected Works of Lincoln*, 5:357, 423; *Detroit Free Press*, July 15, 1862.

21. Dunn, "First Michigan Colored Infantry," 8; Hargrove, "Their Greatest Battle," 26; *Detroit Advertiser and Tribune*, April 15, 1863.

22. Dunn, "First Michigan Colored Infantry," 10–11; Robertson, *Michigan in the War*, 488–89; *Detroit Free Press*, May 29, 1861.

23. Smith, "Raising a Black Regiment," 507.

24. *Detroit Free Press*, August 19 and 21, 1863.

25. McRae, "Camp Ward," 4; in a letter to the editor in the December 28, 1863, *Free Press* regarding the alleged poor condition of the First Michigan Colored Infantry's barracks, Captain George W. Lee, assistant quartermaster, writes of "the quarters furnished the Fifth Cavalry, encamped on [these] same grounds last year."

26. Gilbert and Titus, *Narrative of Sojourner Truth*, 172–73; *Detroit Advertiser and Tribune*, November 24, 1863.

27. Quoted in Woodson, "Century with the Negroes," 45; Dr. Charles Tripler to Bennett H. Hill, December 19, 1863, Records of the Office of the Quartermaster General, box 500, Consolidated Correspondence; McRae, *Negroes in Michigan*, 58–59; *Detroit Free Press*, December 28, 1863.

28. *Detroit Free Press*, January 16, 1864.

29. Joseph R. Smith to Henry Barns, January 20, 1864, Letters Sent by Military Commander at Detroit, Mi., Records of the Provost Marshal General's Bureau, entry 5895; Herek, *These Men Have Seen Hard Service*, 15.

30. *OR*, ser. 3, vol. 3, 252.

31. *Detroit Advertiser and Tribune*, March 7, 1864.

32. Quoted in Dunn, "First Michigan Colored Infantry," 59; *Detroit Free Press*, March 29, 1864.

Chapter 4

1. Sterling, "Civil War Draft Resistance," 51–52; Hubbart, *Older Middle West*, 140–42.
2. James B. Fry report, *OR*, ser. 3, vol. 5, 608–9; Murdock, *One Million Men*, 6; Geary, *We Need Men*, 32–35; Shannon, *Organization and Administration*, 1:260.
3. *Detroit Free Press*, July 13 and 15, 1862.
4. *Detroit Free Press*, July 15, 1862.
5. *Detroit Advertiser and Tribune*, July 16, 1862; Romeyn obituary, *New York Times*, July 23, 1885; Curtis, *History of the Twenty-fourth Michigan*, 26; Mark Flanigan biography, George B. Catlin Papers.
6. *Detroit Free Press*, July 16 and 22, 1862; *Detroit Advertiser and Tribune*, July 16, 1862; Sterling, "Civil War Draft Resistance," 248–49.
7. Fuller, *Messages of the Governors of Michigan*, 2:506.
8. *Detroit Free Press*, July 22 and 23, 1862.
9. *Detroit Free Press*, July 23, 1862; May, *Michigan and the Civil War Years*, 30; Woodford, *This Is Detroit*, 69–70.
10. *Detroit Free Press*, August 19, 1862; Robert Burns to his mother, July 15 and August 24, 1862, Robert Burns letterbook; Henry Billings Brown diary, September 1, 1862.
11. Murdock, *Patriotism Limited*, 6–7; Fry report, *OR*, ser. 3, vol. 5, 609–10; W. A. Faxon to Henry Potter, August 7, 1862, in *Letters of Henry Albert Potter*.
12. Quoted in Moore, *Rebellion Record*, 5:57; quoted in Landon, *Western Ontario*, 223.
13. Schneider, *Detroit*, 29–30.
14. Thomas Blair, A.A.G. to Austin Blair, November 4, 1862, Provost Guard: Enlistment Papers, Discharges, Letters, Regimental Service Records; Robinson, *Michigan in the War*, 745.
15. Warner, *Generals in Blue*, 162–63; Fry report, *OR*, ser. 3, vol. 5, 599. Also see *OR*, ser. 3, vol. 3, 125–46, for detailed regulations regarding the operations of the Bureau of the Provost Marshal General; U.S. Congress, "Report of the Secretary of War," 109–10; Nevins, *War for the Union*, 397.
16. Leach, *Conscription*, 252.
17. James B. Fry to Austin Blair, April 24, 1863, Letters Received in Michigan (1863–1865), Records of the Provost Marshal General's Bureau, entry 5903; *Annual Reunion of the Association of the Graduates of the United States Military Academy*, 93–96; Eicher and Eicher, *Civil War High Commands*, 296; *Detroit Free Press*, May 6, 1863; Bennett H. Hill to James B. Fry, May 11, 1863, Letters Sent by the Acting Assistant Provost Marshal General, Records of the Provost Marshal General's Bureau, entry 5897; Murdock, *One Million Men*, 92–93.
18. Fry report, *OR*, ser. 3, vol. 5, 599; Murdock, *Patriotism Limited*, 7.
19. Fry report, *OR*, ser. 3, vol. 5, 611–12, 616.
20. Marlatt, *Stuart Letters*, 2:984–85; *Detroit Free Press*, March 5, 1863.
21. Dunbar and May, *Michigan*, 379; Murdock, *Patriotism Limited*, 14.
22. Murdock, *Patriotism Limited*, 3, 9–10; Kautz, "Fodder for Cannon," 207–9; also see Murdock, *One Million Men*, 178–96.
23. Quoted in Leach, *Conscription*, 314–15.

24. Murdock, *Patriotism Limited*, 60; McPherson, "Battle Cry of Freedom," 133; *Detroit Free Press*, February 17 and March 18, 1865; *Detroit Advertiser and Tribune*, February 17 and 22, 1865; Kautz, "Fodder for Cannon," 207–10.

25. Cashin, "Deserters, Civilians, and Draft Resistance," 269.

26. Quoted in Brown, *Michigan Men*, 6; Charles Cleveland diary, February 7, 11 and 14, 1865, Cleveland Family Papers.

27. Quoted in Jimerson, *Private Civil War*, 95; Glaza-Herrington, *Dear Brother and Sister*, 278–79.

28. Kundinger, "Racial Rhetoric," 3; *Detroit Free Press*, September 7, 1862.

29. *Thrilling Narrative*, 2; *Detroit Free Press*, February 27 and March 7, 1863; Woodford, *Father Abraham's Children*, 64–65; Quinn, "Detroit Riot," 3.

30. *Detroit Free Press*, March 6, 1863; Woodford, *Father Abraham's Children*, 64–65.

31. *Detroit Free Press*, March 7, 1863; Schneider, *Detroit*, 70.

32. *Detroit Free Press*, March 7 and 22, 1863; Wayne County Historical and Pioneer Society, *Chronography of Notable Events*, 277.

33. Markovitz, *Legacies of Lynching*, xvi.

34. City of Detroit, *Journal of the Common Council, 1863*, 241; *Thrilling Narrative*, 2; *Detroit Free Press*, March 7, 1863; *Detroit Advertiser and Tribune*, March 14, 1863; also see Wells, *With Touch of Elbow*, 68. Wells served in the Eighth Michigan Cavalry and recounts how he and his Company F were detailed to the Detroit Barracks in the winter of 1862–63 to serve provost duty.

35. Joseph R. Smith to Lorenzo Thomas, January 9, 1864, Letters Sent by Military Commander at Detroit, Mi., Records of the Provost Marshal General's Bureau, entry 5895. Thomas was adjutant general of the Union army. *Detroit Free Press*, March 7 and 8, 1863; Woodford, *Father Abraham's Children*, 65–66.

36. State of Michigan, *Annual Report of the Adjutant General, 1863*, 446; *Thrilling Narrative*, 3; Farmer, *History of Detroit*, 577; John A. Warren to Elisha Weaver, March 21, 1863, quoted in Yacovone, *Freedom's Journey*, 69; *Detroit Free Press*, March 7 and 9, 1863; *Detroit Advertiser and Tribune*, March 9, 1863; Woodford, *Father Abraham's Children*, 67; quoted in Winks, *Blacks in Canada*, 288.

37. Roberts, *Sketches and Reminiscences*, 115. Croghan Street was renamed Monroe Avenue on May 4, 1891, in honor of William C. Monroe, who served as the first minister of the Second Baptist Church of Detroit from 1836 to 1846. *Detroit Free Press*, March 7, 1863; Mary E. Bissell diary, March 6 and 7, 1863. In the mid-nineteenth century, "Dutch," meaning "Deutsch," was a common term for Germans or people of German descent. Her belief was incorrect, as most of the rioters were Irish.

38. City of Detroit, *Journal of the Common Council, 1863*, 242; Woodford, *Father Abraham's Children*, 67; Frances Phelps to Joseph R. Smith, March 10, 1863, Joseph Rowe Smith Family Papers.

39. *Detroit Free Press*, March 7 and 8, 1863; Schneider, *Detroit*, 72–73; *Detroit Advertiser and Tribune*, March 9, 1863; William P. Spalding to his wife, March 12, 1863, Spalding Family Papers; quoted in Woodson, "Century with the Negroes," 45; Yacovone, *Freedom's Journey*, 69.

40. *Detroit Free Press*, August 14, 1863; Quinn, "Detroit Riot," 52.

41. Webb, *History*, 38–39.

42. Schneider, *Detroit*, 73.
43. Fannie Wright diary, March 6, 1863; Henry Billings Brown diary, March 6, 1863.
44. Elizabeth Douglass to "My Dear Sam," March 11, 1863, Samuel T. Douglass Papers; *Thrilling Narrative*, 15; City of Detroit, *Journal of the Common Council, 1863*, 256–57.
45. Baker, *Affairs of Party*, 244–45; Katz, *Anti-Negro Riots*, iii; Roediger, *Wages of Whiteness*, 56–58; Jacobson, *Whiteness of a Different Color*, 53.
46. Quaife, *From the Cannon's Mouth*, 168–69.
47. State of Michigan, *Journal of the Senate of the State of Michigan, 1871*, 174–75; Faulkner obituary, *Detroit Free Press*, June 3, 1877.
48. Voegeli, *Free but Not Equal*, 34–35; *New York Times*, July 14, 1863; see *OR*, ser. 1, vol. 27, pt. 2, 875–912, for Union military correspondence pertaining to the New York riots.
49. John Newberry to Bennett Hill, *OR*, ser. 3, vol. 3, 488–89; quoted in Leach, *Conscription*, 327; Farmer, *History of Detroit*, 1066–67. Newberry left his law practice in 1864 to help establish the Michigan (Railroad) Car Works. At the time of his death in 1887, it was the largest manufacturing establishment in Detroit and Newberry was considered one of Detroit's leading industrialists.
50. Bennett Hill to James Fry, *OR*, ser. 3, vol. 3, 551; Herek, *These Men Have Seen Hard Service*, 49–58.
51. Bennett Hill to James Fry, *OR*, ser. 3, vol. 3, 551.
52. Rogers, *Guardian of the Lakes*, 4–5, 149.
53. Ibid., 80, 83–84; John C. Carter to Gideon Welles, U.S. War Department, *Official Records of the Union and Confederate Navies in the War of the Rebellion*, ser. 1, vol. 2, 414–15 (hereafter cited as *ORN*).
54. Chancellor, *Englishman in the American Civil War*, 105.
55. Quinn, *Detroit Riot*, 41–42; Weber, *Copperheads*, 51.
56. Murdock, *Patriotism Limited*, 44–45; Leach, *Conscription*, 258; "Instructions to Enrolling Officers, no. 2" June 10, 1863, Civil War Vertical File—Contemporary Publications; quoted in Sterling, "Civil War Draft Resistance," 211.
57. Bennett Hill to James Fry, *OR*, ser. 2, vol. 6, 231–32; W. P. Anderson to J. R. Smith, *OR*, ser. 2, vol. 6, 231–32; Klement, "Clement L. Vallandigham's Exile in the Confederacy," 151, 155; also see Klement, *Limits of Dissent*, 226–28.
58. *Detroit Free Press*, June 3, 1863; *Detroit Advertiser and Tribune*, October 27, 1863; Fry to Stanton, *OR*, ser. 3, vol. 5, 680.
59. Bennett Hill to James Fry, *OR*, ser. 3, vol. 3, 367.
60. Quoted in Spiro, "History of the Michigan Soldiers' Aid Society," 212. The Detroit Soldiers' Aid Society will be discussed more fully in chapter 6.
61. State of Michigan, *Annual Report of the Adjutant General, 1863*, 484–85; Cimbala, "Soldiering on the Home Front," 191; Pelka, *Letters of Johnson*, 14–15.
62. May, *Michigan and the Civil War Years*, 51, 62; *Detroit Advertiser and Tribune*, November 6, 1863, and September 19, 1864.
63. George D. Converse to "Dear Friends," January 2, 1865, George D. Converse Papers; Murdock, *Patriotism Limited*, 52–53.
64. Weber, *Copperheads*, 154; Abraham Lincoln, "Executive Order," August 8, 1862, Peters and Woolley, *American Presidency Project*; Charles Abbott to Samuel

Abbott, March 16, 1865, Samuel H. Abbott Papers; Sterling, "Civil War Draft Resistance," 261.

65. Morrison, *Garden Gateway*, 51–52; Zachariah Chandler to Henry W. Lord, November 16, 1861, Robert M. Zug Papers; Hamer, "Luring Canadian Soldiers," 150.

66. *Detroit Advertiser and Tribune*, October 1, 1863.

67. *Detroit Advertiser and Tribune*, May 17, 1862.

68. Hoy, *Canadians in the Civil War*, 135–36; Havran, "Windsor and Detroit Relations," 373; Hamer, "Luring Canadian Soldiers," 151–52; Winks, *Canada and the United States*, 194, 196.

69. Hansen and Brebner, *Mingling of the Canadian and American Peoples*, 148–49; quoted in Landon, *Western Ontario*, 223; *Detroit Free Press*, October 1, 1864.

70. *OR*, ser. 3, vol. 5, 905.

71. *Detroit Free Press*, November 8, 1864.

Chapter 5

1. Rips, *Detroit*, 123; Hershock, *Paradox of Progress*, 67–68; Parkins, "Historical Geography of Detroit," 292–93.

2. Crathern, *In Detroit*, 14.

3. Deskins, *Residential Mobility*, 67–68.

4. Schramm and Henning, *Detroit's Street Railways*, 9, 13–14; O'Geran, *Detroit Street Railways*, 21–22.

5. Richards, *Appleton's Illustrated Hand-book of American Travel*, 346.

6. "Detroit Before the War," *Detroit Free Press*, September 26, 1897; Palmer, *Early Days in Detroit*, 233–38.

7. Pisani, *Prince Napoleon in America*, 167; Laugel, *United States during the War*, 121–22. Laugel was a French historian and engineer who wrote this account of his 1864–65 travels in the United States, primarily in the Midwest.

8. Dillon, "A Woman's Place," 7.

9. Lerner, *Majority Finds Its Past*, 16; Holliday, *Woman's Life in Colonial Days*, 293–95.

10. Lerner, *Majority Finds Its Past*, 17–18, 25; Clinton, *Other Civil War*, 40; Diner, *Erin's Daughters*, 84–90.

11. Massey, *Bonnet Brigades*, 24; Dillion, "A Woman's Place," 8.

12. Massey, *Bonnet Brigades*, 6.

13. Ibid., 108–13; Perlmann and Margo, *Women's Work?* 87; *Johnston's 1861 Detroit City Directory*, 22–24; Moehlman, *Public Education in Detroit*, 100–101, 105.

14. Ross and Catlin, *Landmarks of Detroit*, 515–16.

15. Brockway, *Fifty Years of Prison Service*, 68–69; Mary P. Davis to her sister, April 27, 1864, Mary P. Davis Letters.

16. Fite, *Social and Industrial Conditions*, 187; Diner, *Erin's Daughters*, 80–82; DuBois, *Black Reconstruction in America*, 700; Harper, *Women during the Civil War*, 238–39.

17. Giesberg, *Army at Home*, 74–75.
18. *Detroit Free Press*, August 26, 1864; Silber, *Daughters of the Union*, 61.
19. *Detroit Free Press*, November 22 and December 6, 1864; quoted in Foner, *Women and the American Labor Movement*, 117–18; quoted in Baron and Klepp, "'If I Didn't Have My Sewing Machine,'" 24.
20. Hicks, *Life of Trevellick*, 35–38; Blum and Georgakas, *Michigan Labor*, 23.
21. Andrews and Bliss, *History of Women in Trade Unions*, 94–95, 98; *Detroit Free Press*, August 26, 1864.
22. Andrews and Bliss, *History of Women in Trade Unions*, 98–99.
23. Quoted in Lewis, *Lumberman from Flint*, 192; quoted in *Detroit Free Press*, September 16, 1862.
24. Grossman, *William Sylvis*, 22–23, 76.
25. Ibid., 24–25; Woodford and Woodford, *All Our Yesterdays*, 322–23.
26. Blum and Georgakas, *Michigan Labor*, 19–21; *Detroit Free Press*, December 10, 1862; Quinn, "Detroit Riot," 21–22.
27. Quoted in Smith and Judah, *Life in the North*, 221–22; Grossman, *William Sylvis*, 159.
28. Quoted in Smith and Judah, *Life in the North*, 223–24.
29. *Detroit Free Press*, August 23 and September 1, 1862; Lerner, *Majority Finds Its Past*, 22–23.
30. Giesberg, *Civil War Sisterhood*, 199, no. 15; Vinyard, *Irish on the Urban Frontier*, 58.
31. *Detroit Free Press*, May 14, 1863, and April 4, 1865; Spiro, "History of the Michigan Soldiers' Aid Society," 406.
32. U.S. Bureau of Labor, *Report on Condition of Women and Child Wage-Earners*, 236.
33. Thornton and Ekelund, *Tariffs, Blockades, and Inflation*, 68–69; Moehlman, *Public Education in Detroit*, 104.
34. Johann Look to "Dear Children," May 31, 1863, Look Family Papers; *Detroit Free Press*, September 30 and November 11, 1863, March 5, 1864; Woodford, *Detroit and Its Banks*, 96.
35. Thornton and Ekelund, *Tariffs, Blockades, and Inflation*, 68–69; Moehlman, *Public Education in Detroit*, 104.
36. Dunbar and May, *Michigan*, 387.
37. Wilson, *Business of Civil War*, 18.
38. Farmer, *History of Detroit*, 202.
39. Schneider, *Detroit*, 66–67; Silber, *Daughters of the Union*, 107; Woodford, *Father Abraham's Children*, 69; Sears, *For Country, Cause, and Leader*, 4, 14.
40. Lowry, *Sexual Misbehavior*, 90.
41. Lowry, *Story the Soldiers Wouldn't Tell*, 86–87.
42. *Detroit Free Press*, July 27, 1864.
43. Catlin, *Story of Detroit*, 539; Freedman, *Their Sisters' Keepers*, 13, 15; Hershock, *Paradox of Progress*, 71; quoted in Farmer, *History of Detroit*, 204; Schneider, *Detroit*, 95.
44. *Detroit Free Press*, February 4, 1864.
45. City of Detroit, *Journal of the Common Council, 1864*, 317, and *1865*, 227; Farmer, *History of Detroit*, 204; Schneider, *Detroit*, 95.

Chapter 6

1. Giesberg, *Civil War Sisterhood,* 117.
2. Quoted in Spiro, "History of the Michigan Soldiers' Aid Society," 133–34; *Detroit Free Press,* June 8, 1862, and January 10, 1863.
3. *Detroit Advertiser and Tribune,* September 19, 1862.
4. Spiro, "History of the Michigan Soldiers' Aid Society," 404–5.
5. *Detroit Free Press,* May 13, 1863; Massey, *Bonnet Brigades,* 44, 59.
6. *Detroit Free Press,* November 21, 1861; Martin, *St. Mary's Hospital,* 50–57, 64; Lanman, *Red Book of Michigan,* 217; Farmer, *History of Detroit,* 653; St. Mary's Hospital Letterbook, December [no date], 1864, St. Mary's Hospital Records, 4.
7. Woodford and Mason, *Harper of Detroit,* 9–16; Farmer, *History of Detroit,* 657.
8. Woodford and Mason, *Harper of Detroit,* 9–16, 29–38; *Detroit Free Press,* December 20, 1862.
9. Tripler, *Eunice Tripler,* 146–47; Woodford and Mason, *Harper of Detroit,* 74, 306.
10. Adams, *Doctors in Blue,* 155; Joseph Tunnicliff to Austin Blair, October 9, 1863, Harper Hospital Records. Tunnicliff's role as state agent was to assist sick and wounded Michigan soldiers in Washington, or their family members, in all manner of matters such as financial assistance, providing information, arranging transportation, and assisting with discharge, transfer, or furlough papers. State of Michigan, *Annual Report of the Adjutant General, 1863,* 486.
11. Harper Hospital Board of Trustees, *Constitution and Rules of the Harper Hospital,* 21; George W. Lee to Montgomery Meigs, April 11, 1864, Records of the Office of the Quartermaster General, box 500, Consolidated Correspondence; Woodford and Mason, *Harper of Detroit,* 76.
12. *Detroit Free Press,* July 15, 1864, and October 13, 1864; Robertson, *Michigan in the War,* 115; Woodford and Mason, *Harper of Detroit,* 82–84.
13. Immanuel Brown to "Dear Wife and Son," February 6, 7, and 10, 1865, Immanuel Brown Papers; Frank Marsh to "Dearest Mother," February 15, 1865, Edwin Holmes Papers; Rutkow, *Bleeding Blue and Gray,* 26–27.
14. Frank Gross diary, April 6, 1865; Adams, *Doctors in Blue,* 174–75; State of Michigan, *Annual Report of the Adjutant General, 1864,* 867; C. H. Crane to Joseph R. Smith, March 28, 1864, Letters Received from Headquarters, Northern Dept., 1864–65, Records of U.S. Army Continental Commands; Rutkow, *Bleeding Blue and Gray,* 125.
15. *Detroit Free Press,* June 7, 1865.
16. Frank Gross diary, April 6, 1865; Adams, *Doctors in Blue,* 164.
17. Joseph J. Tuttle to "Dear Sister," May 10, 1865, Joseph J. Tuttle Papers.
18. Massey, *Bonnet Brigades,* 153; McTeer and Millbrook, "For Loved Ones Far Away," 113.
19. Massey, *Bonnet Brigades,* 33; Spiro, "History of the Michigan Soldiers' Aid Society," 5, 15–16.
20. Spiro, "History of the Michigan Soldiers' Aid Society," ii, 19–20.
21. Ibid., 21–22, 165–66.
22. E. B. Andrews to Valeria Campbell, August 17, 1863, James V. Campbell Papers. Andrews was the Sanitary Commission representative in the Midwest and

Valeria Campbell (brother of James V. Campbell) was the tireless recording secretary for the Detroit Soldiers' Aid Society.; Brockett and Vaughan, *Woman's Work*, 594.

23. Newberry, *U.S. Sanitary Commission*, 407–10.

24. Ibid.; *Detroit Free Press*, April 22, 1864.

25. State of Michigan, *Annual Report of the Adjutant General, 1864*, 895.

26. *Detroit Free Press*, March 28, 1862; Crathern, *In Detroit*, 25, 27.

27. Fite, *Social and Industrial Conditions*, 299. Also see Holt, *Orphan Trains*, for a discussion of the mid-nineteenth-century orphan trains.

28. Moss, *Annals of the Christian Commission*, 106–7; Rable, *God's Almost Chosen Peoples*, 213–14.

29. Moss, *Annals of the Christian Commission*, 348–49; Ladies Army Committee of the Christian Commission, circular dated Detroit, December 15, 1863; U.S. Christian Commission, *Works and Incidents*, 224–25.

30. Basler, *Collected Works of Lincoln*, 7:254.

Chapter 7

1. Tidwell, *April '65*, 107.

2. Lucas, *Memoir of John Yates Beall*, 296.

3. Robert Minor to Franklin Buchanan, *ORN*, ser. 1, vol. 2, 823. Minor's lengthy report presents a detailed account from the Confederate perspective of the planned expeditions to free Confederate prisoners on Johnson's Island in the spring and fall of 1863.; William Murdaugh to Stephen Mallory, *ORN*, ser. 1, vol. 2, 828–30.

4. Quoted in Foreman, *World on Fire*, 685; Sanders, *While in the Hands of the Enemy*, 70–73; Carpenter, "Plain Living at Johnson's Island," 310; Bush, "*I Fear I Shall Never Leave This Island*," 146–47; Jones, *Northern Confederate*, 148.

5. "Canadian" to James Bennett, *OR*, ser. 2, vol. 3, 657–58.

6. United States Military Academy, Association of Graduates, *Annual Reunion, 1885*, 93–96; Bennett Hill to James Fry, *OR*, ser. 3, vol. 3, 1008; Warner, *Generals in Blue*, 97; Cox, *Military Reminiscences*, 2:57–59.

7. Robert Minor to Franklin Buchanan, *ORN*, ser. 1, vol. 2, 822–28.

8. Quoted in Winks, *Canada and the United States*, 147; Stanton to governors, *OR*, ser. 3, vol. 3, 1013; Robert Minor to Franklin Buchanan, *ORN*, ser. 1, vol. 2, 822–28; *Detroit Advertiser and Tribune*, October 13, 1863.

9. *Detroit Free Press*, November 12 and 13, 1864; Zachariah Chandler to Edwin Stanton, *OR*, ser. 3, vol. 3, 1019; Winks, *Canada and the United States*, 148.

10. Nathan W. Brooks to J. Wilson Brooks, November 19, 1863, Brooks Family Papers; Joseph R. Smith to Lorenzo Thomas, *OR*, ser. 3, vol. 3, 1031–32.

11. *Detroit Advertiser and Tribune*, November 13, 1863.

12. William Sherman to Stephen Burbridge, *OR*, ser. 1, vol. 32, pt. 3, 463.

13. See Coffman, *Old Army*; and Skelton, *American Profession of Arms*, for thorough discussions of antebellum army culture.

14. State of Michigan, *Journal of the House of Representatives*, 28–29.

15. Ibid., 89–90.

16. State of Michigan, *Journal of the Senate of the State of Michigan, 1864,* 232–33.

17. Henry Terry to Northern Department Headquarters, *OR,* ser. 1, vol. 32, pt. 3, 219; Samuel Heintzelman to Henry W. Halleck, *OR,* ser. 1, vol. 32, pt. 3, 218.

18. Joseph R. Smith to Carroll H. Potter, April 9, 1864, Letters Received from Headquarters, Northern Dept., 1864–65, Records of U.S. Army Continental Commands; Carroll H. Potter to Joseph R. Smith, April 21, 1864, Letters Received from Headquarters, Northern Dept., 1864–65, Records of U.S. Army Continental Commands.

19. Cullum, *Biographical Register,* 312.

20. Joseph R. Smith to Carroll H. Potter, March 31, 1864, Letters Sent by Military Commander at Detroit, Mi., Records of the Provost Marshal General's Bureau, entry 5895; Joseph R. Smith to Bennett H. Hill, April 5, 1864, Letters Sent by Military Commander at Detroit, Mi., Records of the Provost Marshal General's Bureau, entry 5895.

21. Mark Flanigan to Joseph R. Smith, April 18, 1864, Letters Received in Michigan (1863–1865), Records of the Provost Marshal General's Bureau, entry 5903.

22. Cullum, *Biographical Register,* 312; Joseph R. Smith to "My Dear Ju[liet]," May 23, 1864, Joseph Rowe Smith Papers; Bennett Hill report, Historical Reports of the State Acting Assistant Provost Marshal General and District Provost Marshals, 1865, Records of the Provost Marshal General's Bureau, M1163, 3.

23. *Detroit Free Press,* September 4, 1868.

24. Lucas, *Memoir of John Yates Beall,* 19–20; John Carter to Gideon Welles, *ORN,* ser. 1, vol. 2, 478–79; Jones, ed., *Northern Confederate,* 146.

25. Lucas, *Memoir of John Yates Beall,* 296; Phillips, "Johnson's Island and the Lake Erie Raid," 249. The author was a Union officer on Johnson's Island at the time of the planned raid. Headley, *Confederate Operations,* 235.

26. Lucas, *Memoir of John Yates Beall,* 33; John Dix to Edwin Stanton, *OR,* ser. 1, vol. 43, pt. 2, 226–28.

27. Headley, *Confederate Operations,* 249, 253.

28. John Dix to Edwin Stanton, *OR,* ser. 1, vol. 43, pt. 2, 227; Headley, *Confederate Operations,* 248–50; Lucas, *Memoir of John Yates Beall,* 33–36, 296.

29. Headley, *Confederate Operations,* 250; Lucas, *Memoir of John Yates Beall,* 39–40.

30. Headley, *Confederate Operations,* 250–51; Winks, *Canada and the United States,* 290.

31. Bennett Hill to John Carter, *OR,* ser. 1, vol. 39, pt. 2, 399; Bennett Hill to C. H. Potter, *OR,* ser. 1, vol. 43, pt. 2, 233–34; Cox, *Military Reminiscences,* 2:61.

32. Phillips, "Johnson's Island and the Lake Erie Raid," 257; U.S. Army, *Trial of John Y. Beall,* 92–94; Goodwin, *Team of Rivals,* 696.

33. Henry Billings Brown diary, September 20, 1864; *Detroit Free Press,* September 21, 1864; *Detroit Daily Advertiser and Tribune,* September 20, 1864.

34. Foreman, *World on Fire,* 689–90.

35. Joseph Hooker General Orders, *OR,* ser. 1, vol. 39, pt. 3, 23–24; Hebert, *Fighting Joe Hooker,* 289; Thompson, *Civil War to the Bloody End.* 308.

36. See Prince, *Burn the Town,* for a modern analysis of the St. Albans affair.

37. *Detroit Free Press*, October 16 and 21, 1864; Benjamin, *The St. Albans Raid*, 78–79.

38. *Richmond Whig*, October 15, 1864.

39. Quoted in Massey, *Bonnet Brigades*, 224.

40. City of Detroit, *Journal of the Common Council, 1864*, 190; October 1864 Post Returns, Returns from U.S. Military Posts, 1800–1916, M617, roll 314, Detroit Barracks, October 1842–May 1866; Flom, "Early Swedish Immigration," 608–9.

41. "Captain Eber B. Ward's Fortress," 21; Farmer, *History of Detroit*, 1234–35; George A. Custer to "My Dear Friend," October 29, 1864, George Armstrong Custer letter.

42. *Detroit Advertiser and Tribune*, November 7, 1864; Hill report, Reports of the State Acting Assistant Provost Marshal General, 7–8; Klement, *Limits of Dissent*, 148; Silvestro, *Rally round the Flag*, 3; Kautz, "Fodder for Cannon," 160–61, 200; also see Gibson, "Lincoln's League," for a thorough analysis of the Union League.

43. *Detroit Advertiser and Tribune*, November 7, 1864; *Detroit Free Press*, October 26, 1864, and November 1, 1864.

44. Joseph Hooker to Edwin Stanton, November 3, 1864, Thirtieth Michigan Regimental Service Records; Edwin Stanton to Joseph Hooker, November 4, 1864, Thirtieth Michigan Regimental Service Records.

45. Joseph Hooker to Austin Blair, November 4, 1864, Thirtieth Michigan Regimental Service Records; *Detroit Free Press*, November 8, 1864.

46. Northern Dept. Headquarters to Joseph R. Smith, April 8, 1864, Letters Received from Headquarters, Northern Dept., 1864–65, Records of U.S. Army Continental Commands; *Detroit Advertiser and Tribune*, November 7, 1864.

47. *Detroit Free Press*, November 17, 1864; quoted in Bahde, "Our Cause is a Common One," 71; George A. Douglas to Michigan adjutant general John Robertson, November 26, 1864, Thirtieth Michigan Regimental Service Records; William S. Atwood to Michigan adjutant general John Robertson, November 30, 1864, Thirtieth Michigan Regimental Service Records; Grover S. Wormer to William E. Christian, December 1, 1864, Slafter Family Papers.

48. Henry Billings Brown diary, August 22–25, 1864; Murdock, *Patriotism Limited*, 211.

49. *Detroit Free Press*, January 10, 1865.

50. *New York Times*, November 27, 1864; Headley, *Confederate Operations*, 323–30.

51. *Detroit Free Press*, December 1, 1864; Francis A. Roe to Gideon Welles, *ORN*, ser. 1, vol. 3, 377; Bennett Hill to Carroll Potter, *OR*, ser. 1, vol. 45, pt. 2, 82–83.

52. Bennett Hill to James Fry, *OR*, ser. 1, vol. 45, pt. 2, 69–70.

53. *Detroit Free Press*, December 7, 1864.

54. Joseph Hooker to Edward Townsend, *OR*, ser. 1, vol. 45, pt. 2, 82.

55. Joseph Hooker to Austin Blair, December 12, 1864, Thirtieth Michigan Regimental Service Records.

56. *Journal of the Senate*, 38th Cong., 2nd sess., December 14, 1864, 26; Raney, "Diplomatic and Military Activities of Canada," 67–68, 79.

57. *Detroit Free Press*, December 16, 1864.

58. *Detroit Free Press*, December 17, 1864.

59. *Detroit Free Press*, December 29, 1864; Winks, *Canada and the United States*, 292; Chambers, *Prince of Wales Regiment*, 62.

60. Winks, *Canada and the United States*, 325.

61. *Detroit Advertiser and Tribune*, February 6, 1865; Hewett, *Supplement to the Official Records of the Union and Confederate Armies*, pt. 2, vol. 31, ser. 43, 571, 576.

62. *OR*, ser. 3, vol. 4, 1020; Raney, "Diplomatic and Military Activities of Canada," 76; quoted in Snell, "H. H. Emmons," 310–15.

63. Eli Strawbridge to James Doolittle, February 11, 1865, "Selections from the Doolittle Correspondence," 104.

64. Edwin Shaw to George Shaffer, February 21, 1865, George T. Shaffer Papers; Silas W. Sadler to his parents, February 5 and April 4, 1865, Silas W. Sadler correspondence; Gardner L. White to friend, January 30, 1865, Gardner L. White Papers; George Campbell to his father, January 30, 1865, Campbell Family Papers.

65. Bennett H. Hill to Henry Halleck, October 14, 1864, J. W. Flanagan Collection.

66. Henry Billings Brown diary, April 3, 1865; *Detroit Free Press*, April 11, 1865.

67. Brunner, "In Detroit When Lincoln Was Assassinated," 77.

68. Morrison, *Garden Gateway*, 53.

69. Silas W. Sadler to his parents, April 27, 1865, Silas W. Sadler correspondence.

Chapter 8

1. Adams, *Letter from Washington*, 263, 267.

2. *Detroit Free Press*, December 19, 1865; Lanman, *Red Book of Michigan*, 217–18; Farmer, *History of Detroit*, 658–59.

3. Robertson, *Michigan in the War*, 85; *Detroit Free Press*, June 5, 1865.

4. Scott, *Forgotten Valor*, 653.

5. Martin, *St. Mary's Hospital*, 64–65; Robertson, *Michigan in the War*, 488–93.

6. Kaplan, *Politics and the American Press*, 29.

7. *Detroit Free Press*, September 26, 1865, September 28, 1866, and July 12, 1867. Quoted in Bukovac, "Michigan Democratic Press," 512.

8. Farmer, *History of Detroit*, 348.

9. Katzman, *Before the Ghetto*, 50.

10. Sumner, *History of Women in Industry*, 230.

11. Ibid, 203.

12. *Detroit Free Press*, September 10, 1868.

13. Amelia Ryerse Harris diary entry, September 15, 1867, in Harris and Harris, *Eldon House Diaries*, 281.

14. Holli, *Reform in Detroit*, 4; Dunbar and May, *Michigan*, 387.

15. *Detroit Free Press*, September 26, 1869.

16. *Detroit Free Press*, September 23, 1866, and May 30, 1869.

17. McConnell, *Glorious Contentment*, 138–65.

18. *Detroit Free Press*, August 5, 1891.

19. *Detroit Free Press,* January 16, 1901; *Detroit News,* January 28, 1997.
20. *Detroit Free Press,* November 3, 2011.
21. *Detroit Free Press,* April 10, 1872.
22. Ibid.; Farmer, *History of Detroit,* 312. In 2005, the Soldiers' and Sailors' Monument was moved several hundred feet from its original location to its current home at Campus Martius Park. A rededication ceremony was held on April 9, 2005.

Bibliography

Manuscript and Archival Sources

Abbott, Samuel H. Papers. Michigan State University Archives & Historical Collections, Lansing.

Beers, Isaac. Letter. Bentley Historical Library, University of Michigan, Ann Arbor.

Bissell, Mary E. Diary. Burton Historical Collection, Detroit Public Library.

Brooks Family. Papers. Burton Historical Collection, Detroit Public Library.

Brown, Henry Billings. Diary. Burton Historical Collection, Detroit Public Library.

Brown, Immanuel. Papers. Burton Historical Collection, Detroit Public Library.

Burns, Robert. Letterbook. Minnesota Historical Society, St. Paul.

Campbell Family. Papers. Michigan State University Archives & Historical Collections, Lansing.

Campbell, James V. Papers. Bentley Historical Library, University of Michigan, Ann Arbor.

Catlin, George B. Papers. Burton Historical Collection, Detroit Public Library.

Chandler, Zachariah. Papers. Library of Congress, Manuscripts Division, Washington, D.C.

Civil War Vertical File—Contemporary Publications. Bentley Historical Library, University of Michigan, Ann Arbor.

Cleveland Family. Papers. Bentley Historical Library, University of Michigan, Ann Arbor.

Converse, George D. Papers. Bentley Historical Library, University of Michigan, Ann Arbor.

Custer, George Armstrong. Letter. Bentley Historical Library, University of Michigan, Ann Arbor.

Davis, Mary P. Letters. Bentley Historical Library, University of Michigan, Ann Arbor.

Digest Journal of Detroit Common Council, 1856–62. Burton Historical Collection, Detroit Public Library.

Douglass, Samuel T. Papers. Burton Historical Collection, Detroit Public Library.

Farr, George. "My Own Life." Michigan State University Archives & Historical Collections, Lansing.

Flanagan, J. W. Collection. Albert and Ethel Herzstein Library, San Jacinto Museum of History, La Porte, Tex.

Gross, Frank. Diary. Bentley Historical Library, University of Michigan, Ann Arbor.

Harper Hospital. Records. Walter P. Reuther Library, Wayne State University, Detroit.

Holmes, Edwin. Papers. Michigan State University Archives & Historical Collections, Lansing.

Humphrey, Willis C. Papers. Burton Historical Collection, Detroit Public Library.

Ladies Army Committee of the Christian Commission (Detroit). Circular. Clarke Historical Library, Central Michigan University, Mt. Pleasant.

Lincoln, Abraham. Papers. Manuscripts Division, Library of Congress, Washington, D.C.

Look Family. Papers. Bentley Historical Library, University of Michigan, Ann Arbor.

McClelland, Robert. Papers. Bentley Historical Library, University of Michigan, Ann Arbor.

Montgomery, Thomas S. "Eleven Months Experience in a Rebel Prison." Clarke Historical Library, Central Michigan University, Mt. Pleasant.

Quinn, Andrew S. "The Detroit Riot of 1863: Racial Violence and Internal Division in Northern Society during the Civil War." Bentley Historical Library, University of Michigan, Ann Arbor.

Randall, William H. Reminiscences. Bentley Historical Library, University of Michigan, Ann Arbor.

Records of the Office of the Quartermaster General. Record Group 92. National Archives, Washington, D.C.

Records of the Provost Marshal General's Bureau. Record Group 110. National Archives, Chicago.

Records of U.S. Army Continental Commands, 1821–1920. Record Group 393. National Archives, Washington, D.C.

Regimental Service Records, 1861–65. Michigan Adjutant-General's Department, Archives of Michigan, Lansing.

Returns from U.S. Military Posts, 1800–1916. Microfilm M617. National Archives, Washington, D.C.

Sadler, Silas W. Correspondence. Bentley Historical Library, University of Michigan, Ann Arbor.

Shaffer, George T. Papers. Bentley Historical Library, University of Michigan, Ann Arbor.

Slafter Family. Papers. Michigan State University Archives & Historical Collections, Lansing.

Smith, Gordon. Collection. Archives of Michigan, Lansing.

Smith, Joseph Rowe. Family Papers. Clarke Historical Library, Central Michigan University, Mt. Pleasant.

Smith, Joseph Rowe. Papers. Burton Historical Collection, Detroit Public Library.

Spalding Family. Papers. Bentley Historical Library, University of Michigan, Ann Arbor.

Spalding, Wilbur. Letters and Diary. Bentley Historical Library, University of Michigan, Ann Arbor.

St. Mary's Hospital Records. Burton Historical Collection, Detroit Public Library.

Thornton Blackburn Fugitive Slave Case File. Archives of Michigan, Lansing.

Tuttle, Joseph J. Papers. William J. Clements Library, University of Michigan, Ann Arbor.

Wallace, Elmer D. Papers. Bentley Historical Library, University of Michigan, Ann Arbor.

White, Gardner L. Papers. Burton Historical Collection, Detroit Public Library.

Wright, Fannie. Diary. Wright Family Papers. Bentley Historical Library, University of Michigan, Ann Arbor.

Zug, Robert M. Papers. Burton Historical Collection, Detroit Public Library.

CITY, STATE, AND FEDERAL GOVERNMENT DOCUMENTS

Bureau of the Census Library. *Population of the United States in 1860: Compiled from the Original Returns of the Eighth Census.* Washington, D.C.: Government Printing Office, 1864.

City of Detroit. *Journal of the Common Council of the City of Detroit: From the Time of Its First Organization.* Detroit: City of Detroit, 1824–.

Fuller, George N. *The Economic and Social Beginnings of Michigan.* Lansing: Wynkoop Hallenbeck Crawford, 1916.

State of Michigan. *Annual Report of the Adjutant General of the State of Michigan for the Year 1863.* Lansing: John A. Kerr, 1864.

———. *Annual Report of the Adjutant General of the State of Michigan for the Year 1864.* Lansing: John A. Kerr, 1865.

———. *Annual Report of the Quarter-Master General, 1861.* Lansing, 1862.

———. *Journal of the House of Representatives of the State of Michigan, Extra Session 1864.* Lansing: John A. Kerr, 1864.

———. *Journal of the Senate of the State of Michigan, Extra Session 1864.* Lansing: John A. Kerr, 1864.

———. *Journal of the Senate of the State of Michigan, Extra Session 1871.* Lansing: W. S. George and Co., 1871.

U.S. Army. *Trial of John Y. Beall: As a Spy and Guerrillero, by Military Commission.* New York: D. Appleton, 1865.

U.S. Bureau of Labor. *Report on Condition of Women and Child Wage-Earners in the United States.* 19 vols. Washington, D.C.: Government Printing Office, 1910.

U.S. Congress. *Journal of the Senate.* Washington, D.C.: Government Printing Office, 1789–.

———. "Report of the Secretary of War," In *Message of the President of the United States and Accompanying Documents to the Two Houses of Congress.* Washington, D.C: Government Printing Office, 1863.

U.S. War Department. *Official Records of the Union and Confederate Navies in the War of the Rebellion.* 30 vols. Washington, D.C.: Government Printing Office, 1894–1922.

———. *The War of the Rebellion: A Compilation of the Official Records of the Union and Confederate Armies.* 128 vols. Washington, D.C.: Government Printing Office, 1881–1902.

NEWSPAPERS

Calhoun County (Mi.) Patriot
Detroit Advertiser and Tribune
Detroit Courier
Detroit Daily Advertiser
Detroit Free Press
Detroit Journal and Advertiser
Detroit Tribune
New York Times
Richmond Whig

DISSERTATIONS AND THESES

Book, Carol A. "Michigan Rescues Its Boys: A Study of Michigan's Efforts during the Civil War to Supply Its Citizen Soldiers When the Federal Government Failed." M.A. thesis, Oakland University, 1995.

Dunn, William. "A History of the First Michigan Colored Infantry." M.A. thesis, Central Michigan University, 1967.

Emmer, Dorothy. "The Civil and Political Status of the Negro in Michigan and the Northwest Before 1870." M.A. thesis, Wayne University, 1935.

Gibson, Guy James. "Lincoln's League: The Union League Movement during the Civil War." Ph.D. diss., University of Illinois, 1957.

Kautz, Craig L. "Fodder for Cannon: Immigrant Perceptions of the Civil War—The Old Northwest." Ph.D. diss., University of Nebraska, 1976.

McRae, Norman. "Blacks in Detroit, 1736–1833: The Search for Freedom and Community and Its Implications for Educators." Ph.D. diss., University of Michigan, 1982.

Parkins, Almon E. "The Historical Geography of Detroit." Ph.D. diss., University of Chicago, 1918.

Raney, William F. "The Diplomatic and Military Activities of Canada, 1861–1865, As Affected by the American Civil War." Ph.D. diss., University of Wisconsin, 1919.

Skavery, Stanley. "A Case Study of the Irish in Detroit, 1850–1880." Ed.D. diss., University of Michigan, 1986.

Smith, Earl O. "The Public Life of Austin Blair, War Governor of Michigan." M.A. thesis, Wayne University, 1934.

Spiro, Robert. "History of the Michigan Soldiers' Aid Society, 1861–1865." Ph.D. diss., University of Michigan, 1959.

Sterling, Robert E. "Civil War Draft Resistance in the Middle West." Ph.D. diss., Northern Illinois University, 1974.

Woodson, June B. "A Century with the Negroes of Detroit, 1830–1930." M.A. thesis, Wayne University, 1949.

PUBLISHED PRIMARY SOURCES

Adams, Lois Bryan. *Letter from Washington, 1863–1865.* Detroit: Wayne State University Press, 1999.

Basler, Roy, ed. *Collected Works of Abraham Lincoln.* 8 vols. New Brunswick, N.J.: Rutgers University Press, 1953.

Benjamin, L. N., comp. *The St. Albans Raid; or, Investigations into the Charges against Lieut. Bennett H. Young and Command.* Montreal: John Lovell, 1865.

Brockway, Zebulon Reed. *Fifty Years of Prison Service: An Autobiography.* New York: Country Life, 1912.

Brodda, O. A. "Letter to the Editor." *Bridgemen's Magazine,* July 1903, 21.

Brunner, J. H. "In Detroit When Lincoln Was Assassinated." *Confederate Veteran* 6 (1898).

Bush, David R., ed. *"I Fear I Shall Never Leave This Island": Life in a Civil War Prison.* Gainesville: University Press of Florida, 2011.

Carpenter, Horace. "Plain Living at Johnson's Island." In *Battles and Leaders of the Civil War,* vol. 6, edited by Peter Cozzens. Urbana: University of Illinois Press, 2004.

Chancellor, Christopher, ed. *An Englishman in the American Civil War: The Diaries of Henry Yates Thompson.* London: Sidgwick & Jackson, 1971.

Clowes, Walter F. *The Detroit Light Guard: A Complete Record of This Organization from Its Foundation to the Present Day.* Detroit: John F. Eby, 1900.

Cox, Jacob D. *Military Reminiscences of the Civil War.* 2 vols. New York: Charles Scribner's Sons, 1900.

Curtis, Orson B. *History of the Twenty-fourth Michigan of the Iron Brigade.* Detroit: Winn & Hammond, 1891.

Elderkin, James D. *Biographical Sketches and Anecdotes of a Soldier of Three Wars as Written by Himself.* Detroit: privately printed, 1899.

Fuller, George N., ed. *Messages of the Governors of Michigan.* Vol. 2. Lansing: Michigan Historical Commission, 1926.

Glaza-Herrington, Linda. *Dear Brother and Sister: Smith-Haviland-Cadwell Fourth Michigan Infantry Civil War Letters.* N.p.: privately printed, 2012.

Granger, L. W. *Wide-Awake! Romanism: Its Aims and Tendencies. The Sentiments of a "Know-Nothing."* Detroit: privately printed, 1854.

Harper Hospital Board of Trustees. *The Constitution and Rules of the Harper Hospital Together with the Report and Statement of the Trustees.* Detroit: William Graham, 1866.

Harris, Robert S., and Terry G. Harris, eds. *The Eldon House Diaries: Five Women's Views of the 19th Century.* Toronto: Champlain Society, 1994.

Harris, Samuel. *Personal Reminiscences of Samuel Harris.* Chicago: Rogerson, 1897.

Headley, John W. *Confederate Operations in Canada and New York.* New York: Neale, 1906.

Hewett, Janet B., ed. *Supplement to the Official Records of the Union and Confederate Armies.* 100 vols. Wilmington, N.C.: Broadfoot, 1994–2001.

Hodge, Robert W., ed. *The Civil War Letters of Perry Mayo.* East Lansing: Michigan State University Museum, 1967.

Husby, Karla Jean, comp., and Eric J. Wittenberg, ed. *Under Custer's Command: The Civil War Journal of James Henry Avery.* Dulles, Va.: Potomac Books, 2006.

Johnston's 1861 Detroit City Directory and Advertising Gazetteer. Detroit: James Dale Johnston, 1861.

Jones, George H., ed. *A Northern Confederate at Johnson's Island Prison: The Civil War Diaries of James Parks Caldwell.* Jefferson, N.C.: McFarland, 2010.

Kamphoefner, Walter D., and Wolfgang Helbich, eds. *Germans in the Civil War: The Letters They Wrote Home.* Chapel Hill: University of North Carolina Press, 2006.

Kidd, J. H. *Personal Recollections of a Cavalryman.* Ionia, Mich.: Sentinel, 1908.

Lassen, Coralou Peel, ed. *Dear Sarah: Letters Home from a Soldier of the Iron Brigade.* Bloomington: Indiana University Press, 1999.

Laugel, Auguste. *The United States during the War.* New York: Bailliere Brothers, 1866.

Lodge, John C. *I Remember Detroit.* Detroit: Wayne University Press, 1949.

Lucas, Daniel B., and John Y. Beall. *Memoir of John Yates Beall: His Life; Trial; Correspondence; Diary; and Private Manuscript Found among His Papers, Including His Own Account of the Raid on Lake Erie.* Montreal, Canada: John Lovell, 1865.

Marlatt, Helen S. M., ed. *Stuart Letters of Robert and Elizabeth Sullivan Stuart and Their Children, 1819–1864.* 2 vols. N.p.: privately printed, 1961.

Middleton, Stephen *The Black Laws in the Old Northwest: A Documentary History.* Westport, Conn.: Greenwood, 1993.

Moore, Frank, ed. *The Rebellion Record: A Diary of American Events.* 12 vols. New York: G. P. Putnam, 1861–65.

Moss, Lemuel. *Annals of the United States Christian Commission.* Philadelphia: J. P. Lippincott, 1868.

Paddock, Benjamin H. *Our Cause, Our Confidence and Our Consequent Duty: A Sermon Preached in Christ Church, Detroit, Sunday After Ascension, May 12th, 1861, before Company A, First Regiment Michigan Volunteers.* Detroit: Daily Advertiser Steam Power, 1861.

Palmer, Friend. *Early Days in Detroit.* Detroit: Hunt & June, 1906.

Pelka, Fred, ed. *The Civil War Letters of Colonel Charles F. Johnson, Invalid Corps.* Amherst: University of Massachusetts Press, 2004.

Phillips, George M. "Johnson's Island and the Lake Erie Raid of 1864." In *Glimpses of the Nation's Struggle: Minnesota MOLLUS,* vol. 3. 1893. Reprint, Wilmington, N.C.: Broadfoot, 1992.

Pisani, Camille Ferri. *Prince Napoleon in America, 1861.* Bloomington: Indiana University Press, 1959.

Quaife, Milo M., ed. *From the Cannon's Mouth: The Civil War Letters of General Alpheus S. Williams.* Detroit: Wayne State University Press, 1959.

Quinby, William. "Reminiscences of Michigan Journalism." *Collections of the Michigan Pioneer and Historical Society* 30 (1906): 507–17.

Richards, T. Addison. *Appleton's Illustrated Hand-book of American Travel.* New York: D. Appleton, 1861.

Roberts, Robert E. *Sketches and Reminiscences of the City of the Straits and Its Vicinity.* Detroit: Free Press Job and Book Printing House, 1884.

Robertson, John. "Brief Military History of Michigan as a Territory and a State." In *The Semi-centennial of the Admission of the State of Michigan into the Union.* N.p.: Detroit Free Press, 1886.

Rowe, James D. *Camp Notes of a Union Soldier.* N.p.: privately printed, [1912].

Scott, Robert Garth, ed. *Forgotten Valor: The Memoirs, Journals and Civil War Letters of Orlando B. Willcox.* Kent, Ohio: Kent State University Press, 1999.

Sears, Stephen, ed. *For Country, Cause and Leader: The Civil War Journal of Charles B. Haydon.* New York: Ticknor & Fields, 1993.

"Selections from the Doolittle Correspondence." *Publications of the Southern History Association* 11 (March 1907): 94–105.

Simon, John Y., ed. *The Papers of Ulysses S. Grant.* 30 vols. Carbondale: Southern Illinois University Press, 1967–2009.

Smith, George Winston, and Charles Judah. *Life in the North during the Civil War: A Source History.* Albuquerque: University of New Mexico Press, 1966.

A Thrilling Narrative from the Lips of the Sufferers of the Late Detroit Riot, March 6, 1863, with the Hair Breadth Escapes of Men, Women and Children, *and Destruction of Colored Men's Property, Not Less Than $15,000.* Detroit: privately printed, 1863.

Tripler, Eunice. *Eunice Tripler: Some Notes of Her Personal Recollections.* New York: Grafton, 1910.

Trowbridge, Charles C. *Circular. Detroit, February 26, 1847: Sir: at an Adjourned Meeting of the Citizens of Detroit, Held on the 25th Instant, the Undersigned Were Appointed an Executive Committee, to Address Their Fellow Citizens . . . in Behalf of the Suffering Poor of Ireland.* Detroit: privately printed, 1847.

U.S. Christian Commission. *Works and Incidents: First Annual Report.* Philadelphia: privately printed, 1864.

Webb, William. *The History of William Webb, Composed by Himself.* Detroit: Egbert Hoekstra, 1873.

Wells, James M. *With Touch of Elbow, or Death Before Dishonor.* Philadelphia: John C. Winston, 1909.

Williams, Newton H. *Michigan First Regiment: Incidents, Marches, Battles and Camp Life.* Detroit: privately printed, 1861.

Withington, W. H. "Michigan in the Opening of the War." In *War Papers Read before the Commandery of the State of Michigan, Military Order of the Loyal Legion of the United States,* vol. 1. Detroit: Winn & Hammond, 1893.

Wood, Bert D. *Franklin's Yesteryear.* Ann Arbor, Mich.: Edwards Brothers, 1958.

Yacovone, Donald, ed. *Freedom's Journey: African American Voices of the Civil War.* Chicago: Lawrence Hill Books, 2004.

PUBLISHED SECONDARY SOURCES

Adams, George Worthington. *Doctors in Blue: The Medical History of the Union Army in the Civil War.* 1952. Reprint, Baton Rouge: Louisiana State University Press, 1996.

Andrews, John B., and W. D. P. Bliss. *History of Women in Trade Unions.* 1911. Reprint, New York: Arno, 1974.

Angelo, Frank. *On Guard: A History of the Detroit Free Press.* Detroit: Detroit Free Press, 1981.

Annual Reunion of the Association of the Graduates of the United States Military Academy. East Saginaw, Mich.: Evening News, 1886.

Babson, Steve. *Working Detroit: The Making of a Union Town.* New York: Adama Books, 1984.

Bahde, Thomas. " 'Our Cause is a Common One': Home Guards, Union Leagues, and Republican Citizenship in Illinois, 1861–1863." *Civil War History* 56, no. 1 (2010): 66–98.

Baker, Jean H. *Affairs of Party: The Political Culture of Northern Democrats in the Mid-Nineteenth Century.* Ithaca, N.Y.: Cornell University Press, 1983.

Baron, Ava, and Susan E. Klepp. " 'If I Didn't Have My Sewing Machine . . .': Women and Sewing Machine Technology." In *A Needle, a Bobbin, a Strike:*

Women Needleworkers in America, edited by Joan M. Jensen and Sue Davidson. Philadelphia: Temple University Press, 1984.

Billington, Ray Allen. *The Protestant Crusade, 1800–1860: A Study of the Origins of American Nativism*. 1938. Reprint, Gloucester, Mass.: Peter Smith, 1963.

Blum, Albert A., and Dan Georgakas. *Michigan Labor and the Civil War*. Lansing: Michigan Civil War Centennial Observance Commission, 1964.

Brockett, Linus P., and Mary C. Vaughan. *Woman's Work in the Civil War: A Record of Heroism, Patriotism and Patience*. Philadelphia: Zeigler, McCurdy, 1867.

Brown, Ida C. *Michigan Men in the Civil War*. Ann Arbor: University of Michigan, 1959.

Bukovac, Janice L. "The Michigan Democratic Press and the Fifteenth Amendment: A Divided Party United." In *The Civil War and the Press*. New Brunswick, N.J.: Transaction, 2000.

Burton, Clarence M., ed. *The City of Detroit, Michigan, 1701–1922*. Detroit: S. J. Clarke, 1922.

Campbell, Helen. *Prisoners of Poverty: Women Wage Workers, Their Trades and Their Lives*. Boston: Little, Brown, 1900.

Campbell, Stanley. *The Slave Catchers: Enforcement of the Fugitive Slave Law, 1850–1860*. Chapel Hill: University of North Carolina Press, 1968.

"Captain Eber B. Ward's Fortress: An Untold Chapter of Civil War Times in Detroit." *Detroit Monthly*, May 1901, 20–21.

Cashin, Joan E. "Deserters, Civilians, and Draft Resistance in the North." In *The War Was You and Me: Civilians in the American Civil War*, edited by Joan E. Cashin. Princeton, N.J.: Princeton University Press, 2002.

Castellanos, Jorge. "Black Slavery in Detroit." *Detroit in Perspective: A Journal of Regional History* 7, no. 2 (1983).

Catlin, George B. *The Story of Detroit*. Detroit: Detroit News, 1926.

Chambers, Ernest J. *The Origin and Services of the Prince of Wales Regiment*. Montreal E. L. Ruddy, 1897.

Cimbala, Paul A. "Soldiering on the Home Front: The Veteran Reserve Corps and the Northern People." In *Union Soldiers and the Northern Home Front: Wartime Experiences, Postwar Adjustments*, edited by Paul A. Cimbala and Randall M. Miller. New York: Fordham University Press, 2002.

Clinton, Catherine. *The Other Civil War: American Women in the Nineteenth Century*. 1984. Reprint, New York: Hill & Wang, 1999.

Coakley, Robert W. *The Role of Federal Military Forces in Domestic Disorders, 1789–1878*. 1988. Reprint, Darby, Pa.: Diane, 1996.

Coffman, Edward M. *The Old Army: A Portrait of the American Army in Peacetime, 1784–1898*. New York: Oxford University Press, 1988.

Coleman, Charles H. "The Use of the Term 'Copperhead' during the Civil War." *Mississippi Valley Historical Review* 25 (1938): 263–64.

Conway, James, and David Jamroz. *Detroit's Historic Fort Wayne*. Mt. Pleasant, S.C.: Arcadia, 2007.

Crathern, Alice. *In Detroit . . . Courage Was the Fashion: The Contributions of Women to the Development of Detroit from 1701 to 1951*. Detroit: Wayne State University Press, 1953.

Dain, Floyd Russell. *Every House a Frontier: Detroit's Economic Progress, 1815–1825*. Detroit: Wayne State University Press, 1956.

Deskins, Donald R., Jr. *Residential Mobility of Negroes in Detroit, 1837–1965*. Ann Arbor: University of Michigan, 1972.

Dilla, Harriette M. *The Politics of Michigan, 1865–1878*. New York: Columbia University Press, 1912.

Dillon, Ruby. "A Woman's Place." In *Michigan Women in the Civil War*. Lansing: Michigan Civil War Centennial Observance Commission, 1963.

Diner, Hasia R. *Erin's Daughters in America: Irish Immigrant Women in the Nineteenth Century*. Baltimore, Md.: Johns Hopkins University Press, 1983.

Douglass, R. Alan. *Uppermost Canada: The Western District and the Detroit Frontier, 1800–1850*. Detroit: Wayne State University Press, 2001.

Driscoll, John K. *Rogue: A Biography of Civil War General Justus McKinstry*. Jefferson, N.C.: McFarland, 2005.

DuBois, W. E. B. *Black Reconstruction in America, 1860–1880*. 1935. Reprint, New York: Free Press, 1998.

Dunbar, Willis F., and George S. May. *Michigan: A History of the Wolverine State*. 3rd rev. ed. Grand Rapids, Mich.: William B. Eerdmans, 1995.

Farmer, Silas. *History of Detroit and Wayne County and Early Michigan*. 3rd ed. Detroit: Silas Farmer, 1890.

Ferrie, Joseph P. *Yankeys Now: Immigrants in the Antebellum United States, 1840–1860*. New York: Oxford University Press, 1999.

Fite, Emerson D. *Social and Industrial Conditions in the North during the Civil War*. 1909. Reprint, New York: Frederick Ungar, 1963.

Flom, George T. "Early Swedish Immigration to Iowa." *Iowa Journal of History and Politics* 3, no. 4 (1905): 583–615.

Foner, Eric. "The Ideology of the Republican Party." In *The Birth of the Grand Old Party: The Republican's First Generation*, edited by Robert F. Engs and Randall M. Miller. Philadelphia: University of Pennsylvania Press, 2002.

Foner, Philip S. *Women and the American Labor Movement: From Colonial Times to the Eve of World War I*. New York: Free Press, 1979.

Foreman, Amanda. *A World on Fire: An Epic History of Two Nations Divided*. London: Allen Lane, 2010.

Formisano, Ronald P. *The Birth of Mass Political Parties: Michigan, 1827–1861*. Princeton, N.J.: Princeton University Press, 1971.

Freedman, Estelle B. *Their Sisters' Keepers: Women's Prison Reform in America, 1830–1930*. 1981. Reprint, Ann Arbor: University of Michigan Press, 1984.

Freidel, Frank, ed. *Union Pamphlets of the Civil War, 1861–1865*. 2 vols. Cambridge, Mass.: Harvard University Press, 1967.

Geary, James W. *We Need Men: The Union Draft in the Civil War*. DeKalb: Northern Illinois University Press, 1991.

George, Mary Karl. *Zachariah Chandler: A Political Biography.* East Lansing: Michigan State University Press, 1969.

Giesberg, Judith. *Army at Home: Women and the Civil War on the Northern Home Front.* Chapel Hill: University of North Carolina Press, 2009.

———. *Civil War Sisterhood: The U.S. Sanitary Commission and Women's Politics in Transition.* Ithaca, N.Y.: Northeastern University Press, 2000.

Gilbert, Olive, and Francis Titus. *Narrative of Sojourner Truth: A Bondswoman of Olden Time.* Boston: privately printed, 1875.

Gilpin, Alec R. *The Territory of Michigan, 1805–1837.* Lansing: Michigan State University Press, 1970.

Goodwin, Doris Kearns. *Team of Rivals: The Political Genius of Abraham Lincoln.* New York: Simon & Schuster, 2005.

Gould, Lewis L. *Grand Old Party: A History of the Republicans.* New York: Random House, 2003.

Gray, Susan E. *The Yankee West: Community Life on the Michigan Frontier.* Chapel Hill: University of North Carolina Press, 1996.

Gray, Wood. *The Peace Movement in the Old Northwest, 1860–1865: A Study in Defeatism.* Chicago: University of Chicago Libraries, 1935.

Grimsted, David. *American Mobbing, 1828–1861: Toward Civil War.* New York: Oxford University Press, 1998.

Grossman, Jonathan. *William Sylvis, Pioneer of American Labor.* New York: Columbia University Press, 1945.

Hamer, Marguerite. "Luring Canadian Soldiers into Union Lines during the War between the States." *Canadian Historical Review* 27, no. 2 (1946): 150–62.

Hansen, Marcus Lee, and John B. Brebner. *The Mingling of the Canadian and American Peoples.* Vol. 1. 1941. Reprint, New York: Arno, 1970.

Hargrove, Hondon. "Their Greatest Battle Was Getting into the Fight: The Michigan Colored Infantry Goes to War." *Michigan History* 75, no. 1 (1991): 24–30.

Harper, Judith E. *Women during the Civil War: An Encyclopedia.* New York: Routledge, 2007.

Havran, Martin J. "Windsor and Detroit Relations during the Civil War." *Michigan History* 38 (December 1954): 371–89.

Hawthorne, Frank W. *The Episcopal Church in Michigan during the Civil War.* Detroit: Wayne State University Press, 1966.

Hebert, Walter H. *Fighting Joe Hooker.* Indianapolis: Bobbs-Merrill, 1944.

Herek, Raymond J. *These Men Have Seen Hard Service: The First Michigan Sharpshooters in the Civil War.* Detroit: Wayne State University Press, 1998.

Hershock, Martin J. *The Paradox of Progress: Economic Change, Individual Enterprise, and Political Culture in Michigan, 1837–1878.* Athens: Ohio University Press, 2003.

Hicks, Obadiah. *Life of Richard F. Trevellick.* 1896. Reprint, New York: Arno, 1971.

Hinton, Richard J. *John Brown and His Men.* New York: Funk & Wagnalls, 1894.

Holli, Melvin G. *Reform in Detroit: Hazen S. Pingee and Urban Politics.* New York: Oxford University Press, 1969.

Holliday, Carl. *Woman's Life in Colonial Days.* Boston: Cornhill, 1922.

Holt, Marilyn. *The Orphan Trains: Placing Out in America.* Lincoln: University of Nebraska Press, 1992.

Holt, Michael F. *The Rise and Fall of the American Whig Party.* New York: Oxford University Press, 1999.

Hoy, Claire. *Canadians in the Civil War.* Toronto: McArthur, 2004.

Hubbart, Henry C. *The Older Middle West, 1840–1880.* New York: D. Appleton-Century, 1936.

Hutter, W. H., and Ray H. Abrams. "Copperhead Newspapers and the Negro." *Journal of Negro History* 20, no. 2 (1935): 131–52.

Hyde, Charles K. *Detroit: An Industrial History Guide.* Detroit: Detroit Historical Society, 1980.

Isham, Frederic S., comp. *History of the Detroit Light Guard: Its Record and Achievements.* Detroit: privately printed, 1896.

Jacobson, Matthew Frye. *Whiteness of a Different Color: European Immigrants and the Alchemy of Race.* Cambridge, Mass.: Harvard University Press, 1998.

Jimerson, Randall C. *The Private Civil War: Popular Thought during the Sectional Conflict.* 1988. Reprint, Baton Rouge, Louisiana State University Press, 1994.

Kaplan, Richard L. *Politics and the American Press: The Rise of Objectivity, 1865–1920.* New York: Cambridge University Press, 2002.

Katz, Irving I. *The Jewish Soldier from Michigan in the Civil War.* Detroit: Wayne State University Press, 1962.

Katz, William Loren, ed. *Anti-Negro Riots in the North, 1863.* New York: Arno, 1969.

Katzman, David M. *Before the Ghetto: Black Detroit in the Nineteenth Century.* Urbana: University of Illinois Press, 1975.

Kenny, Kevin. *The American Irish: A History.* New York: Pearson Education, 2000.

K.G.C.: An Authentic Exposition of the Origin, Objects, and Secret Work of the Organization Known as the Knights of the Golden Circle. N.p., Ky.: U.S. National U.C., 1862.

Klement, Frank L. "Civil War Politics, Nationalism, and Postwar Myths." In *Lincoln's Critics: The Copperheads of the North,* edited by Steven K. Rogstad. Shippensburg, Pa.: White Mane, 1999.

———. "Clement L. Vallandigham's Exile in the Confederacy, May 25–June 17, 1863." *Journal of Southern History* 31, no. 2 (1965): 149–63.

———. *Dark Lanterns: Secret Political Societies, Conspiracies, and Treason Trials in the Civil War.* Baton Rouge: Louisiana State University Press, 1984.

———. "The Hopkins Hoax and Golden Circle Rumors in Michigan: 1861–1862." *Michigan History* 47, no. 1 (1963): 1–14.

———. *The Limits of Dissent: Clement L. Vallandigham and the Civil War.* Lexington: University Press of Kentucky, 1970.

Klunder, Willard Carl. *Lewis Cass and the Politics of Moderation.* Kent, Ohio: Kent State University Press, 1996.

Knobel, Dale T. *Paddy and the Republic: Ethnicity and Nationality in Antebellum America.* Middletown, Conn.: Wesleyan University Press, 1986.

Kundinger, Matthew. "Racial Rhetoric: The *Detroit Free Press* and Its Part in the Detroit Race Riot of 1863." *Michigan Journal of History,* Winter 2006.

Landon, Fred. *Western Ontario and the American Frontier.* 1941. Reprint, New York: Russell & Russell, 1970.

Lanman, Charles. *The Red Book of Michigan: A Civil, Military, and Biographical History.* Detroit: E. B. Smith, 1870.

Leach, Jack F. *Conscription in the United States: Historical Background.* Rutland, Vt.: Charles E. Tuttle, 1952.

Leach, Nathaniel. *Second Baptist Church of Detroit: An Abbreviated History.* N.p., n.d.

Leake, Paul. *History of Detroit: A Chronicle of Its Progress, Its Industries, Its Institutions, and the People of the Fair City of the Straits.* 3 vols. Chicago: Lewis, 1912.

Lerner, Gerda. *The Majority Finds Its Past: Placing Women in History.* New York: Oxford University Press, 1979.

Lewis, Martin D. *Lumberman from Flint: The Michigan Career of Henry H. Crapo.* Detroit: Wayne State University Press, 1958.

Long, Clarence D. *Wages and Earnings in the United States, 1860–1890.* Princeton, N.J.: Princeton University Press, 1960.

Lowry, Thomas P. *Sexual Misbehavior in the Civil War: A Compendium.* Bloomington, Ind.: Xlibris, 2006.

———. *The Story the Soldiers Wouldn't Tell: Sex in the Civil War.* Mechanicsburg, Pa.: Stackpole Books, 1994.

Markovitz, Jonathan. *Legacies of Lynching: Racial Violence and Memory.* Minneapolis: University of Minnesota Press, 2004.

Martin, Edward G. *St. Mary's Hospital, 1845–1945.* Detroit: privately printed, 1945.

Massey, Mary Elizabeth. *Bonnet Brigades: American Women and the Civil War.* New York: Alfred A. Knopf, 1966.

May, George S. *Michigan and the Civil War Years, 1860–1865: A Wartime Chronicle.* Lansing: Michigan Centennial Civil War Observance Commission, 1964.

May, Samuel. *The Fugitive Slave Law and Its Victims.* New York: American Anti-Slavery Society, 1861.

McConnell, Stuart. *Glorious Contentment: The Grand Army of the Republic, 1865–1900.* Chapel Hill: University of North Carolina Press, 1992.

McPherson, James. "Battle Cry of Freedom." In *Justice: A Reader,* edited by Michael J. Sandel. New York: Oxford University Press, 2007.

———. *Tried by War: Abraham Lincoln as Commander in Chief.* New York: Penguin, 2008.

McRae, Norman. "Camp Ward, Detroit." *Detroit Historical Society Bulletin* 24, no. 8 (1968): 4–11.

———. *Negroes in Michigan during the Civil War.* Lansing: Michigan Civil War Centennial Observance Commission, 1966.

McTeer, Frances, and Minnie Dubbs Millbrook. "For Loved Ones Far Away." In *Michigan Women in the Civil War.* Lansing: Michigan Civil War Centennial Observance Commission, 1963.

Metress, Seamus P., and Eileen K. Metress. *Irish in Michigan.* East Lansing: Michigan State University Press, 2006.

Michigan State Administrative Board. *Michigan: A Guide to the Wolverine State.* New York: Oxford University Press, 1941.

Millis, Wade. "Fort Wayne, Detroit." *Michigan History* 20 (1936): 21–49.

Milton, George F. *Abraham Lincoln and the Fifth Column.* New York: Vanguard, 1942.

Mitchell, Robert E. "Civil War Recruiting and Recruits from Ever-Changing Labor Pools: Midland County, Michigan, as a Case Study." *Michigan Historical Review* 35, no. 1 (2009): 29–60.

Moehlman, Arthur B. *Public Education in Detroit.* 1925. Reprint, New York: Arno, 1974.

Moore, Charles. "The Days of Fife and Drum." *Collections of the Michigan Pioneer and Historical Society* 28 (1900): 437–53.

Morrison, Neil F. *Garden Gateway to Canada: One Hundred Years of Windsor and Essex County, 1854–1954.* Toronto: Ryerson, 1954.

Murdock, Eugene C. *One Million Men: The Civil War Draft in the North.* Madison: State Historical Society of Wisconsin, 1971.

———. *Patriotism Limited, 1862–1865: The Civil War Draft and the Bounty System.* Kent, Ohio: Kent State University Press, 1967.

Neely, Mark E., Jr. *The Union Divided: Party Conflict in the Civil War North.* Cambridge, Mass.: Harvard University Press, 2002.

Nevins, Allan. *The War for the Union: War Becomes Revolution, 1862–1863.* New York: Charles Scribner's Sons, 1960.

Newberry, J. S. *The U.S. Sanitary Commission in the Valley of the Mississippi during the War of the Rebellion, 1861–1866.* Cleveland: Fairbanks Benedict, 1871.

O'Geran, Graeme. *A History of the Detroit Street Railways.* Detroit: Conover, 1931.

Parker, William N. "From Northwest to Mid-west: Social Bases of a Regional History." In *Essays in Nineteenth Century Economic History: The Old Northwest,* edited by David C. Klingaman and Richard K. Vedder. Athens: Ohio University Press, 1975.

Pearson, Henry Greenleaf. *An American Railroad Builder, John Murray Forbes.* Boston: Houghton Mifflin, 1911.

Perlmann, Joel, and Robert A. Margo. *Women's Work? American Schoolteachers, 1650–1920.* Chicago: University of Chicago Press, 2001.

Prince, Cathryn J. *Burn the Town and Sack the Banks: Confederates Attack Vermont!* New York: Carroll & Graf, 2006.

Rable, George C. *God's Almost Chosen Peoples: A Religious History of the American Civil War.* Chapel Hill: University of North Carolina Press, 2010.

Rips, Rae Elizabeth, ed. *Detroit in Its World Setting: A 250-Year Chronology.* Detroit: Detroit Public Library, 1953.

Robertson, John, comp. *Michigan in the War.* Lansing: W. S. George, 1882.

Roediger, David R. *The Wages of Whiteness: Race and the Making of the American Working Class.* 1991. Reprint, New York: Verso Books, 2007.

Rogers, Bradley A. *Guardian of the Lakes: The U.S. Paddle Frigate Michigan.* Ann Arbor: University of Michigan Press, 1996.

Romero, Mary. *Maid in the U.S.A.* New York: Routledge, 2002.

Ross, Robert B., and George B. Catlin. *Landmarks of Detroit.* Detroit: Evening News Association, 1898.

Rubenstein, Bruce A., and Lawrence E. Ziewacz. *Michigan: A History of the Great Lakes State.* 3rd ed. Wheeling, Ill.: Harlan Davidson, 2002.

Russell, John A. *The Germanic Influence in the Making of Michigan.* Detroit: University of Detroit Press, 1927.

Rutkow, Ira M. *Bleeding Blue and Gray: Civil War Surgery and the Evolution of American Medicine.* New York: Random House, 2005.

Sandburg, Carl. *Abraham Lincoln: The War Years.* Vol. 2. New York: Harcourt, Brace, 1939.

Sanders, Charles W., Jr. *While in the Hands of the Enemy: Military Prisons of the Civil War.* Baton Rouge: Louisiana State University Press, 2005.

Schecter, Barnet. *The Devil's Own Work: The Civil War Draft Riots and the Fight to Reconstruct America.* New York: Walker, 2005.

Schneider, John C. *Detroit and the Problem of Order, 1830–1880.* Lincoln: University of Nebraska Press, 1980.

———. "Urbanization and the Maintenance of Order: Detroit, 1824–1847." In *Institutional Life: Family, Schools, Race and Religion.* American Cities: A Collection of Essays, vol. 8. Edited by Neil Larry Shumsky. New York: Garland, 1996.

Schramm, Jack E., and William H. Henning. *Detroit's Street Railways,* vol. 1, *City Lines, 1863–1922.* Chicago: Central Electric Railfans' Association, 1978.

Shannon, Fred A. *The Organization and Administration of the Union Army 1861–1865.* 2 vols. Cleveland: Arthur H. Clark, 1928.

Silber, Nina. *Daughters of the Union: Northern Women Fight the Civil War.* Cambridge, Mass.: Harvard University Press, 2005.

Silbey, Joel H. *A Respectable Minority: The Democratic Party in the Civil War Era, 1860–1868.* New York: W. W. Norton & Co., 1977.

Silvestro, Clement M. *Rally round the Flag: The Union Leagues in the Civil War.* Ann Arbor: Historical Society of Michigan, 1966.

Skelton, William B. *An American Profession of Arms: The Army Officer Corps, 1784–1861.* Lawrence: University Press of Kansas, 1992.

Smith, Michael O. "Raising a Black Regiment in Michigan: Adversity and Triumph." In *A Question of Manhood: A Reader in U.S. Black Men's History and Masculinity,* edited by Darlene C. Hine and Earnestine L. Jenkins, vol. 1. Bloomington: Indiana University Press, 1999.

Snell, J. G. "H. H. Emmons, Detroit's Agent in Canadian-American Relations, 1864–1866." *Michigan History* 56, no. 4 (1972): 302–18.

Streeter, Floyd. *Political Parties in Michigan, 1837–1860.* Lansing: Michigan Historical Commission, 1918.

Sumner, Helen L. *History of Women in Industry in the United States.* 1910. Reprint, New York: Arno, 1974.

Swanson, Clifford L. *The Sixth United States Infantry: 1855 to Reconstruction.* Jefferson, N.C.: McFarland, 2001.

Tentler, Leslie Woodcock. *Seasons of Grace: A History of the Catholic Archdiocese of Detroit.* Detroit: Wayne State University Press, 1990.

Thomas, Richard W. *Life for Us Is What We Make It: Building Black Community in Detroit, 1915–1945.* Bloomington: Indiana University Press, 1992.

Thompson, Jerry. *Civil War to the Bloody End: The Life and Times of Major General Samuel P. Heintzelman.* College Station: Texas A&M University Press, 2006.

Thornton, Mark, and Robert B. Ekelund Jr. *Tariffs, Blockades, and Inflation: The Economics of the Civil War.* Wilmington, Del.: Scholarly Resources, 2004.

Tidwell, William A. *April '65: Confederate Covert Action in the American Civil War.* Kent, Ohio: Kent State University Press.

U.S. Military Academy, Association of Graduates. *Annual Reunion, 1885.* East Saginaw, Mich: Evening News, 1885.

Utley, Henry M., and Byron M. Cutcheon. *Michigan as a Province, Territory and State, the Twenty-sixth Member of the Federal Union.* Vol. 3. New York: Publishing Society of Michigan, 1906.

Vander Hill, C. Warren. *Settling the Great Lakes Frontier: Immigration to Michigan, 1837–1924.* Lansing: Michigan Historical Commission, 1970.

Vinyard, JoEllen McNergney. *For Faith and Fortune: The Education of Catholic Immigrants in Detroit, 1805–1925.* Urbana: University of Illinois Press, 1998.

———. *Irish on the Urban Frontier: Nineteenth Century Detroit, 1850–1880.* New York: Arno, 1976.

Voegeli, V. Jacque. *Free but Not Equal: The Midwest and the Negro during the Civil War.* Chicago: University of Chicago Press, 1967.

Volo, Dorothy D., and James M. Volo. *Daily Life in Civil War America.* Westport, Conn.: Greenwood, 1998.

Walsh, Justin E. *"To Print the News and Raise Hell!" A Biography of Wilbur F. Storey.* Chapel Hill: University of North Carolina Press, 1968.

Warner, Ezra J. *Generals in Blue.* Baton Rouge: Louisiana State University Press, 1964.

Wayne County Historical and Pioneer Society. *Chronography of Notable Events in the History of the Northwest Territory and Wayne County.* Detroit: O. S. Gulley, Bornman, 1890.

Weber, Jennifer L. *Copperheads: The Rise and Fall of Lincoln's Opponents in the North.* New York: Oxford University Press, 2006.

Weddon, Willah. *Michigan Governors: Their Life Stories.* Lansing: NOG, 1994.

Wibberly, Leonard P. O. *The Coming of the Green.* New York: Henry Holt, 1958.

Wilson, Brian C. *Yankees in Michigan.* East Lansing: Michigan State University Press, 2008.

Wilson, Mark R. *The Business of Civil War: Military Mobilization and the State, 1861–1865.* Baltimore, Md.: Johns Hopkins University Press, 2006.

Winks, Robin W. *The Blacks in Canada: A History.* New Haven, Conn.: Yale University Press, 1971.

———. *Canada and the United States: The Civil War Years.* Baltimore, Md.: Johns Hopkins University Press, 1960.

Wood, Forrest G. *Black Scare: The Racist Response to Emancipation and Reconstruction.* Berkeley: University of California Press, 1968.

Woodford, Arthur M. *Detroit and Its Banks: The Story of Detroit Bank & Trust.* Detroit: Wayne State University Press, 1974.

———. *This Is Detroit, 1701–2001.* Detroit: Wayne State University Press, 2001.

Woodford, Frank B. *Father Abraham's Children: Michigan Episodes in the Civil War.* Detroit: Wayne State University Press, 1961.

Woodford, Frank B., and Philip P. Mason. *Harper of Detroit: The Origin and Growth of a Great Metropolitan Hospital.* Detroit: Wayne State University Press, 1964.

Woodford, Frank B., and Arthur M. Woodford. *All Our Yesterdays: A Brief History of Detroit.* Detroit: Wayne State University Press, 1969.

General Reference Aids

Cullum, George W. *Biographical Register of the Officers and Graduates of the U. S. Military Academy.* New York: Houghton Mifflin, 1891.

Eicher, John H., and David J. Eicher. *Civil War High Commands.* Stanford, Calif.: Stanford University Press, 2001.

Hathaway, Richard J., comp. *Dissertations and Theses in Michigan History.* Lansing: Department of State, Michigan History Division, 1974.

McDevitt, Theresa. *Women and the American Civil War: An Annotated Bibliography.* Westport, Conn.: Praeger, 2003.

Murdock, Eugene C. *The Civil War in the North: A Selected Annotated Bibliography*. New York: Garland, 1987.

Sprenger, Bernice Cox, comp. *Guide to the Manuscripts in the Burton Historical Collection*. Detroit: Burton Historical Collection, Detroit Public Library, 1985.

INTERNET SOURCES

Letters of Henry Albert Potter. http://freepages.genealogy.rootsweb.ancestry.com/~mruddy/letters.htm.

Peters, Gerhard, and John T. Woolley, eds. *The American Presidency Project*. http://www.presidency.ucsb.edu/ws/?pid=69819.

Index

www.ingramcontent.com/pod-product-compliance
Lightning Source LLC
Chambersburg PA
CBHW070438100426
42812CB00031B/3331/J